JIHAD JOE

RELATED TITLES FROM POTOMAC BOOKS, INC.

Radical Islam in America: Salafism's Journey from Arabia to the West
—Chris Heffelfinger

"My Heart Became Attached": The Strange Odyssey of John Walker Lindh
—Mark Kukis

Virtual Caliphate: Exposing the Islamist State on the Internet
—Yaakov Lappin

JIHAD JOE

AMERICANS WHO GO TO WAR IN THE NAME OF ISLAM

J. M. BERGER

Potomac Books, Inc.
Washington, D.C.

Library of Congress Cataloging-in-Publication Data
Berger, J. M. (John M.)
Jihad Joe : Americans who go to war in the name of Islam / J.M. Berger. — 1st ed.
p. cm.
Includes bibliographical references and index.
ISBN 978-1-59797-693-0 (hbk. : alk. paper)
1. Terrorists—Recruiting—United States. 2. Terrorism—Religious aspects—Islam. 3. Religious militants—United States. 4. Jihad. 5. Islamic fundamentalism—United States. 6. Qaida (Organization) I. Title.

HV6432.B464 2011
363.3250973—dc22

2010053161

Printed in the United States of America on acid-free paper that meets the American National Standards Institute Z39-48 Standard.

Potomac Books, Inc.
22841 Quicksilver Drive
Dulles, Virginia 20166

First Edition

10 9 8 7 6 5 4 3 2 1

CONTENTS

INTRODUCTION

The "New" Problem

In 1979 a motley band of several hundred extremists staged an armed takeover of the Grand Mosque in Mecca, Islam's holiest site. It was an unprecedented heresy, and it marked the dawn of the modern age of terrorism.

They were mostly Saudis, but the terrorists included Egyptians, Sudanese, Kuwaitis, Iraqis, Yemenis, and at least two Americans.[1]

The siege took place during a period of violent change in the Islamic world, soon after the revolution that installed the Ayatollah Khomeini in Iran and just before the Soviet invasion of Afghanistan. As many as six hundred followers of a Saudi named Juhayman Al Otaibi believed they had discovered the *mahdi*, an Islamic messiah figure embodied by Juhayman's cousin. They struck during the Hajj, Islam's most sacred pilgrimage, seizing the Grand Mosque and taking scores of hostages. For two weeks, Saudi Arabia was paralyzed by the siege, which eventually ended with a violent raid that left most of the terrorists dead and the historic mosque smoldering from its minarets.[2]

Juhayman and a handful of his men were captured and publicly executed. One of his American followers was taken prisoner and then secretly whisked home. Weeks after the siege ended, the wife of the other American walked into the U.S. consulate in Jeddah to inform officials that her husband, Faqur Abdur-Rahman, had been killed during the takeover. Saudi police had showed her his picture. His body had been buried in a mass grave, along with everyone else who was killed while taking part in the attack. "She does not desire to attempt to recover her husband's remains," a State Department official reported.[3]

The Siege at Mecca was only the beginning. Thirty years later, after a highly visible series of incidents in 2009 and 2010, U.S. media outlets discovered a new reason to worry. Americans were "suddenly" signing up for violent jihad.

Yet the phenomenon is far from new. Since 1979 American citizens have repeatedly packed their bags, left wives and children behind, and traveled to distant lands in the name of military jihad, the armed struggle of Islam.

Their reasons are as varied as their backgrounds—some travel to defend Muslims in peril, and some fight to establish the reign of Allah on earth. Some are channeling a personal rage that has little to do with religion. Others seek a community where they can belong.

Americans fought the Soviets in Afghanistan, and at least one American citizen was present at the founding of al Qaeda. Americans have gone to jihad in Bosnia, Chechnya, Somalia, and Yemen. Virtually every major terrorist attack against the United States—including 9/11—has included Americans as willful accomplices.

While all major religions have rules that limit or justify war, a small but significant minority of Muslims believe that under the correct circumstances, war is a fundamental obligation for everyone who shares the religion of Islam. When war is carried out according to the rules, it is called military jihad or simply jihad.

"Jihad" is a word that has become contentious, with many Muslims arguing that it is most properly applied to a host of nonviolent activities, such as self-improvement or seeking justice. Although this argument applies in certain contexts, military jihadists do not make such qualifications when they call their work jihad.

"Whenever jihad is mentioned in the [Koran], it means the obligation to fight. It does not mean to fight with the pen or to write books or articles in the press, or to fight by holding lectures." Those are the words of Abdullah Azzam, the spiritual and physical leader of the volunteer jihad against the Soviets in Afghanistan, who was speaking in Brooklyn in 1988.[4] This book will generally follow Azzam's usage, although it will also examine those who use the pen and the lectern to incite others to acts of physical jihad.

I acknowledge that there is a debate in the public square on this issue, but this book defines jihad as jihadists do—as the use of violence to achieve specific goals, usually either the defense of Muslims perceived to be in peril or the advancement of Islam's global position.

Although most religions include guidelines for war and civic defense, the rules of jihad are fundamental to the core texts of Islam. A small minority of Muslims even rate jihad as one of Islam's most basic obligations.

OTHER DEFINITIONS

Throughout this book, I have put a premium on representing the voices of American jihadists and letting their own words explain their actions. This doesn't mean I accept everything they say as being sincere and legitimate. Far from it—there are clear lies in some cases, distortions and misconceptions in others. But regardless of how imperfect these sources are, the words of American jihadists provide a window into their overt reasons for taking up arms and their moral context for the violence they inflict.

In many cases, however, these sources are strong. Some, of course, are statements given in interviews after an arrest—attempts to rationalize or justify violent acts in an effort to win a lighter sentence or to burnish a public image. Yet many of the quotes you will read in these pages were intended for Muslim audiences. Many are taken from surveillance tapes in which these Americans talked with their peers in unguarded moments. Such sources are invaluable windows into why Americans take up the banner of jihad.

What lies in their hearts only Allah knows. One can only work with the sources as they exist. To ignore the stated reasons that jihadists use to justify their actions is, at the least, foolish. To impose imagined reasons without examining the evidence is reckless.

Many labels exist for people who embrace a vision of global jihad or the dream of a world ruled by Islamic law, such as Salafis, Wahhabis, Deobandis, Muslim Brotherhood, and Islamists. For the most part, I have tried to downplay these labels, in part to spare the reader a barrage of unfamiliar and confusing technical terms whose meanings are often disputed.

One area where important definitions can get murky is the distinction between "terrorist" and "jihadist." The two terms have become conflated in recent years, in part due to a deliberate and systematic rebranding of the word by Western diplomatic maneuvers and psychological operations. Here, I think an important distinction can be drawn. Not all jihadists are terrorists, but virtually all Muslim terrorists define their activities as jihad.

No definition of terrorism is universally accepted. For purposes of this book, terrorists are nongovernment actors who engage in violence against noncombatants in order to accomplish a political goal or amplify a message. Noncombatants include political leaders (such as Anwar Sadat) and military personnel not engaged in a conflict (for instance, the victims of the 1996 Khobar Towers bombing). Terrorists may be supported by states, but they have a fundamental quality of independence—or at least of disavowal and deniability.

Under this definition, John Wilkes Booth would be considered a terrorist, as would the Unabomber. The Third Reich would not be considered a terrorist organization, but American neo-Nazis would. The state of Israel is not a terrorist organization, regardless of one's views on the morality of its actions, but the Jewish Defense League was. The label is about describing context and behavior, not about assigning moral judgment. As it is used here, the word "terrorism" is not a moral qualifier or a tool for demonizing individuals or groups; it's an attempt to verbalize the fundamental difference between the actions of an established and recognized nation and what is essentially a vigilante mentality targeting noncombatants.

A key term in this book is "jihadist." Generally, anyone characterized as a jihadist will fit into one of the following categories:

- Someone who travels abroad to fight in a foreign conflict specifically in the name of Islam.
- Someone who takes part in terrorist activities that are explicitly defined by the participants as a form of military jihad or that are explicitly motivated by jihadist ideology.
- Someone who actively finances, supports, advocates, or provides religious justification for explicit military jihad as described previously.

Not all jihadists are terrorists or even criminals. Not everyone profiled in this book is a terrorist or a criminal, although many are. The sample of people discussed in these pages is skewed toward terrorists because those cases are better documented and because, in the post–September 11 environment, many American Muslims who took part in jihad but not in terrorism are understandably reluctant to draw attention to themselves. I can sympathize with their reasons, but I wish

I could have found more people who would step forward for this discussion in order to present a more balanced point of view. Anyone with this kind of history should feel free to contact me—there will be other opportunities to tell those stories, and I think it's important.

A few other useful terms to consider:

***Radicals*:** For purposes of this book, radicals are people or institutions that advocate an ideology with clear connections to nonstate violence, whether by justifying it or by providing rationalizations that are clear precursors to action.

***Conservative and/or fundamentalist*:** Wherever possible, I prefer the former term to the latter. In discussing Muslim terrorism, the discussion of religious views and social mores is unavoidable. Muslims or people who adhere to forms of Islam described herein as conservative tend to be communities that strictly enforce such Islamic or Arab cultural practices as covering women's faces, banning music, or criminalizing homosexuality.

***Jihadist incitement*:** When people in this book are called jihadists even though they have not committed violence, this refers to those who make explicit and unqualified calls to take part in violent acts specifically described as jihad.

WHAT WENT INTO THIS BOOK

I documented more than 240 American citizen jihadists while researching this book. About half of them were born in the United States. I also examined 41 legal long-term residents of the United States. For every case we know about, there are a certain number of cases that have never become public, particularly those concerning Americans who fought overseas in Afghanistan during the 1980s. Based on an extensive review of court records, interviews, and witness accounts, as well as informal conversations with intelligence and law enforcement officials and private experts working in the field of counterterrorism, my best guess is that at least 1,400 Americans have taken part in some form of military jihad over the last 30 years. However this number should be treated with extreme caution. We simply don't know for certain.

I performed about one hundred interviews with current and former intelligence, law enforcement, military, and diplomatic officials; Muslim radicals and counterradicals (including former jihadists and al Qaeda members); the families and the associates of former jihadists; and academics who study Islam and Islamic radicalism as well as some third-party accounts.

I mined tens of thousands of pages of court records and drew on dozens of intelligence and diplomatic documents obtained under the Freedom of Information Act (FOIA), as well as material generously shared by sources and colleagues. Included in the data set are more than one thousand pages of FBI records pertaining specifically to September 11, which I obtained through the FOIA and which can be viewed on my website, Intelwire.com.

I also reviewed scores of hours and thousands of pages of jihadist and Salafist propaganda, as well as al Qaeda internal records and documents captured in the process of prosecuting the war on terrorism. A more complete description of this material and its sourcing can be found in the acknowledgments.

WHAT IS NOT INCLUDED IN THIS BOOK

This book is primarily concerned with who American jihadists are, how they are recruited and indoctrinated, and why they do what they do. In order to maintain that focus, I have deliberately downplayed terrorist tradecraft, except where it is exceptionally relevant.

The World Trade Center bombing and the September 11 attacks have been covered in lavish detail elsewhere. I made a conscious decision to avoid rehashing the details of those attacks at length, except where I felt I could add something new and distinctly American to the record. After wrestling with the question, I also decided to devote relatively little time to Hamas, Hezbollah, and Palestinian Islamic Jihad activities in the United States.

This decision should not be read as a dismissal of the importance of Palestinian jihadist groups in the fabric of American jihadism. Although the U.S. activities of these organizations are important and represent a serious challenge for law enforcement, they exist on a slightly different plane from the broader global jihad movement, which is most dangerously represented by al Qaeda.

The involvement of foreign jihadists as fighters in Israel and Palestine is relatively limited. Most Americans involved with Hamas and Hezbollah have been fundraisers and propagandists, with a handful of arms traffickers and an even smaller number who have actually tried to go to the Holy Land to fight.

Finally, the Palestinian political issue is very complex, especially as it plays out among Americans, both Muslim and otherwise, and condensing the topic into one or two chapters would require more simplification than I was prepared to accept.

CLOSING THOUGHTS

American politicians habitually describe al Qaeda's motive as the creation of a global caliphate—a world-spanning Islamic state with dreams of conquest. Although this does reflect the view of certain Islamic thinkers and fringe Muslim leaders, jihad is most often characterized as defensive in nature. When Muslims are imperiled, other Muslims are urged to wage jihad in their defense.

Bosnia is one of the most obvious examples of this line of thought. Serbian assaults on Bosnian Muslims provided a clear rationale for why Muslims from around the world should lend assistance, whether directly by fighting or indirectly by financially supporting Muslim fighters.

The definitions of when Muslims are being attacked and what type of attack justifies a military response, however, are extremely fluid and subject to manipulation by cynical and ambitious figures such as Al Qaeda's top leaders, Osama bin Laden and Ayman Al Zawahiri.

The Soviet invasion of Afghanistan in 1979, with its clearly imperialist intentions, was deemed sufficient to justify jihad and even for some scholars to declare jihad mandatory for all able-bodied Muslims. Yet the American invasion of 2001—vastly different in its intent and execution—was also characterized by some scholars as a justification for jihad. And the persecution of Muslims need not be military. Much of Al Qaeda's ideological justification is based on American and Western economic and (to a lesser extent) cultural hegemony.

It's not surprising that American Muslims would take part in the jihad against the Soviets when Ronald Reagan was denouncing communism and pronouncing the mujahideen heroes and freedom fighters. It may be harder to see why Americans go to Somalia and kill fellow Muslims.

American jihadists are an incredibly diverse group. They include all levels of economic success and failure and every sort of background and ethnicity, including blacks and whites, Latinos, women, and even Jews. They come from big cities and small towns and every part of America, including the East and West Coasts, the Deep South, and the Midwest.

These are their stories.

1
The Early Years

Islam has been a significant part of the American fabric since at least the days of the slave trade, when African Muslims were forced from their homes and brought to the United States to labor in the fields. Perhaps one in ten slaves was Muslim—maybe more, maybe less. No record was made. Most Muslim slaves lost their traditions; some were forced to convert under duress.[1]

Bilali Muhammad was one such Muslim slave, captured in North Africa in the late eighteenth century, who tried to keep the traditions of Islam alive on the Sapelo Island plantation where he was enslaved in Georgia. He wrote about the Islam he remembered, using the Arabic alphabet but not the Arabic language, and kept the document close to his heart until he died. Although he did not ultimately succeed in preserving the religious tradition he had chronicled, traces of Islam pervade the Christian and cultural practices of his descendants. Black churches on the island face east toward Mecca.[2]

"We were Christian by day and Muslim by night," one former Sapelo slave told her daughter.[3]

Other traces of Islam lingered like a half-forgotten dream. The "Levee Camp Holler," an early blues song whose roots stretch back to slave music in Mississippi, is strikingly reminiscent of the Islamic call to prayer, which sounds five times a day from minarets around the world.[4] For the most part, however, the memory of original Islam faded over decades of slavery and Christianization.

Yet those origins influenced the shape of Islam in America for many years after the Civil War. Although orthodox Sunni Islam was represented by a few individuals and small, isolated congregations in the young United States, the dominant expression of Islamic thought in the twentieth century came from African American communities, whose interpretations often differed greatly from the original traditions.

The Moorish Science Temple, founded in New Jersey and later established in Chicago, was one of many early groups claiming to be part of an Islamic tradition. In reality, it was a barely recognizable amalgamation of theosophical beliefs revolving around a book called the *Seven Circle Koran*, which was derived from the incipient New Age movement.[5]

Later, the Nation of Islam channeled Black Nationalism through a filter of Islamic rhetoric, making significant alterations in the process. Malcolm X led many African Americans into a more orthodox understanding of Islam after completing the Hajj—a ritualistic trip to the holiest site in Islam, the Grand Mosque in Mecca, Saudi Arabia, that all Muslims are required to make at least once if they are able.

Starting in the 1960s, these indigenous Islamic communities were joined by increasing numbers of orthodox Muslim immigrants from Egypt, Iraq, and elsewhere in the Muslim world. The immigrants initially organized under the banner of the Muslim Brotherhood and established a beachhead on college campuses, where many of its members were students.[6]

Around the same time, the Saudis began to take an interest in American Islam. With its de facto control over Hajj pilgrims and a massive reservoir of oil money, the Saudi government had struck a long-time deal with its extremely conservative clerical establishment. In exchange for political backing from the religious authorities, the government would provide all of the support needed to spread the Saudi interpretation of Islam to every corner of the world.

The primary vehicle for this support was the Muslim World League (MWL), founded in 1962 with help from several major Brotherhood figures. One of the league's founders and at least one other member of its leadership council were also CIA intelligence assets.[7] The MWL was richly subsidized by the Saudi government, and it passed along that subsidy to Islamic organizations around the world, including those in the United States. Of course, the support came with strings attached.

The MWL's scholars were out to "correct" Muslims whose practices did not fall in line with the ultraconservative beliefs of the Saudi establishment, often referred to as Wahhabism, after its founder, an eighteenth-century cleric named Muhammad Ibn Abd Al Wahhab. Starting in the mid-1970s, the MWL began an aggressive campaign to take control of American Islam under the guise of "coordinating" the Islamic work. The league directly hired top leaders away from American-based groups such as the Muslim Students Association and used a variety of means to install Saudi-influenced imams in mosques around the country.[8]

The Saudis were especially concerned with reforming the beliefs of African American Muslims under the influence of the Nation of Islam and eventually pulled its leader, W. D. Muhammad, into their orbit. The group's internal political struggle gradually splintered the Nation of Islam along fault lines that dated back to the assassination of Malcolm X.

Factions emerged, which aligned at various points on the spectrum between religious and Black Nationalist orientations. Sometimes these conflicts broke out in violence. In January 1973 members of the Nation of Islam from Philadelphia brutally executed seven relatives of Khaliffa Hamaas Abdul Khaalis, the African American leader of a Sunni-oriented breakaway sect who had written scathing letters attacking the character and religious beliefs of NOI leaders. Four of Khaalis's young children—one just a baby—were among the victims.

Unsatisfied with the justice of the courts, Khaalis and several followers responded by laying siege to Washington, D.C., in March 1977, killing one person, wounding several more, and taking more than a hundred hostages. Khaalis demanded that the men who had killed his family, by then in prison, be delivered to him for execution, along with prominent members of the national Nation of Islam who had no clear connection to the case.

Khaalis also demanded that movie theaters boycott the film *Mohammad, Messenger of God*, a biographical drama directed by Syrian American Moustapha Akkad. Although widely considered respectful of Islam, the film's depiction of Muslims offended Khaalis's sensibilities.

It is difficult to look at the unthinkable tragedy that devastated Khaalis's family and conclude that the siege was primarily an act of religiously motivated jihad. Yet the protest against the movie foreshadowed later controversies, and Khaalis framed much of his rhetoric in terms of broad Islamic principles. The siege was broken during its second day, and Khaalis and his accomplices were arrested and imprisoned. Today the incident is largely forgotten.[9]

Such moments of high drama were relatively few. The unfolding tension between NOI and the growing Sunni-influenced African American community simmered but seldom boiled over. The Saudis patiently and steadily supported the conversion of Black Nationalist Muslims into Sunni Muslims, equipping many communities with imported Egyptian and Saudi imams.

In 1978 the Muslim World League sponsored a massive convention in Newark, New Jersey, attended by virtually every Muslim organization with an address in the United States, including several members of the American branch of the Muslim Brotherhood. Speakers at the convention urged the participants to take part in the Saudi desire to "coordinate the Islamic work" in North America and dangled financial enticements for those who would take part.[10] The Saudis also paid to fly prominent African American converts to Saudi Arabia for extensive religious indoctrination.

At the end of 1979, three events in the Islamic world coalesced into a multifaceted crisis that would reverberate for decades. In Iran, Ayatollah Ruhollah Khomeini came to power after months of political crisis, transforming the secular government into an Islamic republic and displacing the Shah of Iran, who had been installed in power and supported for decades by the United States. Because of America's support for the Shah, anti-American sentiment quickly built to a fever pitch and culminated in the seizure of the U.S. embassy in Tehran in November. Sixty-six American hostages were captured, launching an international crisis that would eventually bring down the presidency of Jimmy Carter.[11]

Within a few short weeks of the embassy disaster, a group of several hundred armed militants seized the Grand Mosque in Mecca, the holiest site in Islam, in the middle of the annual Hajj pilgrimage. The Saudis were already tense. Khomeini—a Shi'ite Muslim—had inspired an exciting new fervor for Islamic revival that threatened the Saudi-Sunni dominance of Islam around the world.[12]

When news broke that militants had seized the Grand Mosque, many in both Saudi Arabia and the West assumed the attack must be the work of Iran, but it quickly became clear that the threat was homegrown. Most of the militants were from Saudi Arabia, but the group included Egyptians, Kuwaitis, Yemenis, Iraqis, Sudanese . . . and at least two African Americans.[13]

The Americans had been brought to Saudi Arabia through one of the exchange programs specifically targeting African American Muslims. One American was killed during the siege, Faqur Abdur-Rahman, about whom little is known except his name.[14] The second was captured by the Saudis after French commandos stormed the mosque on the government's behalf. He was later released and repatriated. The name of the second American remains unknown.[15]

The story was covered up by both the Saudis and the United States. At the beginning of the two-week siege, the Iranian government fired off a scathing accusation that the United States was behind the assault. Rumors of American involvement sparked rioting and a mob attack on the U.S. embassy in Islamabad, Pakistan. Any credible evidence that Americans had been involved in the attack—even acting on their own initiative—would have dramatically escalated the situation.

The militants, led by a radical Saudi named Juhayman Al Otaibi, were a motley crew of messianic believers trying to act out a prophecy regarding the Islamic version of Armageddon, which included the start of an apocalyptic war against Christians and Jews. Otaibi's writings had a strident anti-Western, anti-Christian tone, and they condemned the Saudi regime as well for a perceived failure to enforce the original traditions of the Prophet Mohammed.[16]

In some ways, Otaibi's message foreshadowed the thinking of the not-yet-imagined al Qaeda. The parallel may be the result of both groups following similar traditions and sources, but there may be more to it. Otaibi's group preached on the grounds where Osama bin Laden attended college, at King Abdul Aziz University in Jeddah, and the group's members were known in bin Laden's social circle.[17]

Otaibi's followers were not the first terrorists or even the first jihadist-terrorists, but they were the vanguard of the modern age of terrorism, foreshadowing what would follow in both tactics and message.

The third event of the winter of 1979 would spread an evolving, radicalized vision of Islam on the wind like a puff of breath dispersing dandelion spores.

At the end of December, a few days before the Mecca siege ended, the Soviet Union invaded Afghanistan. The Muslim world was infuriated by the invasion, and within weeks, the Saudis were calling on Islamic nations to unify their efforts to support the country's Muslim freedom fighters, known as the mujahideen.

From the Saudi perspective, the invasion couldn't have come at a better moment. For years, the Saudis had bought into their own mythology, coming to see the kingdom as a perfected Islamic state where crime, radicalism, and evil in general could hold no sway.

That assumption had been undermined in the most dramatic way possible, with an assault on the country's most precious asset—its religious credibility. The Saudis were not merely the masters of the Grand Mosque; they were its protectors, and they had failed spectacularly.

In the aftermath, the leaders of the security apparatus took a hard look at what they had wrought and began to worry that it could happen again. One possible solution would have been to steer their religious program into a more moderate zone. Instead, they took a quicker and easier route: if the kingdom was plagued with angry, religiously fervent young men, the kingdom would simply send them away . . . to Afghanistan.

The Saudi decision to support the Afghan mujahideen was based on a complex stew of foreign and domestic concerns and was supported by both the political and religious establishments. The American decision to do the same was a much simpler Cold War calculation. As National Security Adviser Zbigniew Brzezinski told President Carter, "We now have the opportunity of giving to the USSR its Vietnam war."[18]

Cold warrior Ronald Reagan would up the ante. Calling the mujahideen "freedom fighters," he embarked on a campaign of support that included covert arms and training. The State Department's United States Information Agency produced hours of propaganda films promoting the mujahideen and their struggle, which the videos sometimes referred to as "jihad." The videos even showed mujahideen operations against the Russians, a style of presentation that jihadists would soon emulate.

One American government video showed Afghan children in school being indoctrinated into the jihadist lifestyle. Ironically, those children would reach prime fighting age just in time for U.S. forces to arrive twenty years later, and they would remember the lessons that the United States had forgotten.

VOICEOVER: In the towns and the camps of the 3 million [Afghan refugees] is a generation born with this national holy war burning in their hearts and minds. Their own number is in the hundreds of thousands, and they all learn one thing more important to them than these word drills. The Afghan has never been conquered. Afghanistan can be destroyed, but the Afghan will never submit.

CHILD: Right now, of ten brothers, only two brothers are left. And they have gone to jihad.

VOICEOVER: How many sisters?

CHILD: I had three sisters, and all three are dead.

VOICEOVER: When you grow up, what will you do?

CHILD: I will go on jihad.[19]

The Reagan administration also turned a blind eye to a parade of fire-breathing Islamic clerics and Afghan fighters who toured the United States seeking support from Muslims and non-Muslims alike.

The Virginia-based World Anti-Communist League, a right-wing organization, sponsored mujahideen leaders on tours of the United States and helped provide money and aid supplies.[20] Delegates from the Anti-Communist League met with top officials from the Muslim World League at a summit in Malaysia just one month after the Soviet invasion and agreed on a "joint effort . . . to combat all atheistic cults and movements."[21]

The fight against communism made for strange bedfellows. Mujahideen leaders would sometimes share the podium with Nicaraguan contras at WACL events, cheered on by the future leaders of right-wing, antigovernment militia groups.[22]

Support from the American Muslim community ultimately proved to be more significant. During the course of the Afghanistan war, the Muslim World League and its American affiliates sent emissaries to encourage contributions, financial and otherwise, to the Afghanistan jihad. The most persuasive of these speakers was the man in charge of coordinating all the Arab volunteers who traveled to Afghanistan as volunteer fighters: Abdullah Azzam.

Azzam was a Palestinian Islamic scholar who had made a new home in Saudi Arabia, teaching in the universities there and studying in Egypt, where political and religious forces also fostered such committed jihadist thinkers as the "Blind Sheikh" Omar Abdel Rahman and a young firebrand named Ayman Al Zawahiri.[23] Even before the Afghanistan war broke out, Azzam was a familiar figure to American Muslims, having traveled during the late 1970s to Indianapolis, Indiana, where he met with MWL-linked figures associated with the Muslim Students Association.[24] On at least one trip, Azzam was accompanied by one of his young college students from Saudi Arabia named Osama bin Laden.[25]

After the invasion, with financing from the MWL, Azzam set up shop in Pakistan, first in Islamabad and later in Peshawar, where he coordinated the flow of money and volunteers into Afghanistan. The volunteer fighters, known as Arab Afghans, came from all over the world but especially from Saudi Arabia. During the war, Azzam and other prominent clerics traveled to raise money and invite Muslims to join the fight in person. They recruited from all walks of life but especially valued volunteers with military experience. In the early phase of the jihadist movement, many experienced soldiers came from Egypt.

America was one of Azzam's favorite destinations. During the 1980s, as the jihad against the Soviets heated up, Azzam set up outposts around the United States under the banner of the Al Kifah Refugee Services Center, starting in Brooklyn and then expanding into Atlanta, Boston, Chicago, Pittsburgh, and Tucson. The function of the centers was to recruit Americans for the jihad and to ensure that they had the right connections to meet up with the Afghan mujahideen once they got to Pakistan. Azzam spoke in Arabic, which was translated into English in real time for the benefit of American converts.[26]

No one kept track of how many Americans answered the call, and no one in or out of the U.S. government would venture a guess on the record. More than 30 documented cases were examined for this book. Based on court records and intelligence documents, a conservative estimate might be that a minimum of 150 American citizens and legal residents went to fight the Soviets. The reality is probably much higher, but any estimate (including mine) should be treated with great skepticism.

The Brooklyn center was located at the Al Farook Mosque on Atlantic Avenue, home to a loose collection of angry young (and not-so-young) men who gathered to focus their rage through a religious filter and receive guidance about where, how, and at whom to unleash rough justice. They learned from a number of teachers.

"There are so many miracles like this, I can talk about miracles ten hours, if you want," said Tamim Adnani, a popular speaker who was fluent in English and one of Azzam's top deputies in Afghanistan.

Adnani told tales of American journalists who had been moved to abandon their posts, convert to Islam, and join the mujahideen at the sight of Muslim martyrs. Russians would lay down their arms and surrender to the mujahideen without a shot being fired. The bodies of martyred mujahideen did not decay.

He explained to his audience that it was good to come and fight the Russians but even better to stay and see the struggle through to the creation of an Islamic state in Afghanistan. And after Afghanistan, he vowed, then on to Moscow and Palestine. "Nothing but jihad . . . Even after liberation of Afghanistan, even after the Islamic government, [the mujahideen] will not stop."[27]

Another frequent headliner was Omar Abdel Rahman, the firebrand Egyptian cleric who would figure significantly in the American jihad movement during the 1990s. Rahman's speeches tended to emphasize Islam first, last, and in the middle. Stern and alarmist, his appeal to join the mujahideen relied heavily on ideology and his interpretation of Islam. Rahman was blind, so he had no tales of combat to share, but he had traveled to Afghanistan anyway to show his support, an effort that was viewed as heroic.[28]

Yet Abdullah Azzam stood head and shoulders over the rest. At least dozens and as many as hundreds of Muslims living in America heard his call and were moved to action. Azzam toured the world propounding the jihad in Afghanistan, leveraging his scholarly credentials to argue for the legitimacy of the Afghan jihad as an act of defense against outside aggression. He also wrote books and produced videos exhorting Muslims to the cause. Although he frequently invoked the struggle of the Palestinians against the Israelis, most of his energy and direct efforts were reserved for Afghanistan. It was easier to get there and fight, thanks in no small part to the covert helping hand provided by the United States and the generous financing of the Saudi government.

Although one can find arguments in favor of offensive jihad (that is, attempting to conquer non-Muslims without provocation), most jihadist ideologues find it easier to persuade audiences of the need for defensive jihad, which allows Muslims to conduct war in certain circumstances. In Afghanistan few could argue against the right of Muslims to fight the Soviets. Azzam's 1984 book, *Defense of Muslim Lands*, lays out some of this rationale.

> Defensive Jihad: This is expelling the *Kuffar* [infidels] from our land, and it is *Fard Ayn*, [Arabic for] a compulsory duty upon all. It is the most important of all the compulsory duties and arises in the following condition: if the *Kuffar* enter a land of the Muslims.
>
> We have to concentrate our efforts on Afghanistan and Palestine now, because they have become our foremost problems. Moreover, our occupying

> enemies are very deceptive and execute programs to extend their power in these regions. The people of Afghanistan are renowned for their strength and pride. It seems as if the Glorified and Exalted prepared the mountains and the land there especially for jihad.[29]

Azzam advanced the same line of thought in his lectures, often with stirring effect.

> In situations like Afghanistan and Palestine, [the scholars] have all ruled that jihad becomes an individual obligation, that if the enemy enters a Muslim land by as much as a hand span, jihad becomes the personal duty of every Muslim man and woman in that territory. [. . .] And if the people of that land are incapable, or negligent, or lazy, or refrain, the individual obligation expands in a circular fashion to include those nearest to them. And if they are also negligent, or lazy, or refrain, and so on, until the entire earth is included in the individual obligation. [. . .] All of [the scholars] stated this fundamental, that the individual obligation becomes, in this situation, like prayer and fasting—an obligation which cannot be abandoned.[30]

The latter point is among the most controversial positions taken by jihadist thinkers. Daily prayer and the annual Ramadan month of fasting are among the "Five Pillars" of Islam, the baseline obligations that every Muslim is required to meet. Jihad is notably absent from that list, an omission that many jihadist scholars have tried to rectify. Although such rhetoric is largely rejected by mainstream Islamic scholars, it can have a profound effect on individuals looking for an excuse to fight—even those who neglect the actual pillars, as many jihadists do.

One of Azzam's best-known books was *Join the Caravan*, which was published a few years after *Defense of Muslim Lands*. This work showed a distinct expansion of the author's jihadist vision. The war with the Soviets was winding to a close, and the mujahideen were poised to claim victory over the world's most fearsome superpowers. Azzam had assembled a force of fighters, many of whom had been trained by experts and hardened in combat. Where would they go once the Soviets were defeated?

Azzam presented a sweeping list of reasons why jihad would continue to be mandatory for all Muslims who were able.[31] The list included:

- *To keep the "disbelievers" from dominating the world.* To justify this rather broad motive, Azzam quoted an infamous passage from the Koran that orders believers to fight until all *fitna* has ceased. Azzam and other jihadist ideologues translate *fitna* as "disbelief," although it is more often defined as "internal conflict among Muslims."
- *Because God wants you to.* This motive doesn't require much explanation, but it's noteworthy in that the injunction lacks a specific provocation. Azzam cited several different variations on this theme, including fear of hell, desire for heaven (via martyrdom), and following the example of the Prophet and his companions.
- *Scarcity of men.* The global Muslim community, known as the *Ummah*, was sorely lacking in capable fighters who were also fully committed to religion, in Azzam's estimation. "We will pass through Afghanistan so that you see for yourself an entire regiment, in which not a single person among them is proficient in the recitation of the Koran," he lamented.
- *Protecting the* Ummah. This extended to protecting both the lives and the "dignity" of Muslims around the world and protecting Muslim resources and houses of worship. Although this message was key to Azzam's appeal, its importance had been significantly demoted during the course of the war against the Soviets. As seen in the previous rationales, the jihad had become to a large extent self-justifying. Once drawn in by an arguably legitimate defensive need, the world's most influential jihadist was now fighting for more esoteric reasons.
- *Establishing a solid foundation as a base for Islam.* Azzam also expounded on this idea in a 1988 article for his *Al Jihad* magazine, titled "The Solid Base." The use of the word "base" here is highly significant—in Arabic, the word is "al Qaeda." According to Azzam, the Muslim community must wage jihad from an "area of land." This base would be "like the small spark which ignites a large keg of explosives, for the Islamic movement brings about an eruption of the hidden capabilities of the *Ummah*."

Azzam's lectures and videotapes of battles fought by the mujahideen against the Soviets were often shown at mosques around the greater New York area. One

American who was captivated by the videos and the talk of jihad was Abdullah Rashid, an African American born in Brooklyn under the name Clement Hampton-El.[32]

His father was a Christian preacher, and his mother was deeply involved with the Moorish Science Temple, raising her son in the same tradition. Young Clement inherited from them both an intensity of belief and a propensity for persuasive talk—the "gift of gab," as his wife put it.[33]

Hampton-El had served in the U.S. Army during the 1950s. After being discharged for fighting over a racial incident, he was swept up into the rush of Black Nationalism that erupted during the 1960s. He was headstrong and passionate, even from an early age, and would wax on about the coming Revolution, which never came. He loved all kinds of music, and he loved women, remaining an inveterate womanizer even after becoming a Muslim.

One day in 1967, Hampton-El was walking past the Islamic Mission of America, a Sunni mosque on State Street in Brooklyn, while sporting the distinctive maroon fez commonly worn by Moorish Science adherents. ("He was a man of hats," his wife remarked dryly.) Several Muslims standing outside the mosque took him to task.

"They said what you are practicing is not really true Islam, and they told me what I should do," Hampton-El recalled. He converted to Islam the year he got married, changing his name to Abdullah Rashid.

His twenty-one-year-old wife, then known as Elsie, was a Methodist and was not so fast to convert. Rashid was always rushing headlong into a new idea. Elsie took her time, investigated and considered, but eventually joined her husband in his new faith, taking the name Alia.

Rashid studied zealously under Shaykh Daoud Ahmed Faisal, a Moroccan immigrant and the founder of the State Street Mosque. He learned how to pray in Arabic and studied the rules and the rituals of Islam. Among them was the concept of jihad. Rashid understood jihad to be fighting in self-defense, but the definition of what constituted self-defense wasn't always clear.

Rashid was a restless soul, but for a time he was content with adventuring at home, immersing himself in books about ninja techniques and idolizing martial arts superstar Bruce Lee. He once told an acquaintance that Lee's meditative techniques were very similar to Islamic prayer—both called for clearing the mind in order to take focused action.[34]

During the day, he worked as a medical technician, surrounded by the seriously ill and dying, which earned him the nickname "Doctor Rashid," or simply "Doc."[35] He tried to comfort those he met. At night, he and Alia were active in their community, struggling to clear their neighborhood of drug dealers and muggers who menaced the neighborhood's children. Colorful stories circulated about Rashid's nighttime patrols of the community in ninja attire. His wife recalled that the reality was more like a highly organized neighborhood watch.

"And we did, did little patrols, you know. I had sometimes the observation thing up by the window, and we'd check it out," she said. "But it wasn't like we were out there like those gangbusters. It was just we live here."

According to investigators, Rashid found other, less innocuous outlets for his adventurous streak, which he kept from his wife. He was known as someone who could obtain guns and other weapons, which he trafficked among his associates in the Black Nationalist movement in Philadelphia and among Brooklyn Muslims, who were stockpiling arms on the pretext of providing security at Al Farook and other area mosques.

Even that was not enough to sate his desire for action. In 1988, after a conversation with a friend about the jihad in Afghanistan, Rashid decided that he wanted to get involved. "What made me go was a combination of things. The killing of innocent people. [It] just seem[ed] right," he recalled during an e-mail interview in 2010.[36]

His first challenge was convincing Alia. "I don't see why you should go there and go to jail," she said. Rashid was undeterred and continued to bring it up. In his dramatic but questionable account, he remembered telling her, "You can't outrun death. You got to die. So you best try to go back to Allah, with all of the good deeds that you can, sincerely."[37]

Alia was unconvinced and looked into it further. Her main concern was that Rashid was going to end up in jail. What did the U.S. government think about the jihad? After she read about the issue extensively, it seemed to her that the government approved of the fight. It also seemed to be acceptable from an Islamic standpoint. Her husband became single-minded about the subject, and eventually Alia capitulated.

With the decision made, Rashid arranged for some time away from his job and went to the Al Kifah office on Atlantic Avenue. There, he spoke with Fawaz Damra, the imam of the affiliated Al Farook mosque. A Palestinian, Damra had come to the United States in 1984 and took over at Al Farook in 1986. He helped establish the Al Kifah office there on behalf of Abdullah Azzam.[38]

Rashid gave Damra $500 and got a green light for the trip. He still had to buy his own airline ticket, which he did with Alia's assistance. In June 1988 he left the United States and flew to Pakistan. With his typical enthusiasm and love of theater, Rashid boarded the flight dressed in full army fatigues. When he disembarked at the airport in Islamabad, a Pakistani approached him and suggested he switch to more discreet apparel.

From Islamabad, Rashid caught a connecting flight to Peshawar, where Al Kifah had an office. The chief of the Al Kifah guesthouse enthusiastically welcomed Rashid and recommended an extensive program of religious study. Rashid explained that he didn't have much time and that he had already been trained by the U.S. military. He asked to be shown to the front lines. After haggling with various people, he was taken to the front lines and arrived at a camp equipped with Stinger missiles, courtesy of the CIA. Rashid was immediately smitten with the life of the mujahideen.

"It was every denomination that you could think of over there, young, old, rich and poor," he recalled. "We had some kids that ran away from Kuwait, from Saudi, from Abu Dhabi, who had money to throw out the window, but their desire was to go to jihad."[39]

There were also other Americans. One of them had traveled from New York with Rashid, a striking red-haired man with a long beard and a broad smile named Mohammed Zaki, who went by the nom de guerre of Abu Umar Al Amriki ("the American"). Zaki, whose family tree had roots in Egypt, had been born in Washington, D.C., and later lived in San Diego.[40]

Despite his dreams of glory, Rashid's trip to the front lines was fraught with problems. First he was stricken with malaria and spent long days lying in bed. When he recovered, he joined the battle. Carrying a rocket-propelled grenade launcher and a Kalashnikov rifle (the Soviet-made gun of choice for mujahideen around the world), he ventured onto the battlefield in search of glory . . . and promptly stepped on a land mine. He recounted the ordeal on a videotape made just weeks after the incident.

> It was pitch black, and we could see almost like it was daylight. So we got to the opening, and it was an opening, say, about 15 feet by 8. And we figured

> we'd go in here, hit them with the rockets, the bazooka grenade launchers, machine gun fire, and as they tried to escape, we had grouped the brothers over here to get them over there. […]
>
> [T]he brothers stepped in before me, about six, seven of them. And as I stepped in, 'cause I had taken the combat boots off now, we all had on sneakers so we could move, I felt that I had stepped on a rock. And as I raised my foot up, BOOM. I went flying up in the air, because it was a mine.
>
> There was a bright, white light, and blue. And I saw, as I went up in the air, my leg say POP. And I went flying behind a rock wall, WHOP, on the ground. And machine gun fire went POP, POP, POP, POP, POP, POP, POP, POP. And more mines, BOOM, BOOM. And then my reality, the impact hit me, and I grabbed my leg. I said, "Oh." I said, "My leg is off." And it was just dangling, hanging.[41]

It took eighteen hours for Rashid's fellow combatants to get him to a medical facility. The battlefield medics, such as they were, wanted to amputate the leg, but Zaki, the American, fought to keep the limb.[42]

"They carried us by stretcher for a while, first on their backs, then on stretchers, then on mules," Rashid said. "Nobody ever immobilized my leg. All the way there, for 14 hours, just flop, flop, flop, flop. Blood comin' in and out, in and out. I was yelling and screaming."[43]

Rashid spent the next three weeks in a Saudi-run hospital in Peshawar before flying home to complete his recovery in the United States. Zaki flew back with him. Rashid experienced serious pain for months afterward; his leg would never be the same. Yet he had no regrets. Far from it. Just a few weeks after he returned to the United States, he recorded an impassioned speech exhorting other Americans to join the fight.

> My stay in Afghanistan was tremendous. And my reason for telling you this is, is because I want you to feel, and perhaps to seek, to be warriors, [. . .] blessings from Allah, just for your efforts and endeavor to fight for the cause of Allah, with your wealth, with your life. [. . .] Now, I've been away from Afghanistan now, approximately, 40 days now. I miss it dearly. It's wonderful, fighting for Allah. You may think that sounds a little strange. My leg here was blown off, just about. [. . .] In my love for him, this means nothing.

> And *inshallah* [God willing], it's a blessing, 'cause we're supposed to fight in war, we're told this here.[44]

The video recording was made by new friends. On his return from Afghanistan as a wounded warrior, Rashid became an instant celebrity in the Brooklyn Muslim community centered at the Al Farook Mosque. Chief among his patrons was Mustafa Shalabi, the Egyptian who headed the Al Kifah jihad recruiting station attached to the mosque.

Shalabi visited Rashid in the hospital and convinced him that his story could inspire other Muslims. In addition to the videotape, Shalabi wanted him to travel around the country, talking about jihad. The attention was exactly what Rashid craved.

"Becoming a mujahideen just swelled his head," Alia recalled. "They said go here to Canada, and speak to the students, he would go to Canada. He loved to travel, he would go to Canada. They said, go to Mexico, and tell them about what mujahideen is about, he would go there." [45]

Rashid did little to refute the "swelled head" theory, inflating his fifteen minutes of fame into an epic tale about a man of consequence.

> The word had spread pretty far and wide, who I was and what my experience was, because the videotape went throughout the world. I used to hear from people in Egypt and Yemen, and people coming from Saudi Arabia I never even met would tell me we saw your film. And people who were not Muslims would say we saw your films.[46]

Although the scope of his stardom was exaggerated, Rashid did achieve a certain notoriety within the growing circle of Americans enamored of jihad. Within days after his release from the hospital, Shalabi gave Rashid a ticket to Boston, where he spoke at the Massachusetts Institute of Technology in Cambridge and at other events in the area.

Despite the fairly short and inglorious reality of his mujahid career, word spread around town that "Doctor Rashid" was the real deal, and he would soon find other ways to make himself useful. When Abdullah Azzam next came to America, Rashid and several other members of the Brooklyn community accompanied him on recruiting trips around the United States. Even though the Soviets were now on the run, the Al Kifah operation was still going strong.[47]

2
Al Qaeda's Americans

August in Peshawar is hot by any measure, but it's relatively dry and about 20 degrees cooler than the 110-degree days typical of June.

On one such August day in 1988, a small group of Arab men who had fought the Soviet Union in Afghanistan gathered in the dusty border town to discuss the future of jihad.

Among those attending were the legendary Abdullah Azzam, father of the global movement to support the Afghanistan jihad; his protégé, Osama bin Laden; and a handful of bin Laden's closest followers. Azzam and bin Laden agreed the time had come to form a new group. The question at hand: what would that group set out to accomplish?[1]

One man furiously scratched out a few sparse pages of notes to memorialize the meeting. He was known in the room as Abu Rida Al Suri, but his real name was Mohammed Loay Bayazid, and he was an American citizen from Kansas City.

From its very first day, the newly christened group, al Qaeda, would include American citizens at its highest levels.

Bayazid had arrived at this momentous day through Abdullah Azzam. He was born in Syria, and his family moved to the United States while he was in his teens.[2] Bayazid was not particularly religious, but he encountered a handout written by Azzam that described miraculous happenings in Afghanistan and decided he had to see for himself.[3]

Azzam was prone to sweeping and poetic descriptions of the lightly armed and vastly outnumbered mujahideen who were prevailing over elite Russian soldiers thanks only to their faith in God.[4] There were stories about the *shahid*, or martyrs killed in the line of action, whose bodies were said to give off a sweet perfume.[5]

In 1985 Bayazid decided to fly to Afghanistan and ask questions later. After making contact with Azzam's organization through a phone number printed on the handout, he found himself thrust into a world unimaginably different from his fairly typical American life back in Kansas City. The enormous culture shock dislocated him from his old life.[6]

Bayazid fought alongside Azzam and later Osama bin Laden during the jihad against the Soviets. Earning bin Laden's trust over time, by 1987 he had been put in charge of managing the Saudi's finances and other war assets. Records maintained by al Qaeda give a glimpse into Bayazid's routine duties—bin Laden fired off memo after memo to the American mujahid, requesting inventories of weapons and instructing him to distribute money and arms to other bin Laden allies.

In the spring of 1987, bin Laden wrote to Bayazid, summoning him from Karachi to take part in a battle against the Soviets. "[I hope] that you move toward us immediately in anticipation of the attack on the Russians as the time has come," bin Laden wrote. Bayazid was told to research whether bin Laden needed a visa to travel to Yemen, then visit one of bin Laden's sick friends, and then come to the front lines with money and men.[7]

Bayazid went to meet bin Laden for a strike against an Afghan government installation in Khost, just over the border from Pakistan. When he got there, he found bin Laden ill and the Arabs in disarray. The battle went badly, and the Arab fighters were humiliated in front of their Afghan counterparts. Bin Laden learned from his mistakes, though, and the group did better next time, engaging in more and more ambitious attacks.[8]

By 1988 bin Laden and Azzam were deep into planning the next phase of the jihad. The war against the Soviets was clearly coming to an end, and the mujahideen were emerging victorious. Yet the Afghan factions were poised to start a bloody civil war over who would run the country when the Soviets left. Azzam wanted the Arab volunteers to stay out of that conflict.

These deliberations set the stage for the August 1988 meeting, recorded by Bayazid.[9] The idea was to start a new organization from scratch, or "below zero," as the American wrote it, but the nature of the organization was a point of contention. Bin Laden was moving into waters that Azzam saw as extreme, and tension between the two had been building.

"Disagreement is present," Bayazid noted laconically. Bin Laden had several bullet points he wanted to achieve, which included inserting himself into the struggle for Afghanistan in opposition to local warlord Ahmad Shah Massoud, a veteran of the Soviet jihad whom Azzam supported.[10]

Bin Laden also argued that the jihad organization owed a debt to its Egyptian faction, led by Ayman Al Zawahiri of the Egyptian Islamic Jihad, whose ultimate goal was to overthrow the Mubarek regime back home and install an Islamic state. Again Azzam pushed back. One year earlier the Palestinian scholar had helped create Hamas.[11] Why would the organization tackle Egypt when the Palestinians were suffering under Israeli occupation?

Finally, bin Laden wanted to run the jihad with an open door recruiting policy in order to increase the numbers available for the newly minted al Qaeda. At the time of the meeting, bin Laden had identified a little more than three hundred candidates for specialized training with the new group. Azzam favored a more discriminating approach that would rely on trusted, proven brothers.[12]

Some days later the conversation resumed. This time the meeting included a core of eight or nine bin Laden loyalists, and Azzam was not invited. The first day was consumed with complaints about Azzam and his organization. On the second day, the conversation turned pragmatic. The men discussed which training camps would be controlled by al Qaeda and how to direct fighters from one to the other, along with the requirements for new members, which included "obedience," references, and "good manners."

On the third day, the minutes read, "the work of al Qaeda commenced."[13]

Americans were easy to find among the first recruits. Bin Laden seemed strangely enamored of Americans and people who had spent time in the United States, but the first consideration was practical. Someone with a U.S. passport could travel anywhere in the world without arousing suspicion, and bin Laden needed couriers to ferry money and information for his increasingly global operation.[14]

One of the first American recruits was Wadih El Hage. He must have read the memo about obedience, because on his application to join al Qaeda, he listed as his sole work qualification "carrying out orders."[15]

El Hage was born into a Catholic family in Lebanon. They moved to Kuwait when he was two. He learned about Islam as a teenager and converted shortly after he moved to the United States to attend the University of Southwestern Louisiana in 1978. El Hage had spent three years involved with the jihad against the Soviet, starting in 1982, when he took a job with the Muslim World League's office in Peshawar. He returned to America in 1985, married an American convert to Islam, and became a U.S. citizen in 1989. After getting married, El Hage took a job directly under Abdullah Azzam in Quetta, Pakistan, starting in 1987.[16]

In Quetta he met Osama bin Laden, and the following year he applied to join al Qaeda. According to his wife and his attorney, El Hage was never a combatant, and he suffered from a congenitally deformed arm that would have put a crimp in his military aspirations. Nevertheless, his application to join al Qaeda stated that he had been trained on "most types of weapons, mines, explosives and booby traps."[17]

Another of Al Qaeda's early members was Jamal Al Fadl, a young Sudanese man who spent time in Saudi Arabia in his youth but was forced to leave after he narrowly escaped being caught smoking pot. He moved to Brooklyn in 1986, where he worked as a grocery bagger and eventually found Allah at the radical Al Farook mosque.[18]

Al Fadl began to volunteer in his spare time at Abdullah Azzam's Al Kifah Center in Brooklyn. At first, he raised money and recruited members locally. Toward the end of 1988, not long after the founding of al Qaeda, Al Kifah's emir, Mustafa Shalabi, decided it was time for Al Fadl to join the fight. Unlike some other would-be jihadists, Al Fadl got the full ride. Shalabi gave him his ticket and some spending money.

Al Fadl's experience—recounted in noteworthy detail during the 2001 East African Embassy bombings trial—was typical for new recruits in the early days of al Qaeda and bears a strong, noncoincidental resemblance to a cult indoctrination. When he arrived in Peshawar, Al Fadl and several other recruits were taken to a guesthouse and instructed to give up their money, their personal effects, their passports, and even their names. Al Fadl was rechristened Abu Bakr Al Sudani.

With these indoctrination techniques, al Qaeda removed the trappings of the outside world, physically severing new recruits from their previous lives. The method mentally dislocated the recruits and forced them to reorient in a totally new world. The method had been tested and refined by Azzam's organization on hundreds, perhaps thousands, of fighters who went before Al Fadl during the war against the Soviets.

"I went to Afghanistan with a blank mind and a good heart," Loay Bayazid told journalist Lawrence Wright many years later. "Everything was totally strange. It was like I was born just now, like I was an infant, and I have to learn everything new. It was not so easy after that to leave and go back to your regular life."[19]

At the guesthouse, Al Fadl went through two days of basic indoctrination about the concept of jihad and conditions inside Afghanistan. Then he and his fellow recruits were shipped off to an al Qaeda–controlled training camp in Afghanistan. They started with small arms—including the classic terrorist weapon of choice, the Kalashnikov rifle—and rocket-propelled grenades.

This phase of the training lasted forty-five days, then he was sent to another guesthouse inside Afghanistan for ten more days of religious training, some of which was provided by Osama bin Laden himself, who spoke about the obligatory jihad to defend Muslim lands that had been invaded. According to bin Laden, this obligation eclipsed all other obligations, such as family, business, and school, reinforcing the recruits' emotional disconnect from the outside world with a religious dimension.

The third phase was combat. Al Fadl and his fellow recruits spent two months on the front lines, fighting in some of the lingering conflicts with the occupation government and getting involved in the factional disputes that were just starting to crystallize.

After this, the recruits were formally part of the organization. Following a brief leave in Peshawar, Al Fadl was sent to a succession of camps for additional training. He was always on the move and adjusting to new environments while being fed a constant diet of religious indoctrination and being trained in improvised explosives, booby traps, and advanced weaponry.

Al Qaeda's young army of volunteer jihadists came from everywhere in the world, including the United States. Many American volunteers were first- or second-generation immigrants of Arab descent, but not all of them.

Daniel Boyd was one of the recruits who stood out from the crowd, a tall, white American with a baby face and a lion's mane of blond hair, looking other-worldly in traditional Arab dress and taking the name "Saifullah."[20] Boyd arrived at the tail end of the jihad against the Soviets and managed to log some combat hours before it was over, including an attack on a Russian plane.[21]

"Man, it hit the ground. It was an ammunition plane," he told a government informant in 2009. "Son, you had to see the explosion on that thing. Everybody getting down. [. . .] Now that explosion filled the horizon. [. . .] I was high, high, higher."[22]

Boyd stayed on for advanced training, spending about three years in Afghanistan and Pakistan. The jihadists he spent time with were closely linked to al Qaeda. He returned home to North Carolina after a run-in with the law in Pakistan, where he had been robbing banks. Although outwardly he seemed to resume a normal life, he was quietly raising a family inculcated with his strict, militaristic reading of Islam, stocking his home with weapons and ammunition for what he saw as his inevitable return to jihad.

"One day, *inshallah* [God willing], Allah's going to put me back. I saw the *deen* [Islamic way of life in practice]," he told some friends, years later. "I saw the *deen*."[23]

Another dabbler in jihad was Khaled Ibrahim, an Egyptian-American living in Newark. Ibrahim was moved to join the armed struggle in Afghanistan after hearing a speech by Azzam, but he wanted to be trained before he left. Ibrahim signed up for firearms instruction after seeing a poster at the As-Salaam mosque in Jersey City. That decision brought him into contact with one of the most dangerous operatives in the history of terrorism—Ali Abdelsaoud Mohamed, the most formidable of al Qaeda's Americans.

Mohamed had been an Egyptian army officer during the early 1980s. As part of his military training, he had been selected to take part in a joint exercise that brought Egyptian commandos to Fort Bragg for the same unconventional warfare drills practiced by the U.S. Army's elite Green Berets.[24] Around this time, Mohamed was recruited into the hard-core radical group known as Egyptian Islamic Jihad (EIJ) by its emir, Ayman Al Zawahiri.[25]

Linked to the assassination of Anwar Sadat in 1981, EIJ was hell-bent on overthrowing the secular Egyptian government and replacing it with an Islamic state. Zawahiri was a cell leader in EIJ at the time, and he had recruited a number of members from the military, with the idea of staging a coup. That idea failed, but

Sadat was ultimately assassinated by military officers connected to EIJ. Zawahiri and hundreds of others were indicted for conspiracy in the killing. Zawahiri was released after three years and fled Egypt for Afghanistan, where he set up an EIJ operation in exile, contributing valuable military expertise to the Arab mujahideen gathered by Azzam.[26]

There, Zawahiri met Osama bin Laden and forged an alliance that continues until this day. Zawahiri was deeply involved in al Qaeda operations from day one. EIJ was nominally a distinct organization under Zawahiri's leadership, but for most practical purposes, al Qaeda and Islamic Jihad were one and the same. They shared payroll, personnel, and facilities, and sworn al Qaeda members answered to Zawahiri as readily as to bin Laden himself.[27]

Conversant in Arabic, English, Hebrew, and French, Ali Mohamed fancied himself a spy, and a spy was exactly what Zawahiri wanted, especially one who could infiltrate the American intelligence services. Zawahiri and other Egyptian radicals blamed the United States for supporting Egypt's brutal dictatorship and sneered at what they perceived as America's corrupt and decadent morality. The Egyptians were ahead of the curve, eyeing the United States as a potential enemy even as the CIA was helping arm the mujahideen in Afghanistan.[28]

Infiltrating the CIA was Mohamed's first assignment from Zawahiri. Mohamed began by simply walking into the U.S. embassy in Cairo and asking to talk to the CIA case officer stationed there. Skeptical but eager for Arabic-speaking sources, the agency tried him out in Germany, assigning him to infiltrate a mosque whose head cleric was connected to Hezbollah. What the CIA didn't tell him was that the agency had already infiltrated the mosque.

Mohamed's first act as a CIA asset was to tell the target of the investigation that he was working for the CIA and had been ordered to spy on him. The agent already in place reported this back to the agency, and Mohamed's CIA career came to an abrupt halt. The CIA issued a burn notice to U.S. and allied intelligence services that Mohamed was not to be trusted. He was not told why he was released.[29]

Mohamed spent the next several months working as a counterterrorism adviser for Egypt Air, where he gained valuable information about airline security that would come into play years later. The ultimate target remained the United States, however, and in 1986 Mohamed hopped on a plane for New York.

How he got his visa is a mystery—the burn notice added Mohamed's name to a visa watch list. At the time, however, the United States was still trying to work out whether it could leverage Islamic extremists to fight communism more broadly than in Afghanistan, and Mohamed was not the only dangerous person to slip across the border. Whether by oversight or strategic miscalculation, the State Department let a walking time bomb enter the country.[30]

Wasting no time, Mohamed proposed to a woman he had met on the flight into New York, and they were married in Reno six weeks later. Now secure in his ability to stay in America for an extended period, he turned to his assignment. First, he set up a communications hub near his wife's home in California. Joining him there was Khalid Abu El Dahab, an Islamic Jihad operative whom Mohamed had personally recruited. "Be patient," Mohamed told his protégé. "There is a bigger plan."[31]

Mohamed walked into an army recruiter's office in Oakland, California, and enlisted.[32] Still extremely fit at age thirty-two, he aced basic training and soon scored an assignment at Fort Bragg at the John F. Kennedy Special Warfare Center, which trains elite Special Forces soldiers in conventional and unconventional warfare, including psychological operations.

Initially, Mohamed worked as a supply sergeant, but with his unique background and strong language skills, he was tapped to serve as assistant director of the Middle East Seminar for the Special Operations and International Studies Department in the school. Ayman Al Zawahiri's trusted spy was now educating the U.S. Army about the Middle East.

Mohamed's tenure at Fort Bragg was a comedy of errors. He seemed to relish the role of spy but somehow remained oblivious to the fact that spies are not meant to be seen. In his spare time, he rifled through any loose papers he could find on the base, taking copies of maps and army training manuals that might be useful to Zawahiri's Islamic Jihad down to the local Kinko's to make copies.

He also copied dozens of documents marked "top secret," which must have delighted him. Many of these were actually simulated secret documents used in a training exercise, listing fictitious fleet positions and containing little intelligence of value.[33] Other material was more sensitive. Eventually Mohamed's paper sweeps raised the suspicions of his commanding officer, who took steps to secure genuinely classified information, but he didn't know the full extent of Mohamed's espionage, and no further action was taken.

Mohamed's indiscretions became even more indiscreet. At one point, while discussing Anwar Sadat with a superior officer, Lt. Col. Robert Anderson, Mohamed volunteered that Sadat "was a traitor and he had to die." In 1988 he informed Anderson that he was planning to travel to Afghanistan to take part in the jihad during his annual leave.

Anderson was appalled, pointing out that there could be tremendous ramifications if a U.S. Army soldier was exposed while killing Russians. Mohamed shrugged it off. After a month of leave, Mohamed returned looking like he had been to war. He gave Anderson a souvenir—the belt from a Russian Special Forces soldier's uniform—and a debriefing on the action, including maps of the combat. He told another officer that he had given U.S. Army maps of the region to warlord Ahmad Massoud, the ally of Abdullah Azzam.

Anderson filed an eight-page report outlining his concerns about Mohamed's freelance adventuring. It disappeared into the black hole of army bureaucracy, and he never heard back from his superiors.[34]

Where Anderson saw cause for alarm, retired colonel Norvell Deatkine saw opportunity. A civilian instructor in Middle East studies at the school, Deatkine helped train Special Forces members in "Civil Affairs," a nebulous department purportedly focused on community relations overseas that often served as a cover for psychological operations and intelligence works.

Deatkine drafted Mohamed as a Middle East specialist. At one point, he convened a panel discussion that was videotaped as an educational aid. Mohamed was the star of the show, fielding questions from a motley handful of army wonks whose expressions ranged from pained to dazed to disinterested. Of the five panelists, Mohamed cut the most formidable picture of a soldier by far.[35]

Animated and basking in the spotlight, Mohamed was remarkably candid during the ninety-minute talk, providing a window into the viewpoint of the hardened jihadists who would soon target America. If only anyone had been paying attention.

Many American jihadists of the period were motivated by a mix of understandable emotions and rationalizations, including the impulse to defend Muslims in peril and a craving for adventure in a venue that had been blessed by both Muslim religious authority and American patriotism.

Mohamed cared nothing for America. His loyalty lay with a radical version of

Islam reflecting the sophisticated and ambitious thinking of his mentor, Zawahiri, and a core ideology that would soon become part and parcel of the newly formed al Qaeda.

Mohamed's views came from established jihadist ideology—specifically the writings of Egyptian Muslim Brotherhood ideologue Sayyid Qutb, which had deeply influenced Azzam, Zawahiri, and bin Laden. These views included the separation of the world into a war between Islam and non-Islam, and the overwhelming imperative to create Islamic states ruled by shariah law. Sitting in the heart of one of the most important military installations in the United States, Mohamed told the panel,

> I cannot consider Islam a religion without political domination. So what we have, what we call *Dar Al Harb*, which is the world of war, and *Dar Al Islam*—the world of Islam. And *Dar Al Harb*, the world of war, it comprises all the territory [that] doesn't have Islamic law. [. . .] So as a Muslim, I have an obligation to change *Dar Al Harb* to *Dar Al Islam*.

When asked about the rise of Islamic fundamentalism in the Middle East, Mohamed replied that there was no such thing as a Muslim fundamentalist—"just ordinary Muslims." All Muslims were, by definition, fundamentalists, he explained.

> If you look at the religion, the religion, we do not have moderate, we do not have extremist, we do not have people between. You have one line. You accept the one line or not. [. . .] I accept everything, and this is my way. In the religion I can't compromise. [. . .] I will accept the whole part of the religion, or I will not accept the whole part of the religion. So the fundamentalist, it mean that the people they try to establish an Islamic state based on the Islamic *shariah* for every aspect in the life.

Ominously, Mohamed predicted that the mujahideen would not stay inside Afghanistan. They would spread around the world, take the war to Russia on its own soil, and transform strategic parts of the Middle East into Islamic states where Christians and Jews would be tolerated but "without power."

> [In Egypt], the religious people, they are calling and they [are] trying to change the system now. And most is the young people. Most is a new generation. They left the country. They are fighting, especially in Afghanistan. So the experiment will repeat again a hundred percent, maybe in Egypt and Algeria.

All of this was happening in plain sight. The underground aspect of Mohamed's activities was even more damaging. It's not clear whether Mohamed actually saw combat during his trip to Afghanistan, but we do know now what he didn't tell his commanding officer then—Mohamed had been providing professionalized, American-style military training to the mujahideen during his trip at camps affiliated with Abdullah Azzam that would soon become the property of al Qaeda.[36]

It was the start of an illustrious terrorist career, which would span at least three continents and encompass some of al Qaeda's most deadly terrorist attacks—the 1993 World Trade Center bombing, the East African Embassy bombings, and perhaps even September 11.

Several Americans were present at the camps during the time that Mohamed was there. Among them were Abdullah Rashid, the African American from Brooklyn who nearly lost his leg during combat, and Fawaz Damra, the imam at Brooklyn's Al Farook mosque.

Perhaps the most important figure in Afghanistan around the time that Mohamed was working in the training camps was Mustafa Shalabi, a fellow member of Egyptian Islamic Jihad who had been personally recruited by Zawahiri. Now a naturalized American citizen (through fraud), Shalabi answered to Azzam, at least on paper, and ran the Al Kifah Center in Brooklyn on his behalf.[37]

If Mohamed and Shalabi hadn't met before Afghanistan, they certainly knew each other afterward. Shortly after they returned to the country, Shalabi invited Mohamed to bring his training skills to the New York area. Mohamed handed out copies of the maps, the training manuals, and the documents he had stolen from Fort Bragg, which served as the foundation for the world's most dangerous book, the *Encyclopedia of Jihad*, a terrorist training manual without parallel.

Mohamed began work on the *Encyclopedia* by translating the stolen army training manuals into Arabic, then enhancing them with his own specialized knowledge. He carefully redrew illustrations of U.S. soldiers handling heavy arms, replacing the Western figures with cartoonish mujahideen fighters. Sometimes he simply inserted a page from a U.S. army manual and added annotations in Arabic. Mohamed's diagrams showed how to field-strip weapons, create improvised explosives, operate rocket-propelled grenades, and target Soviet tanks.[38]

He also added material not found in any army manual, such as instructions on how to create terrorist cells, surveillance and the selection of terrorist targets, how to create deadly poisons and other methods of assassination, and how to manipulate authorities if arrested. The book grew over the years, existing first on paper and later in electronic formats. The core text still exists today and circulates on the Internet. Copies of the book were captured in Afghanistan after the U.S. invasion in 2003.[39]

Mohamed took copies of both his edited manuals and the army originals to Brooklyn and Jersey City, where they were made available as part of the library at the Al Kifah Center and the As-Salaam mosque.[40] He wasn't only providing reference works, however. By early 1989 Mohamed was traveling on weekends from Fort Bragg to New Jersey to conduct hands-on training for a select group of about ten aspiring American jihadists.

The group predated Mohamed's arrival. Its informal leader was a naturalized American citizen from Egypt named El Sayyid Nosair. After earning his degree in industrial design and engineering from Helwan University in Egypt, Nosair's life had become tumultuous. He had dabbled with terrorism, reportedly training under the infamous Abu Nidal.

Not long afterward, in 1981, he moved to the United States, settled in Pittsburgh, and married an Irish American convert to Islam. Nosair lived a short walk from the University of Pittsburgh in a mildly seedy neighborhood with a handful of cockroach-infested bars and low-end strip clubs but relatively safe streets.[41]

His time in Pittsburgh was troubled. He was badly injured while working as an electrician, and he was eventually fired from his job after trying to convert his coworkers to Islam on company time. Allegations of sexual assault dogged him. Seeking a clean start, he packed up his wife and children and moved to Jersey City, where he found a job working at a power plant and began to attend the Masjid As-Salaam.

Around the same time he discovered the Al Kifah Center. Like so many others, he was drawn in by the powerful charisma of Abdullah Azzam. He began to spend more and more time at the center.

Family and health considerations prevented him from going to Afghanistan, but he began to organize an informal training program for those who might succeed where he could not.

It was Nosair's poster that had been spotted at As-Salaam by Khaled Ibrahim. A small group with a rotating membership of about six to twelve local Muslims began to practice shooting at a gun club in Calverton, New Jersey. Initially they were coached by an African American Muslim from Brooklyn, an ex-marine suspected of being involved in a series of bank robberies. His name is unknown because he was never charged, and the case remains open.[42]

The Brooklyn fighter, Abdullah Rashid, who had by now mostly recovered from nearly losing his leg in Afghanistan, joined the group. Hoping to prevent future jihadists from suffering premature injuries like his own, he had become a zealous advocate of training.[43]

Two other African American Muslims took part in the training, along with recent Palestinian immigrant Mohammed Salameh and Egyptian immigrant Mahmud Abouhalima, who had come to the United States a few years earlier. Both men would later be implicated in the World Trade Center bombing.

Members of the group came and went over time. Authorities suspected at one point that Wadih El Hage had trained with the men but never proved it; however, El Hage did once sell a gun to Abouhalima.[44] The target-practice sessions in Calverton were frequent but irregular. The men sometimes brought their children along. Nosair's son, Zak Ebrahim, remembered one trip to the shooting range when he was only six years old:

> My father seemed to be having almost as much fun as I was, if not more. Using a fully automatic weapon, he shot the legs out from under one of the larger targets. The men all shot it and had a laugh. Trying to emulate him on the next turn, I held the trigger back on a fully automatic rifle. I fired one bullet after another in quick succession. [. . .]
>
> Besides the five or six men, there were just as many of their kids waiting to take their turn. By late morning, it began to softly drizzle and I knew our time at the range was coming to an end. On what I figured would be my last turn at shooting, I took aim at my target and let each bullet fly. The last one hit the small orange light that sat on top of the target, and to everyone's

> surprise, especially mine, the entire target exploded, black smoke billowing into the sky.
>
> My uncle turned to the rest of the men and in Arabic said *ibn abu*, which means, "Like father, like son." They all seemed to get a very good laugh out of that comment. It wasn't until a few years later that I fully understand, understood what they thought was so funny. They thought they saw in me the same destruction my father was capable of.[45]

The men were wrong. Zak turned his back on his father's name and views and grew up to be an antiviolence advocate.

It was Nosair who brought Ali Mohamed into the circle, introducing him to the other trainees as "Abu Omar." The first classes were held in Jersey City at the apartment of one of the students.

"It was about navigating in areas like if you are lost in a desert area or a jungle," Khaled Ibrahim recalled, "or you are part of a group and you want to find your way, how to use a compass, how to find your way by looking at the stars, and survival things, and how to recognize some of the weapons if you see them, like tanks, stuff like that."[46]

Yet there were other lessons, which seemed less oriented toward Afghanistan. Mohamed showed them diagrams on the construction of pipe bombs, how to make and use the most effective Molotov cocktails, how to mix chemicals and build detonators for homemade bombs, and even how to build "zip guns"—crude homemade pistols that could not be traced by law enforcement.

He also taught cell structure and operational security. To keep communications away from their home, members of the group rented mailboxes near the mosque from a check-cashing company called Sphinx Trading.[47] In 2001 mailboxes at this location would be used by some of the 9/11 hijackers.

The cell attracted the attention of the Joint Terrorism Task Force, a cooperative investigation unit with members from both the NYPD and the FBI. The first investigation was spurred by a bomb threat against Atlantic City casinos, but it continued as a Neutrality Act case after it became clear that the men were at least nominally training to fight in Afghanistan. The act—rarely enforced—makes it illegal for Americans to fight in foreign wars.[48]

During the 1980s the FBI had little interest in pursuing cases related to Afghanistan, although bits of intelligence sometimes came up during other investigations. People from the United States were going over there to fight, and Afghan and Arab mujahideen came to the United States to raise funds and train in relative safety outside the war zone. None of this was considered fair game for investigation.[49]

For instance, a large number of foreign mujahideen flew to Plainfield, Indiana, for an extended stay at a facility controlled by the Islamic Society of North America (ISNA) during the late 1980s. ISNA's foreign financing was already the subject of a separate investigation, so the agent in charge sent a memo to headquarters about the mujahideen. There was no obvious case to prosecute. The president had deemed the mujahideen "freedom fighters," and it was widely known that the United States was supporting their jihad against the Soviets.[50]

The case against ISNA was largely dead in the water anyway. The organization and other connected groups had sponsored hundreds of Muslim students for visas. Many of the students lacked documentation, and some brought significant amounts of money into the country. At the field-office level, a few agents investigated the origins of the money, but when someone left the jurisdiction of one field office and entered another, the case was usually lost. Washington wasn't interested in coordinating the complicated interstate investigation, especially when the Bureau could be accused of religious profiling. Field agents who lobbied for a more aggressive approach to the visa violations were ignored at best and even reprimanded when they persisted.[51]

Aside from the religious complications and a general lack of institutional resolve, the cases involving American mujahideen were often muddy. For instance, noncitizen immigrants were not technically in violation of the Neutrality Act, a federal law that prevents U.S. citizens from taking part in foreign wars. And the Reagan administration had made an inconvenient habit of using private citizens for covert military missions in South America. Because the United States also supported the mujahideen, it was hard to muster enthusiasm for prosecutions.[52]

In the case of the Calverton training, the suspected connection to a bombing plot, along with the fact that the trainees were Americans with roots in the local community, helped overcome some of these hurdles, at least for a short while. The FBI surveilled the Calverton group for a few consecutive weeks, photographing the participants and attempting to establish some basis for further action. In the end, the investigation was shelved. The photographs were filed away, only to emerge years later—after several of the participants had been implicated in terrorist acts.[53]

The FBI surveillance did not capture any images of Ali Mohamed, who was expanding his reach from the Egyptian Islamic Jihad organization and moving deeper into the center of al Qaeda.

The United States had played host to a significant number of jihadists, many of whom were now contemplating life after the Soviet Union. In order to accomplish bin Laden's goal of taking the jihad global, al Qaeda would have to establish a formal presence on American soil. Before that could happen, blood would flow.

3
The Death Dealers

Rashad Khalifa was a rising star in the Islamic world. An Egyptian scholar raised in the Sufi tradition, he moved to the United States in 1959 to study biochemistry. Khalifa decided to stay and raise his family in Tucson while working in his field. His son was the first American of Egyptian descent to play major league baseball.[1]

An obsessive student of the Koran, Khalifa used computers in his day job and was inspired to apply them to analyzing the holy book. He discovered an arcane pattern within the Koran that revolved around the number 19—as seen in the number of chapters and verses, the occurrences of references to numbers within the Koran, and other, even more complicated, derivations.

Based on his writings and translation work, Khalifa became a spiritual leader in his own right. At first, his "mathematical miracle" of the Koran was warmly received by Muslim scholars as proof of the uniqueness and the divine creation of the Koran. But Khalifa didn't stop there.[2]

Over time, his studies led him to conclude that the *hadith* and Sunnah—Islamic traditions about the life of the Prophet Mohammed—were not reliable sources for Islamic practice. Many of the more socially restrictive practices in Islam are supported by these traditions. Eliminating the *hadith* and Sunnah from the mix led Khalifa into an increasingly liberal interpretation his faith. At the Masjid Tucson, where his followers gathered, Khalifa permitted men and women to pray together, and he didn't require women to cover their heads. Word of these practices started to spread.

Worse still, the mathematical analysis of the Koran didn't add up perfectly. According to Khalifa's calculations, one small section of the Koran was illegitimate—written by a human hand and not the living word of Allah. This proclamation was the final straw. The suggestion that even one word of the Koran should be changed or deleted was considered heresy by many Muslims. Khalifa's critics charged he was setting himself up as a prophet, in contradiction of Islamic teachings that state Muhammad is history's final prophet.[3]

In 1985 a group of scholars led by the Grand Mufti of Saudi Arabia, Abdullah Bin Baz, issued a fatwa declaring Khalifa an apostate, a religious crime for which he could be killed under a strict reading of Islamic law.[4]

One Tucson resident who looked on Khalifa with disapproval was Wadih El Hage, one of the first wave of American al Qaeda operatives (see chapter 2). El Hage agreed with the conservatives—Khalifa was not following the true teachings of Sunni Islam and "in general behaved like an infidel."[5]

As word of Khalifa's liberal views and his more esoteric heresies spread further, Islamic radicals in Brooklyn took notice. The anti-Soviet jihadists at the Al Kifah Center were now hardening into wild, undirected radicals, and their influence was growing.

In late 1989 the head of the Al Kifah Center, an al Qaeda–linked Egyptian named Mustafa Shalabi, sent an envoy from New York, an Egyptian, to investigate the Rashad Khalifa situation.

The envoy met up with El Hage, who helped him confirm the liberal cleric's teachings. The envoy went to Masjid Tucson to witness Friday prayers but was turned away because of his long beard, which Khalifa's followers correctly interpreted as a sign of conservatism. Peering in the windows, the envoy saw that men and women were indeed sitting together.

The man returned to New York to report his findings. The bloody response came within a couple of months. On January 31, 1990, a group of men broke into the Masjid Tucson and stabbed Khalifa repeatedly.[6] His body was drenched in a flammable paint thinner. The valves had been opened in a gas stove on the premises, but the fumes had not ignited.[7]

When asked about the killing years later, El Hage said simply, "I think it was a good thing." El Hage was investigated but never charged for the murder—in the end, there would be plenty of other things to charge him with. Yet because of El

Hage's involvement, the killing of Rashad Khalifa is considered the first act of al Qaeda–linked violence in the United States.[8]

Khalifa had already seen how he would die. In September 1989 police in Colorado Springs investigating a series of robberies raided a storage locker being used by members of a radical Islamic fraternity known as Al Fuqra. They found a cache of homemade explosives, military equipment, and training manuals. They also discovered a detailed plan for murdering Rashad Khalifa, including surveillance notes on his movements. The plan was nearly identical to Khalifa's ultimate fate.[9] Police warned the imam of the plot two weeks before he was killed.[10]

One of the alleged killers, a Trinidadian Muslim who went by the name of Benjamin Phillips, had gotten close to Khalifa by posing as a student. He fled the country and escaped prosecution for nearly 20 years before finally being apprehended.[11] Several Al Fuqra members were also convicted of conspiracy in the killing.[12]

AL FUQRA

It's hard to imagine how an Islamic sect with a history of extreme violence and dozens of armed compounds all over the United States stays out of the headlines. Yet that is the story of Al Fuqra.

In 1980 a Pakistani sheikh named Mubarek Ali Gilani came to the Yasin Mosque on Herkimer Street in Brooklyn.[13] He was looking for men to go to Afghanistan to fight the Soviet Union. Gilani was one of the first non-Afghans to join the battle, but his dream went beyond the conflict with communism.

A mystic and an Islamic faith healer of some renown, Gilani had a vision of a purified Islam, purged in fire and blood, with Muslims being segregated from the world of "*kaffirs*" (infidels) and living day to day, according to the precepts of their religion.[14] His followers referred to themselves as Jamaat al Fuqra—the Society of the Poor. The group later changed its name to the Muslims of the Americas.[15]

Gilani's message resonated with African American Muslims, and he began to attract adherents, first in Brooklyn and soon throughout the country, including significant centers of gravity in Virginia, Pennsylvania, and Colorado. Some of Gilani's new American recruits were brought to Pakistan to train in insurgent techniques with mujahideen factions fighting India in the disputed border region of Kashmir. American members of Al Fuqra would eventually take part in other jihadist conflicts, from Chechnya to Lebanon.[16]

Members of the group segregated themselves from Western influences, moving into rural compounds and small private villages in the United States and Canada with names like "Islamberg" and "Islamville." The group also had outposts in Jamaica and Trinidad.[17] Some of the communities aspired to be self-sufficient. Others were financed by "security" firms run by the sect, enterprises that tended to be a mix of bodyguard services and illicit arms trade.[18]

By the mid-1990s there were about thirty such communities in various parts of the United States, in addition to what investigators called "covert paramilitary training compounds" in several remote locations. Most of these communities still exist today.[19]

During the group's thirty-year history, members of Al Fuqra filled a scorecard with crimes of shocking violence, including at least thirty-four incidents that ranged from bombings to kidnappings to murder, but the government has never moved against the group in an organized manner.[20]

Members of Al Fuqra were threaded through the Brooklyn Muslim community, but they stood apart from the hierarchy of scholars and fighters that was, around the same time, crystallizing at the Al Farook Mosque and the Al Kifah Center. A number of news stories during the 1990s, citing multiple anonymous sources, claimed that Abdullah Rashid, the African American mujahid who almost lost his leg in Afghanistan, was closely linked to Al Fuqra.

Michael Scheuer, a CIA analyst who tracked Rashid during the early 1990s, said that Rashid and some of his associates were "at least tangentially involved" in the group. But Tom Corrigan, a member of the New York City Joint Terrorism Task Force (JTTF) who investigated Rashid in the United States, said he wasn't aware of any connection and that Rashid didn't seem to know what the group was in a conversation between the two men during the mid-1990s.[21]

AZZAM'S MAN IN NEW YORK

The murder of Rashad Khalifa was eerily echoed in Brooklyn one year later, but this time the victim was one of the radicals' own—Mustafa Shalabi, the red-headed American citizen from Egypt who headed the Al Kifah Center.[22]

Shalabi had worked in Brooklyn as an electrical contractor during the 1980s. Like so many other Americans, he had become entranced with the jihad against the Soviets through the writings and speeches of Abdullah Azzam. Shalabi traveled to Pakistan and Afghanistan to fight and help raise funds for the mujahideen. He returned to Brooklyn as Azzam's trusted lieutenant, in charge of the American Al Kifah operation. His deputies included the imam of Al Farook, Fawaz Damra, and another naturalized Egyptian American, Ali Shinawy, who had come to the United States during the 1970s and worked repairing trains for the New York City Transit Authority.[23]

In addition to providing Azzam with an operating base in the United States, the Al Kifah Center had quickly evolved into a transit station for the jihad, helping would-be jihadists find transportation and secure visas while providing support for those left behind.

Shalabi was an entrepreneur. In order to support Al Kifah's operations, he employed a number of for-profit criminal enterprises, including gunrunning, arson for hire, and a counterfeiting ring set up in the basement of the jihad office.[24]

Al Kifah also provided training for jihadists in the United States, nominally as preparation for Afghanistan. The Calverton gun club visits organized by Pittsburgh transplant El Sayyid Nosair were part of this program, as were the advanced training sessions conducted by Ali Mohamed. All of this activity was undertaken in the service of Azzam. As the 1980s wound to a close, Azzam remained the shining star of the jihadi world.

The war against the Soviets was finally coming to an end, largely due to the efforts of the native Afghan mujahideen. Yet in the wider Muslim world, a healthy dose of spin transformed the victory of the Afghan resistance into a victory for pan-Islamic jihad, the confluence of foreign money and imported Muslim fighters, with Azzam at the center, managing, inspiring, and holding the whole effort together.

The end of the war posed a powerful question, however. Azzam was heir apparent to a substantial fund-raising operation and an army of irregulars who hung on his every word. Where would this army go? The battle over direction raged on two fronts: in Pakistan, where Azzam tussled with his fellow war veterans, and in the United States, where it took a different form.

Although Azzam was the most influential figure in the jihad machine, he was not the only one. Another prominent scholar with a significant following in the United States was an Egyptian named Omar Abdel Rahman. Blind since childhood, Rahman had managed to memorize the entire Koran, an impressive act of scholarship even for the sighted.

He earned a degree from Cairo's Al Azhar, the most prestigious Sunni Islamic university in the world, and lectured there on the fundamentals of Islam. He also became embroiled in the seething cauldron of the Islamic movement in Egypt and eventually emerged as a spiritual guide to the Islamic Group and the EIJ organization led by Ayman Al Zawahiri.[25]

The relationship between Rahman and Zawahiri was close and operational but riddled with rivalry and animosity. At one point, Zawahiri sided with a faction that sought to remove Rahman from his position on the grounds that blindness made him an unfit leader for the jihad. Nevertheless, they were both potent figures who commanded substantial resources, and ultimately an uneasy accommodation was reached. Rahman continued to lead the Islamic Group, while Zawahiri established a branch of EIJ in exile. Each man exerted significant influence within the other's circles, despite the tensions.[26]

Rahman was arrested after the assassination of Egyptian president Anwar Sadat by EIJ in 1981 and accused of having foreknowledge of the attack and having provided a fatwa to justify the killing on religious grounds. He was acquitted, but Egypt became unfriendly ground for him. Despite his blindness, he made his way to Afghanistan to "see" the war for himself and soon became one of the most vocal supporters of the mujahideen.[27]

Some people in the United States looked on Rahman favorably because of his support for the CIA-backed jihad in Afghanistan. He made several trips to the United States to raise funds for the mujahideen and call American Muslims to join the fighting, attracting a large number of followers. Although Afghanistan was a strong focus for his speeches, Rahman roused a different sort of inspiration than Azzam and attracted more of a hardcore radical audience.

Azzam, in his rhetoric, had a tendency to lead with the glories of jihad, leveraging the spectacle to introduce ideological aspirations more subtly. His writings and speeches still contained plenty of blood and fire, and his goals were unabashedly those of Islamic supremacism. The Azzam style, however, was to first entice new recruits to Afghanistan to see the miracles and later inculcate them with ideology—that approach had drawn in Loay Bayazid, the mostly secularized Muslim from Kansas City, among others.

If Azzam used jihad as the carrot, for Rahman it was unquestionably the stick. The blind sheikh was more vocally—or at least more visibly—critical of

Western and American morals than many of his contemporaries. Yet much of his venom was reserved for Muslim leaders. As the incendiary nature of his rhetoric became clear, Rahman was added to a State Department watch list that barred him from entering the United States.

Soon afterward, he wrote a scathing commentary questioning whether the leaders of Arab countries could be considered Muslims. His arguments were consistent with the radical Islamic movement known as *takfir*—Arabic for "excommunication"—claiming that only leaders who conformed to the strictest interpretation of Islam should be considered Muslims. Leaders who adopted secular legal systems, instead of shariah law such as the government of Egypt, could legitimately be killed in the name of jihad and "must not remain unopposed even for a moment."

> How could a Muslim be so bold, after all we have seen, as to replace even one part of the Shariah? How could a ruler claim to follow Islam, and still do such a thing? Wouldn't he be aware that by giving preference to his own legislation over that of Allah he would inevitably have excluded himself from the Islamic Community? [. . .] The common people and their rulers, the educated and the ignorant, the cultured and the illiterate, all agree that these things are fundamental to Islam. Someone who denies any part of this has left Islam, and must perish in the mire of apostasy.[28]

In April 1989 Rahman was arrested by Egyptian authorities on charges of provoking an antigovernment riot. A few days later, the Islamic Group began to make tentative overtures to the U.S. government, a delicate proposition given American support for Sadat's successor, Hosni Mubarak, an ironclad dictator.

One of Rahman's disciples secretly came to the U.S. embassy in Cairo and met with State Department diplomats to spin the Islamic Group as a legitimate political organization, rather than a terrorist gang. Rahman, he explained, was innocent of the instigation charge that had been leveled against him, and the group was inclined to work with the government to make Egypt more Islamic and less secular. During the long conversation, the IG operative also assured the diplomats that the blind sheik's organization had not attacked U.S. citizens, and he dangled the prospect of cooperation with the Americans where mutual interests could be found.[29]

The embassy officers were intrigued but cautious. The approach seemed like a "desperate outreach effort," one of them wrote in a cable back to Washington. The Islamic Group operative "has revealed much more than we would have considered prudent. [. . .] We deduced that [name redacted]'s willingness to meet with embassy officers, most recently at the embassy itself, is motivated [by] a desperate hope of securing U.S. 'support.'"

The meetings apparently took place without the knowledge of U.S. ambassador to Cairo Frank Wisner, who was aware of the Islamic Group as an Egyptian opposition movement involved with the assassination of Sadat. Wisner said he was unaware of the contacts that were being cultivated within the embassy. Any formal asylum request would have had to go to Wisner for his signature, and he said that no such request was ever filed. An embassy official directly involved in the meetings refused to be interviewed for this book.[30]

A little more than a year after this meeting, in July 1990, Omar Abdel Rahman moved to the United States via a circuitous route from Egypt to Pakistan to Sudan. Despite the presence of his name on a watch list, Rahman's visa to enter the United States was signed by a CIA officer assigned to the embassy in Khartoum who was pulling duty as a consular officer. The government characterized the decision to allow the visa as a simple oversight. The CIA's involvement, investigators said, was merely coincidental.[31]

Even as Rahman's visa was working its way through the system, the blind sheikh was openly telegraphing his hostile intent toward the United States. In early 1990, Rahman gave a speech in Denmark:

> If Muslim battalions were to do five or six operations to the Americans in surprise attacks like the [1983 terrorist bombings] in Lebanon, the Americans would have exited [the Persian Gulf] and gathered their armies and gone back [. . .] to their country.[32]

POWER STRUGGLE

As Rahman was preparing to leave Egypt, a dramatic development in Pakistan changed the course of the jihad movement with a literal explosion. In the wake of the August 1988 creation of al Qaeda, the unified jihad front created by Azzam started to crumble.

Osama bin Laden wanted to expand the movement into a wide-ranging global jihad with aspirations to reclaim Muslim lands in the Middle East from "corrupt" Muslim rulers, with Egypt near the top of the target list. Included in this global jihad would be Egypt's most important patron, the United States.

Azzam, by most accounts, had little interest in fighting fellow Muslims, which he saw as counterproductive. His strategic vision for the long term was attuned more toward lands that had historically been Muslim, such as Spain, the Balkans, and especially Palestine, where Muslims faced a clear external enemy in Israel. His short-term strategy was to consolidate his power base in Afghanistan and help stabilize the political situation there in the wake of the Soviets' departure. To accomplish this, he appealed to the elders of the community.[33]

The passion of youths might be enough to win a war, but to create an Islamic revolution in Afghanistan required serious thinkers, and Muslims fully committed to the propagation of Islam. Azzam was interested in nation building. In December 1988 Azzam wrote:

> It is possible for Muslims to obtain many benefits from the school of the Afghan Jihad. It is also possible for more distinguished models, people with mature abilities and wiser, more mindful propagators to come to the land of jihad. Thousands of such people could bring about a tremendous revolution in the reality of Afghanistan, and in the inhabited regions thereafter. Those thousands may change history.
>
> Mature propagators are still the talk of the hour in the Islamic jihad of Afghanistan, and the subject of pressing necessity and glaring need. There are still many solutions which lie in the hands of those who are not playing the roles they should.[34]

In the months after al Qaeda was established, Azzam used his considerable influence in an effort to seize control of the copious amounts of Saudi money flowing into Peshawar under the pretext of humanitarian relief. He strong-armed former friends, spread nasty rumors about those who didn't play ball, and even called in favors with bank officials to have strategic accounts frozen. When persuasion and politics failed, he turned to force, sending loyalists to beat his opponents and seize their assets. Yet the al Qaeda faction committed to bin Laden was growing in influence. The Saudi had friends in high places, in Afghanistan and back in Saudi Arabia, where donors were becoming concerned about the infighting and the lack of direction. Azzam was forced to create a committee to explore the possibility of exporting jihad to other fronts around the world.[35]

In late 1988 Azzam was dragged into arbitration over one of these disputes, involving a project account worth hundreds of thousands of dollars. The deck was stacked against him. The chief arbitrator was Sayyid Imam Al Sharif, a legendary jihadist ideologue known best by his pen name, Dr. Fadl. Sharif was an Egyptian, a longtime friend of Zawahiri, and a member of the Islamic Jihad. One of Azzam's trusted lieutenants, a financier with close ties to bin Laden, testified that Azzam had falsified evidence in the case. In the end, Azzam suffered a humiliating loss; he was ordered to relinquish the funds and return the materials he had seized during the dispute.[36]

The situation continued to deteriorate. Sometime in 1989 his enemies planted dynamite under the pulpit in a Peshawar mosque where Azzam preached every Friday. That improvised bomb failed to detonate, but the next one succeeded. On November 24, 1989—just days after a contentious meeting about money with bin Laden's supporters—Azzam's car was bombed.[37]

The founding father of the Afghan Jihad had been assassinated, quite possibly by one of his former friends. Exactly who did it remains unknown to this day. There were a multitude of suspects, including the CIA and the Mossad, but Osama bin Laden and Ayman Al Zawahiri certainly had means, motive, and opportunity.[38]

Whoever was responsible, bin Laden took advantage of the situation and began to consolidate his control of the Afghan fund-raising apparatus. In subsequent issues of *Al Jihad* magazine, which Azzam had founded, the father of the Afghan jihad's history was rewritten to tell the tale of his support for the global jihad. His death was portrayed as having united the fractious mujahideen factions in Afghanistan—their continued internecine bloodshed notwithstanding.[39]

Back in Brooklyn, Mustafa Shalabi was caught in the middle of this breaking storm. Although he had long-standing ties to Zawahiri and kept an open channel with bin Laden, he wanted Al Kifah to continue in the direction Azzam had started, specifically by cultivating the Afghan refugees and working to consolidate Afghanistan as a base for future operations.[40]

Things got worse when Omar Abdel Rahman arrived in New York. Shalabi and El Sayyid Nosair picked up Rahman at the airport when he arrived in 1990. Nosair smelled trouble immediately.

"Each one of them has a different view for the Islamic war," Nosair told a friend. "They are going to have a clash someday." Nosair wanted to stay out of it.[41]

Although Azzam's rhetoric was sometimes harsh and always focused on jihad, he was also inspiring and gregarious, offering his vision with a wide smile and a sense of humor. Rahman was an entirely different sort of figure, perpetually angry, delivering fiery speeches that skewed heavily toward the negative. His ambitions went well beyond reclaiming historically Muslim lands. He was intensely focused on expanding the reach of Islam, and anyone who was not with him was against Islam.

> The obligation of Allah is upon us to wage jihad for the sake of Allah. It is one of the obligations that we must undoubtedly fulfill. And we conquer the lands of the infidels and we spread Islam by calling the infidels to Allah. And if they stand in our way, then we wage jihad for the sake of Allah.[42]

The dark tenor of Rahman's rhetoric began to inspire dark thoughts in his followers. Nosair was especially captivated by Rahman's increasingly violent message. His son, Zak Ebrahim, described one Friday service during a speech against violence delivered in 2010:

> [Rahman] began his *khutba*, or oration, and I sat there trying my best to mimic my father as he listened intently to his words. That day, the sheikh argued that Western culture was corrupting Muslims all over the world, that the consequences of American democracy were materialism, sexual perversion and idolatry, meant to distract believers from the true word of God, laying blame for the Muslim world's ills on many of the same groups that Jerry Falwell blamed for 9/11: pagans, feminists and gays. But the sheikh saved his most venomous words for those of the Jewish faith.
>
> On the drive home that afternoon, I wondered to myself, "What made the sheikh and his followers so intensely devout?" I asked my father, "When did you become such a 'good' Muslim?" and he replied, "When I came to

> this country and I saw everything that was wrong with it." And in that instant, I recognized the same look on his face that I had seen on the sheikh.[43]

Nosair wasn't content with ideology. On November 5, 1990, he shot and killed Meir Kahane, a radical Jewish leader, during a conference for a Zionist group at the New York Marriott East Side. The controversial founder of the Jewish Defense League, a terrorist organization based in New York, Kahane had an FBI file more than a foot thick. A rabid, over-the-top Zionist and a member of the Israeli parliament, he was considered a racist and an extremist by most Israelis, let alone by anyone else.[44]

After Kahane's speech, Nosair, wearing a skullcap to appear Jewish, approached Kahane and extended his hand. When Kahane reached to return the handshake, Nosair shot him in the neck with a .357 magnum handgun. Kahane died at the hospital a short while later.

"The son of a bitch killed the Rabbi," someone yelled. "See if you can catch him!" "Stop, murderer!" shouted another. Nosair shot one bystander fleeing the room, then shot an off-duty postal inspector while trying to escape. Unfortunately for the assassin, the inspector was wearing a bulletproof vest and returned fire, taking Nosair down.[45]

Nosair lay on the ground with his arms outstretched and a smile on his face. If he was dreaming that he had achieved martyrdom, he was destined to be disappointed. The killer was taken to the hospital and soon recovered.[46]

Investigators hauled boxes of documents out of Nosair's apartment. Most were in Arabic, but the stash included military training manuals and documents given to Nosair by Sergeant Ali Mohamed, the jihadist mole at Fort Bragg. The material went into storage without close examination. The NYPD's chief of detectives decreed that Nosair had acted alone.[47]

Kahane was widely loathed by Muslims and non-Muslims alike. In a room full of people, no one had gotten a good-enough look to clearly identify Nosair as the man who fired the killing shot. Between those who didn't think he was guilty and those who didn't mind if he was, Nosair became a local hero, especially among the more radical segment of the Muslim community.

Supporters showed up at his hearings and trial proceedings in large and often loud numbers. The hat was passed, and money was raised. One large contribution to Nosair's defense fund came from abroad—Osama bin Laden sent $20,000 for the cause.[48]

Because of the lack of eyewitnesses, Nosair was acquitted of murder and escaped life in prison, but he went to jail on a handgun charge. Crowds cheered outside the courtroom when the verdict was announced. Later, Nosair would receive a stream of visitors in prison, including many of his friends in the blind sheikh's circles.

In this air of increasing violence, Mustafa Shalabi tried to make things work with the blind sheikh. He helped Rahman get an apartment in the Bay Ridge neighborhood of Brooklyn. He hosted gatherings at his home, where he introduced Rahman to his circle of followers. Some of them swore *bayat*—an oath of allegiance—to the sheikh. An Egyptian named Abdo Haggag entered the inner circle, serving as Rahman's speechwriter. Unlike his peers, Haggag found Rahman to be a hypocrite and eventually turned against him, spying on Rahman for the Egyptian government and (much later) becoming a cooperating witness for the United States.[49]

The conflict that had played out in Afghanistan between bin Laden and Azzam was repeating itself in Brooklyn through their respective proxies. Rahman was involved with bin Laden. It's not entirely clear how solid that relationship was, but it was strong enough that bin Laden sent several $5,000 payments to help cover Rahman's living expenses in the United States.[50]

Shalabi was sitting on a significant amount of money, at least tens of thousands of dollars, and some reports put the total as high as $2 million. Rahman wanted the money for the global jihad, including Egypt specifically, but with an eye toward a widening conflict that would soon encompass the United States. Shalabi remained focused on Azzam's vision—Afghanistan first and the rest of the world later.[51]

Shalabi had also taken money out of the center and opened a shop, with the apparent intention of rolling the profits back into the jihad. Yet questions about Shalabi's honesty had persisted for years, and some called this theft. In a 1989 memo sent to Al Kifah officers in the United States and abroad, Fawaz Damra, one of the founders of the Brooklyn office, accused Shalabi of embezzling $1 million from the center.[52]

Damra was forced out of his post as imam of the Al Farook Mosque and sent into exile in Ohio. Omar Abdel Rahman replaced him, but he, too, began to bitterly criticize Shalabi, first for his handling of Al Kifah's funds and then for his religious inadequacy. The two issues were inextricably linked, as far as the sheikh was concerned, and both were matters of life and death.

Rahman did not enjoy unequivocal support from the community. Al Farook members suspected that he himself was funneling Al Kifah funds for his own purposes, such as supporting his family back in Egypt. Shalabi again won the power struggle, and Rahman was dismissed from his duties at Al Farook. Unlike Damra, however, he would not go quietly.[53]

Rahman's loyalists began a whisper campaign against Shalabi that soon grew to a roar. They passed pamphlets around the community warning local Muslims not to trust their money to the Al Kifah Center.

At the beginning of 1991, the tide began to turn against Shalabi. Fearing for his life, he called Ali Mohamed, the jihadist Special Forces sergeant who worked for Ayman Al Zawahiri, and asked him to take Shalabi's wife and son to the airport, where they flew back to Egypt. Shalabi intended to leave the country himself within a few days, but his time had run out.[54]

Enter Wadih El Hage, the al Qaeda member from Tucson who had been mysteriously linked to the brutal killing of liberal imam Rashad Khalifa little more than a year earlier.

According to El Hage, Shalabi called the Arizona Muslim and invited him to New York to look after the Al Kifah office while Shalabi flew to Pakistan, possibly to make his case with what remained of Abdullah Azzam's organization back in Peshawar.[55]

On March 1 neighbors found Shalabi dead in his South Brooklyn apartment, a stain of dried blood beneath him. His death had been extraordinarily violent—he had been shot in the face but somehow survived and tried to fight back against his killers, who then stabbed him to death.[56]

The investigation into Shalabi's assassination was hampered by the standards of the day. At the time, both the NYPD and the FBI were prohibited from conducting investigations predicated on religion. Although Shalabi's killing had clear connections to his religious community, investigators weren't even allowed to use the word "Muslim" in their reports.[57]

Within the local Muslim community, rumors flew hard and fast. Some said the CIA had killed Shalabi; others suggested a Jewish conspiracy. In 2005 New York City detectives extracted a confession that confirmed what had long been suspected: the killing was carried out by the increasingly fanatical followers of Omar Abdel Rahman. According to the confession, three men, all American citizens, took part in the murder—Bilal Alkaisi, Mohammed Salameh, and Nidal Ayyad. None were ever prosecuted for the crime.[58]

As in the Khalifa case, El Hage told investigators he knew nothing about the murder. He claimed that Shalabi had failed to pick him up at the airport as they had arranged, and he had hitched a ride with another Al Kifah official, only to hear about the murder days later.[59]

With Shalabi out of the way, there were few personalities who could draw focus away from the blind sheikh, and the local jihadists either lined up in his camp or dropped out altogether. Rahman had a galvanizing effect on the Brooklyn jihadists who, under Shalabi, had mostly confined themselves to training on weekends.

"He was like a major league ballplayer that wound up playing in a minor-league stadium. He made everybody else around him better," said Tom Corrigan, an NYPD detective who worked with FBI agents on New York's Joint Terrorism Task Force (JTTF), which had taken an interested in Rahman's circle after the Kahane killing.[60]

The energy generated by Rahman was building to a peak. Shalabi's killers were not sated; they desired more violence and were now plotting as a terrorist cell.

Goaded by Nosair, whom they had visited in prison, Salameh and Ayyad settled on the strategy of bombing Jewish targets in New York City. Alkaisi, a Palestinian American who had trained in explosives in Afghanistan, broke with the group after an argument over money. The remaining plotters now lacked expertise.[61]

The cell sought help from overseas, and in September 1992 Ramzi Yousef and Ahmad Ajaj flew into New York City from Peshawar, Pakistan.[62]

Yousef, a Pakistani, was an explosives genius who had refined his craft at Khaldan, an al Qaeda training camp in the vicinity of Khost, Afghanistan, and at the University of Dawa and Jihad in Pakistan. He spent several months shuttling between Khost and Peshawar, extending his own knowledge to others. Ajaj was one of his students.

At the camps, Yousef, Ajaj, and unknown accomplices had been discussing a plot to bomb the World Trade Center in New York. When Salameh's cell called for help, it was the perfect opportunity to make his scheme a reality.[63]

Investigators do not know exactly how the New York conspirators managed to secure Yousef's participation in the plot, but several of the New York plotters—including Salameh, Ayyad, and Egyptian immigrant Mahmud Abouhalima—had been trained by Ali Mohamed, al Qaeda's mole at Fort Bragg.[64]

Mohamed was in Afghanistan when the connection was made, training al Qaeda commanders in military tactics while working on his *Encyclopedia of Jihad*. For the flight to America, Ajaj had packed a collection of terrorist and military manuals in Arabic and English. The books were virtually identical to those Mohamed had given Nosair in New Jersey a few years earlier.[65]

Was Mohamed the link between the New York cell and Ramzi Yousef? The evidence is lacking, but the circumstantial case is intriguing.

"That would make more sense than anything I've heard before," said Corrigan, the JTTF investigator, when asked whether Mohamed could have arranged for Yousef to join the cell. On the other hand, Andrew McCarthy, a federal prosecutor who investigated Ali Mohamed and convicted Omar Abdel Rahman, argues there is "not a shred of evidence" that Mohamed had any prior knowledge of the World Trade Center bombing. Without new evidence, the issue must remain in the realm of speculation.[66]

Yousef took command of Salameh's cell. The conspirators included Abouhalima, Ayyad, and Abdul Rahman Yasin, an American citizen of Iraqi descent born in Bloomington, Indiana, and raised in Iraq. He returned to the United States in 1992 to join family members living in New Jersey. Yasin had been living on welfare when he encountered Yousef, who was renting an apartment downstairs from him. Eyad Ismoil, a Jordanian in the United States on a visa, joined the plot late, as a driver.[67]

With Yousef's arrival, the plans rapidly moved into high gear. Under Yousef's expert supervision, the crew built a devastating and sophisticated truck bomb. Salameh rented the truck, and Ismoil drove it into position—a parking garage under the World Trade Center. Shortly after noon on February 26, 1993, Yousef used a cigarette lighter to ignite a simple fuse. It took twelve minutes to burn down.

The explosion left a crater one hundred feet wide, gouging a hole in the building several stories deep and several more high. The epicenter was the parking garage beneath the World Trade Center. Flames and fumes shot up through the building. People who weren't trapped soon poured out of the building, panic-stricken and covered in soot. More than a thousand people were injured, some seriously, with crushed limbs, fractured skulls, burns, and bleeding wounds. Six died almost instantly.

It was a stunning act of terrorism and mass murder but less than Yousef had desired. His plan was that the explosion would topple one of the towers onto the other, killing thousands.[68]

Ajaj, who had traveled to the United States with Yousef, was already in prison on immigration charges. Salameh was arrested when he tried to recover the deposit on the rental truck used in the attack. Ayyad was next. Yousef, Yasin, and Abouhalima fled the country. Abouhalima was soon captured in Egypt and returned to the United States for trial. Yousef would remain free for two years before being captured in Pakistan. Yasin was detained in Iraq for years. His current whereabouts are unknown. Except for Yasin, everyone in the cell was eventually convicted for the bombing, and all are in prison today.[69]

Investigators knew that Salameh and Ayyad were followers of Omar Abdel Rahman, and they began to increase their scrutiny of the blind sheikh's other followers. What they found was a second wave in the making, an even more ambitious plan to wreak havoc on New York, camouflaged by the jihadists' new cause: the genocidal war raging in Bosnia.

4
Project Bosnia

When he was in high school, Dennis Philips fronted a rock band emulating Jimi Hendrix.

Philips was Jamaican by birth, but his Protestant parents had moved to Canada when he was very young, and that was the culture he knew. Caught up in the turmoil of the sixties, Philips dropped out of college and began to travel through America, bouncing around the drug scene and toying with communism and Black Nationalism, before converting to Islam in the early 1970s and taking on the name Bilal.

He had encountered Islam several times in his travels, but the book that won him over was *Islam, the Misunderstood Religion*, penned by the younger brother of Muslim Brotherhood ideologue Sayyid Qutb. Muhammad Qutb served a crucial role in widening the appeal of his brother's ideas by massaging them into a less overtly incendiary form.[1]

In his quest to understand his new religion better, Philips went to study Islam at the University of Medina in Saudi Arabia and afterward earned a master's in Islamic theology in Riyadh. He began to write and teach about Islam, viewing every engagement as *dawah*—an opportunity to call his students to Islam.[2]

In 1992 U.S. forces deployed to Saudi Arabia to defend the country against Saddam Hussein, whose army had seized neighboring Kuwait and was menacing Islam's heartland.

The Saudi government saw an opportunity in the deployment. In an open field next to the main U.S. encampment, an impromptu bazaar had sprung up. The

Saudi military requested permission from the U.S. military to set up a "Cultural Information Tent" on the site so that the troops could learn more about Saudi culture.[3]

Although Saudi officials assured U.S. commanders that the program was a simple introduction to Arab culture, it was in reality an epic-scale evangelical effort.[4] Leading this revival was Bilal Philips, now a member of the Saudi Air Force's religion brigade. As Philips recalled it, the intent of the program was simply to provide information about Islam.

> In the course of time, a number of people after listening decided to accept Islam, and that number started to increase and increase 'til we were averaging something around twenty converts per day. And, uh, the tent quickly became to be known amongst the chaplains as the Conversion Tent. Although this was not specifically our intention, was not necessarily to convert them but to convey information.
>
> But it just so happened that the number of those who were interested or those who had come and got information, either they had previously investigated something about Islam and, you know, this further information just completed what they were looking for and this convinced or they came and were open-minded enough, they heard this and felt this is what they believed or something closer or made more sense to them or whatever.[5]

That was how Philips remembered the program in 2010 during an interview with the author. In 2003 he had told a somewhat different story to an Arabic-language newspaper based in London.

> [A Saudi official] had a strong urge to convert U.S. soldiers into Islam. But, he did not speak English well. So he sought my help in Saudi Arabia, Qatar, and Bahrain. Since that date, I began giving religious lectures to U.S. soldiers on Islam.[6]

Philips helped assemble a team that spoke English fluently. The Camp for Cultural Information operated twenty-four hours a day for nearly six months, with imams living on-site and working a rotating schedule.

"At first we prepared the soldiers mentally," Philips said in the 2003 interview. One of the team's members "with experience in broadcasting and American psychology" addressed groups of 200 to 250 soldiers at a time, preparing the ground.[7]

The team also arranged for soldiers to visit Saudi families and witness group prayers in Saudi mosques. Some were even taken to see government-sanctioned beheadings (part of the Saudi criminal system). All of this activity was made possible by a standing order from one of the U.S. base's commanders that allowed Muslim soldiers—including the newly converted—to take a four-day pass to visit Mecca through the program. Expenses were covered by the Saudi government.[8]

During one of these field trips, Philips ran into an African American Muslim named Tahir who "just happened" to be in Mecca performing the Umrah, a lesser pilgrimage to the Grand Mosque. Tahir was a Vietnam veteran who later fought alongside jihadists in Afghanistan and had a natural affinity for his fellows in the military.[9] Tahir joined the Saudi camp and helped preach about Islam to the soldiers.

The program was a resounding success. By Philips's account, the team converted about three thousand U.S. soldiers to Islam, collecting names and addresses of converts and steering them toward Islamic centers back in the United States.[10] Other sources pegged the number at sixteen hundred.[11] It was an impressive tally either way.

In 1992 Philips was asked to deploy his U.S. military contacts for an "off the books" mission on behalf of Muslims in Bosnia who had become embroiled in a civil war.

> I was approached by a couple of military people and asked if I knew of any of the troops that had accepted Islam, gone back to the States and had left the American military, you know, who might be willing to go to Bosnia to help train the Bosnians. What they said they were looking for was something like an A-Team of specialists who would then go and train them to help them in resisting the Serbian slaughter.[12]

That request marked the start of a program that would soon spiral out of control, embroiling U.S. military veterans in a jihadist circle with links to al Qaeda and to a stunningly ambitious homegrown plot to kill thousands of innocent victims in New York City.

THE WAR IN BOSNIA

Bosnia-Herzegovina had a long and storied relationship with Islam, going back to its conquest by the Ottoman Empire in the fifteenth century. The official religion of the empire was Sunni Islam, which was broadly adopted, but Bosnian Jews and Christians were permitted to maintain their practices, resulting in a cosmopolitan mix of religions that worked successfully for centuries.

After the fall of the Ottomans, religion and ethnicity became hot issues. A Bosnian Serb, motivated by ethnic nationalism, fired the shot that started World War I. As part of Nazi-occupied Yugoslavia during World War II, Croatian Catholics and Bosnian Muslims took part in the extermination of Jews and Romany populations.

After World War II, Yugoslavia was united in large part by force of will—a cult of personality built around Communist strongman Josip Broz Tito, who suppressed religious expression and raised a generation of secular Slavs for whom the word "Muslim" was mainly an ethnic identifier.

The Muslims of Yugoslavia became perhaps the world's most secular. They drank—a lot. They smoked—a lot. They gambled, ate pork, neglected prayers, and charged interest at their banks. Men's faces were clean shaven, and women's clothes were low cut.

For more than three decades, Tito's iron grip held Yugoslavia together. His death in 1980 was the start of a long and agonizing collapse. In 1991 Croatia and Slovenia peeled away from Yugoslavia, while Serbia and Montenegro maintained most of the infrastructure of the former state under a new flag.

All of these machinations left Bosnia with a mixed population that rapidly and violently separated along "ethnic" lines, even though members of the three main groups—Croats, Serbs, and Muslims—had intermarried, spoke the same language, and looked alike.

There were a few who had kept the Islamic flame alive despite severe state repression. After Tito's fall, longtime Islamic activist Alija Izetbegovic took over the presidency of Bosnia on behalf of the Muslim-controlled Party of Democratic Action (SDA in the Bosnian language) after the country's first multiparty election in 1990.

Izetbegovic hadn't won the election. The actual winner was a charismatic businessman named Fikret Abdic whose appeal cut across ethnic lines. Abdic declined to take the presidency as the result of political machinations that have never been disclosed. Izetbegovic—perceived by many Western leaders as a moderate and secular Muslim—later commissioned a fatwa against Abdic, declaring him an infidel and offering the rewards of martyrdom to anyone who was killed fighting his supporters.[13]

Izetbegovic's personal beliefs are unclear—he was a cipher to his closest associates, as well as to international intelligence agencies—but his actions soon demonstrated that he had no problem wrapping himself in Islam if it provided some benefit.

The new president and his cabinet were unusually well connected in the Muslim world, keeping up strong ties in both Saudi Arabia and Iran despite the sectarian antagonism between the two countries. As civic chaos gave way to a three-way civil war among Bosnia's Serbs, Croats, and Muslims, these international connections came into play.

The Iranians chipped in with direct shipments of arms and elite intelligence operatives to assist the Muslims. The Saudis provided copious funds from the kingdom's coffers but also used their religious leverage to internationalize the conflict.

As part of the latter effort, Izetbegovic was obliged to accept an influx of mujahideen fighters. Between 1,000 and 2,000 foreign fighters took part during the course of the conflict, and they led about 3,000 Bosnians who opted to fight as mujahideen rather than as part of the regular army.[14]

The most prominent leaders of the Bosnian mujahideen were Egyptians associated with Omar Abdel Rahman's Islamic Group and the Egyptian Islamic Jihad.[15] Bosnian president Izetbegovic was allied with these leaders, even consenting to be videotaped during a grip-and-grin meeting with fighters closely tied to Osama bin Laden and Omar Abdel Rahman.[16]

Bin Laden sent several al Qaeda members to Bosnia in an effort to exploit the conflict. The mastermind of September 11, Khalid Shaikh Mohammed, also traveled to Bosnia looking for recruits he could turn from military jihad to terrorism, and two of the 9/11 hijackers fought in Bosnia. However, the majority of the mujahideen were not overtly connected to al Qaeda (see chapter 5).[17]

THE VIEW FROM AMERICA

The Saudi government had invested tremendous resources into shaping the opinions and the organizations of American Muslims. Its most overt tool for this purpose was the New York office of the Muslim World League.

As the war in Bosnia heated up, the English-language *MWL Journal* placed the conflict front and center, with dozens of articles and cover stories focusing on the Muslims' disadvantages in terms of arms and training, compared to the Serbs and the Croats.

The journal also chronicled the impotent rage of the Islamic Conference states over a UN arms embargo that covered the conflict zone. The embargo was widely perceived by Muslims and non-Muslims alike to provide a devastating advantage to Bosnian Serbs by preventing Muslims from defending themselves.

> The Muslim States and communities have been patient. For months on, they have been watching with their hands on their hearts Bosnian Muslims being mercilessly butchered and their children and women being ruthlessly evicted from their homes and farms as Serbia occupies more land and gains more ground.[18]

Others were steering the narrative in American policy circles. Abdurrahman Alamoudi was a player who had over the years worked for several mainstream U.S. Muslim organizations before founding the American Muslim Council in 1990. He was also wired into the Muslim underground. According to an informant, he carried regular payments of $5,000 from Osama bin Laden to Omar Abdel Rahman in New York to cover the cost of Rahman's rent and expensive international phone bills.[19]

Articulate and media-savvy, Alamoudi was a regular presence on television and in newspapers, always ready to provide a quote or a sound bite when journalists needed someone to represent the voice of mainstream American Islam. Alamoudi was an advocate of U.S. intervention in Bosnia, staging protests and rallies for the cameras and writing op-eds for both Muslim and mainstream publications:

> Candidate Clinton called for increased U.S. involvement in the Balkans designed to halt Serb aggression and violations of human rights. President

> Clinton, however, has dithered and drifted, abdicating his responsibilities as leader of the free world and ignoring the considerable powers of his office.[20]

These lobbying efforts were helped by a combination of pragmatism and idealism on the part of the mainstream media. Pragmatically, it was extremely unsafe to report firsthand on the unfolding war, so journalists frequently relied on official pronouncements from Bosnian Muslim officials as to what exactly was going on. Idealism was an even more powerful force—CNN's Christiane Amanpour flatly stated that attempts to report on the conflict from a neutral perspective would have made reporters "complicit in genocide."[21]

Few other reporters would go that far in public, but most Western coverage clearly favored the Muslim side in the war. And in many important respects, the narrative was correct—the Muslims were, by and large, the victims of Serbian aggression, and they endured horrifying war crimes in Bosnia. Nevertheless, most reporting tended to neglect important complexities, such as atrocities and war crimes committed by Bosnian Muslim factions, including the mujahideen, about whom little was known.

On the policy side, things were no better. Top administration officials were either oblivious to the mujahideen or dismissive of their importance. Although Clinton could not be moved to overturn or violate the UN embargo directly, his administration quietly opted to turn a blind eye toward illegal arms shipments to the Bosnian government from Muslim countries, including Iran and Turkey.[22]

As the crisis dragged on, Alamoudi rallied a diverse, media-friendly collection of religious leaders to join his "American Task Force on Bosnia." Despite his support for radicals such as the blind sheikh, Alamoudi won strong backing from American Jews, in part thanks to frequent comparisons between the actions of Bosnian Serbs and the Holocaust:

> Our children and their children will not forgive this generation, will not forgive us, all of mankind, for allowing this genocide—and if I may respectfully call it the second Holocaust of this century. The mass rape, the destruction that went on for more than a year must not be forgiven. We have allowed the destruction not only of life, of property, but of cherished principles of international law, the bedrock of the United Nations itself.[23]

The comparison was profoundly ironic, given that Izetbegovic reportedly collaborated with the Nazis during World War II.[24]

In American mosques, Friday *khutbas* (sermons) increasingly concerned the slaughter of Muslims in the former Yugoslavia, and speakers recounted lurid reports of atrocities—especially allegations about the rape of Muslim women, a frequent theme in jihadist propaganda.

Under the influence of the "blind sheikh" Omar Abdel Rahman, the Al Kifah operations in Brooklyn and Boston had also started to focus heavily on Bosnia. Al Kifah's newsletter, which was personally supervised by Rahman, exhorted readers to provide both "money and men," ruling that jihad in Bosnia was obligatory for all Muslims:

> We help the mujahideen in Bosnia so the [infidels] won't spread in the region. [. . .] We help the mujahideen in Bosnia just to protect this *Ummah* [the community of Muslims] and to return the torturing of the enemy after the backing off of many of the Muslim leaders and their begging the United States to lift the weapon embargo.[25]

Rahman himself echoed these sentiments in extravagant speeches around the New York area.

> Where's virtue? Where is loyalty which remained with the Muslims? . . . They find the women as their honors were violated, and the Bosnian women ask in some conferences what do we do with our pregnancies what do we do? And what should we do? They ask while they are crying. . . . Have the eyes cried? Have the tears shed? Have the hearts been broken? For what is happening to our sisters there? While their honors are violated and they became pregnant out of wedlock, no one lifts a finger.[26]

Siddig Ibrahim Siddig Ali, a bespectacled Sudanese immigrant who worked as Omar Abdel Rahman's translator in New York, echoed his spiritual leader's outrage in speeches around New York.

> We cannot announce and pronounce [Koranic verses about] Jihad, even when we come to America here, because we are still afraid that the CIA or

> the FBI or the authorities of countries are going to be behind us. Therefore, we still have to stay in our shells, and not come out and confront the idea or confront the disease, confront the humiliation, confront the oppression, and confront the [infidels] who has taken our own sisters, our brothers, as slaves in Bosnia.[27]

Siddig should have taken the threat of FBI surveillance more seriously, as will become clear.

THE A-TEAM

Thanks to these public sympathies and his excellent social network, Bilal Philips was making rapid strides in his program to recruit U.S. soldiers who could help train Bosnia's besieged fighters in their efforts against the Serbs. The first step was to secure financing and support for the plan, so Philips flew to Switzerland to meet with a representative of the Bosnian government.

Hasan Cengic was an imam, an official in the Bosnian army, and a notorious gunrunner. Cengic and Izetbegovic had served time in prison together under Tito for their Islamic activism. A trusted confidant, Cengic had been appointed to help manage the torrent of donations flowing to Bosnia's Muslims from around the world, especially from Saudi Arabia.[28]

Izetbegovic and Cengic funneled the donations through a fake charity called the Third World Relief Agency (TWRA), which was for all meaningful purposes a branch of the Bosnian government. The organization's titular head was a Sudanese national named Fatih El Hassanein, whom one al Qaeda informant called "Osama bin Laden's man in Bosnia." Cengic ran the day-to-day operations, deciding how the money would be spent.[29]

"Cengic was a very interesting guy that we followed for a long time, but we really couldn't put a nail into him," recalled Mike Scheuer, who led the CIA's Sunni extremist analysis team during the Bosnian war. "But he was clearly able to supply an awful lot of guns into Bosnia. He was a very important gunrunner."

As the Saudis aimed their substantial financial resources at Bosnia, Izetbegovic charged Cengic with receiving the money through TWRA and transforming it into weapons, in defiance of the UN embargo. During the course of the war, TWRA would take in at least $300 million in funds, raised mostly by Saudi citizens and royals.

Although TWRA does appear to have carried out some actual charity work, it spent far more of its cash on illicit activities. It was, at its core, a criminal organization. TWRA employees—including some of Bosnia's most notorious and violent mobsters—dealt drugs and committed murder, in addition to purchasing weapons and ammunition for the Bosnian army. Much of the money collected had simply disappeared by the time the war ended.[30]

The charity supported Islamic extremism with whatever was left over after lining the pockets of its principals. Omar Abdel Rahman was closely tied to TWRA, which distributed his sermons on tape in Europe. In at least one instance, Rahman appears to have sent a New York–based operative to Bosnia through TWRA's office in Austria (the operative was turned away at the border). Later, investigators would be told by an informant that TWRA was a front for Osama bin Laden. There appears to be some truth in this claim, although the full scope of the linkage is unclear.[31]

Cengic agreed to provide Philips with funds to recruit military veterans who would come to Bosnia in what would end up being a largely futile effort to give the mujahideen a dose of U.S. military professionalism. TWRA funds would be used to pay for the vets' travel and expenses. Although the mission was said to be strictly for training, Cengic also agreed to compensate the families back home should any of the volunteers be killed.[32]

After the meeting, Philips started to canvass his military friends back in the United States. Two proved exceptionally helpful. One was Tahir, the Vietnam vet who had helped convert U.S. soldiers back in Riyadh. His connection to that program meant he had strong ties to new Muslim converts with military experience who could be swayed to help the Bosnians. Now living in the New York area, Tahir quickly took charge of the initial recruitment program and helped prepare the Muslim trainers with equipment such as rifle scopes and night-vision goggles.[33]

The second contact was an African American convert to Islam named Archie Barnes, who had changed his name to Qaseem Ali Uqdah. A marine since 1975 and a Muslim since his teenage years, Uqdah held the rank of gunnery sergeant when he retired around 1991 and became executive director of Muslim Military Members (MMM), an organization that arranged access to literature and places of worship for Muslim soldiers around the United States.[34] Philips had been involved in MMM from its inception.

Uqdah maintained a roster of the names of U.S. servicemen who had converted to Islam during the Gulf War. His younger brother was one of them. The former marine helped Philips identify Muslim soldiers who were close to finishing their obligation to the U.S. armed forces—newly minted veterans who would form the core of the Bosnia training brigade.[35]

According to Philips, about a dozen soldiers were recruited through the end of 1992, including several Special Forces veterans. Tahir personally escorted the vets to Bosnia in two groups of five or six people at a time. The American trainers did not go unnoticed in Bosnia, although the secret of how they got there was known to only a few.[36]

The Americans set up shop outside of Tuzla, the third largest city in Bosnia and home to a retired airfield used during the communist era to train fighter pilots, one of the few usable airstrips remaining in the country. Most of the trainers apparently left after instructing a small group of mujahideen, but some stayed to fight.[37]

In the fall of 1992, Philips and Tahir were trying to gather a third group of American military veterans to make the journey, but Tahir had to drop out. His reasons are unknown, but the next stop on his journey is not. He showed up on the doorstep of Osama bin Laden.

Tahir was believed to be a member of al Qaeda. He had gone to Afghanistan originally under the aegis of Mustafa Shalabi and trained in an al Qaeda camp. He was soon promoted to be a trainer himself, instructing recruits in weapons and close-quarters combat, according to an al Qaeda informant. Bin Laden had sent him to Bosnia on a scouting mission.[38] In New York, Tahir had been responsible for targeting African American Muslims on behalf of al Qaeda, in response to bin Laden's strong interest in recruiting U.S. citizens.[39]

Sometime after Tahir left the Bosnia training project, he showed up in Sudan with his children in tow, according to the informant. He believed—correctly—that he was under investigation in the United States and that he could not safely return. He was promptly escorted into a meeting with Osama bin Laden and Abu Ubaidah al Banshiri, who was al Qaeda's military commander at the time.

Tahir was rumored to have been involved in Al Qaeda's first official terrorist attack, a hotel bombing in Aden, Yemen, in December 1992, not long after he left the Bosnia project. Al Qaeda subsequently sent him to Somalia, the informant said, in response to an American humanitarian mission that would go disastrously wrong, thanks in part to the terrorist group's intervention (see chapter 6).

Bilal Philips, interviewed in 2010, strongly disputed the informant's claim that Tahir was a member of al Qaeda.

> From what I understand, people who, I've heard, had links or whatever, there's a mindset you know, an approach to life and the role of Muslims, and jihad, and this kind of thing. And I never heard Tahir speaking that way. So, I don't believe so. Because, see, when you're locked into that, you know, then it's gonna come out in your conversation.
>
> You know, you feel close to somebody, somebody you can trust, and we were fairly close. I mean, for that limited period of time. So, I think that if this was the idea, I think they were involved in recruiting people. So I would think that he would have tried to recruit me, if that were the case. And there was nothing, nothing of that nature at all. So I think that is really a red herring.[40]

Intelligence sources are sometimes weak, sometimes strong. The intelligence connecting Tahir to al Qaeda was strong. In 1996 U.S. prosecutor Patrick Fitzgerald went to meet the aforementioned al Qaeda informant with a book full of photographs. The informant identified Tahir from one of the photographs and provided biographical details that matched information from other sources. A source familiar with the case confirmed that the man described in the debriefing was the same man who worked on the Bosnia project with Philips.[41] In 2010 I developed a possible lead on Tahir's whereabouts, but several efforts to reach him through intermediaries were unsuccessful.

Before he left the United States, Tahir handed the Bosnia project over to a trusted friend whom he had met during his time in Afghanistan: Abdullah Rashid, the mujahid from Brooklyn who had nearly lost his leg fighting the Soviets.

PASSING THE BATON

Rashid had been watching the developments in Bosnia with great interest. Afghanistan was being "squashed" by intra-Muslim warfare, in his opinion. Bosnia was the new front for Islam and a clear moral imperative, in his view.

> I think it was a disgrace in the sight of humanity that these people was under the heading of ethnic cleansing, setting up rape camps, raping women and killing, killing children, and I looked at it in the same form of genocide that was going on with the Germans that killed the Jews, that people would kill the Africans that came here, before they came here and any other form of genocide, what happened in Afghanistan and everything else. So I thought it was my duty to try to do something as an individual.[42]

In August Rashid was offered an opportunity to act by Tahir. At first, Tahir tried to recruit Rashid into the program as a trainer himself. Rashid's spirit was willing, but his injured leg was weak. Instead, they agreed, he could serve the cause by training others before they left U.S. soil.

When Tahir left the United States in late 1992, he asked Rashid to take over. In December he called Rashid and sent him to Washington, D.C., to meet Bilal Philips and receive further instructions.

When Rashid arrived in Washington, he was met by a U.S. Marine sergeant roughly matching Qaseem Uqdah's description. Rashid would not reveal the man's real name, but Philips confirmed that Uqdah was part of the project in a role similar to that described by Rashid. Uqdah refused to be interviewed for this book but did not deny his involvement in the program when given the opportunity (see details at the end of this chapter).[43]

As Rashid told the story, the two men drove to the embassy of Saudi Arabia, where they were searched twice before being escorted inside to meet with Philips and a Saudi prince. Philips did not recall this event and felt that it was unlikely to have happened, given the nature of the program, which he said had no official sanction.[44]

According to Rashid, he chatted with the prince for a while, then Philips entered the room and explained the project. After the meeting, Rashid visited the marine's home. The soldier gave him army training manuals on combat, sniper techniques, and machine gunnery. The next day the marine showed Rashid around Fort Belvoir.

As Rashid described it, the marine's role in the project was to obtain the names of U.S. soldiers who would be leaving the military soon and could be approached to go on the next mission to Bosnia, corresponding to the role Philips described for former marine Uqdah.[45]

Rashid returned to New York with an agenda and a promise of financing to come. He also had help from another former marine named Abu Ubaidah Yahya, whom Tahir had recommended.

But there were obstacles ahead.

Despite significant bureaucratic hurdles, the Joint Terrorism Task Force was by now actively circling the group of radicals who had gathered around Omar Abdel Rahman. And Rashid was at the center of the storm.

"The name of Abdul Rashid had come up to us, 'Doctor' Rashid," recalled Tom Corrigan, an NYPD detective on the JTTF. "We went out to our sources, the people knew him, but we couldn't get an address on him or a location or a phone number on him. He was kind of famous in the community because any time you mentioned that name, the first thing that came up was he's a guy who fought overseas. He went overseas, he had been wounded overseas."

On his return to New York, Rashid reached out to Garrett Wilson, an imposingly large veteran who worked as a Defense Department police officer by day and a security consultant and trainer by night. Unfortunately for Rashid, Wilson was also a government informant.

Wilson had become concerned about the paramilitary nature of the requests he was receiving from Black Muslim clients in New York and elsewhere. He started running his business contacts past the Naval Intelligence Service, which eventually loaned him out to the JTTF in New York.

The JTTF team had been trying to penetrate the intrigues whirling around the Al Kifah Center. Wilson arranged a meeting with Rashid in late December 1992—a watershed moment because Rashid left his home phone number on Wilson's pager. With that number, the JTTF investigators discovered Rashid's real name and his address, opening the door on new leads and enabling more aggressive surveillance.

Ubaidah and Rashid met with Wilson because they wanted to buy untraceable handguns and shotguns. They wanted training in how to neutralize guards, how to escape surveillance, rappelling, the construction of booby traps, and the use of chemical weapons. Rashid also asked for bomb detonators.

Although Ubaidah told Wilson that the training and the supplies were for Bosnia, Corrigan and other JTTF members were alarmed by the urban warfare element in Rashid's requests and suspected that a campaign of domestic terrorism was in the works.

Many of the requests were, in fact, consistent with operations being staged in Bosnia, a real-life urban war zone. Rappelling, for instance, was prominently featured in propaganda videotapes produced in Bosnia, and there were reports of chemical weapons being used on the ground by both sides.

The guns and the detonators were a different matter. Corrigan's sense of urgency was merited. Just how much would soon become clear.

TRAINING THE TRAINERS

Rashid returned from the Washington, D.C., meeting with new energy and a packed schedule, but his efforts to replicate Tahir's program ran into trouble. Although he had received several leads on veterans who might be able to serve as trainers, he wasn't able to close the deal and put together a team.

Rashid called Philips with a counterproposal—he would train nonveteran Muslim volunteers in the United States, then send the trainees along to Bosnia. Philips agreed and provided him with money to get started. "It was left for him to handle," Philips said.[46]

That may not have been the wisest decision. Rashid's first step was to open a martial arts dojo in a windowless, decrepit Brooklyn studio. With more enthusiasm than pragmatism, he lined the walls with exotic weapons: crossbows, ninja throwing stars, swords, blowguns, and nunchucks.

Out of sight, behind the flashy toys, he stockpiled rifle and shotgun ammunition and equipment for detonating explosives—but no guns or assembled bombs. He also kept a library of military manuals, including those that the marine had provided in Washington.

The search for recruits began. Siddig Ali was a skinny, fired-up Sudanese immigrant who worked as a translator for Omar Abdel Rahman. In late 1992 Siddig had been tapped to give a speech about jihad to area Muslims. After the speech, he was approached by Saffet Catovic, an American citizen of Bosnian descent with ties to Hasan Cengic. Through Catovic, Siddig was introduced to another Bosnian, who brought him to meet Rashid.[47]

With Siddig's help, Rashid organized a training camp in rural Pennsylvania, where recruits from New York and Philadelphia practiced for several weekends in the frigid winter air. The group was a mix of immigrants and Americans, and they trained in martial arts, rappelling, and light weapons, including grenades and assault rifles. There were about forty members to start, which Rashid and Siddig winnowed down to ten men sufficiently fit and competent to go to Bosnia.

Although Rashid was the nominal head of the program, most of the trainees answered to Siddig Ali and also had individual allegiances to Omar Abdel Rahman—which is not to say that the sheikh was particularly pleased about the program.

Rahman grumbled to one of the trainees that he didn't trust Siddig's religion or his money. Unhappy about being upstaged by Rashid's wealthy Saudi patrons, Rahman encouraged his followers to stay away from the program, without success. He also expressed skepticism that Siddig—or anyone else—was actually going to Bosnia.[48]

Rahman's suspicions on the last point were well founded. Although Siddig talked about Bosnia obsessively, he was planning to take action closer to home.

Regardless, thanks to Rashid's influence, the training was intensely focused on Bosnia at every turn. Lectures discussed the challenges of warfare on Bosnian terrain and what the trainers imagined might be useful skills over there. In one exercise, the trainees practiced storming a "Serbian" power plant, using a local facility.

"He gets his training, he goes to Bosnia, I mean he relies on Allah and see, Allah may improve it for the Muslims through them," Siddig said on a surveillance tape. "He who will be a martyr, thank Allah the Lord of the universe and he who stays alive, he still will be trained!"[49]

Rashid's top trainer, Abu Ubaidah, ran some of the sessions. Rashid himself was often absent, although he had arranged the location and outfitted the participants with guns and other military supplies.

Unbeknownst to Siddig and his friends, others were in attendance for the camp's inaugural session: a five-man FBI surveillance team tracking the group. The surveillance was short-lived, terminated due to a lack of support from headquarters—an unfortunate decision.[50] On a subsequent trip, Siddig carried out a little "experiment" for a friend named Mahmud Abouhalima—a key player in the World Trade Center bombing, which was still in the planning stages.

Although Siddig and Abouhalima moved in many of the same circles, they were pursuing their projects independently. In early 1993 Abouhalima asked Siddig for a favor: would he test-explode a bomb design Abouhalima was working on? After consulting with Rashid, Siddig agreed to conduct the experiment, and some of the Pennsylvania trainees may have detonated the test bomb in January 1993.[51]

The bomb's design came from Ramzi Yousef. While the JTTF was working on the visible fringes of the New York jihad operation, Yousef, Abouhalima, and at least five other coconspirators were quietly planning a terrorist attack that would shake the nation.

When Yousef's bomb went off on February 26, 1993, it had a dramatic effect on the Project Bosnia jihadists. Siddig and Abouhalima were friends, if not partners. Both men were devoted to Sayyid Nosair, and both were egged on in their ambitions during visits with Nosair in prison. Rashid also knew both Abouhalima and Nosair from the Calverton training in 1989.

After the Trade Center bombing, Abouhalima turned to Siddig for help getting away. When he explained what he had done, Siddig hugged him and exclaimed, "God is greatest and thanks to God. God is greatest, my God, my God, my God, God is greatest."

Siddig gave Abouhalima letters of introduction to friends overseas who would help him hide and drove him to the airport for his flight out of the country. All of this assistance was for nothing; Abouhalima was arrested in Egypt a few weeks later.

After Abouhalima left, Siddig was emboldened to put his own plans into action. For months, he had been talking with Nosair about possible terrorist plots that he could execute, sometimes using Bosnia as a pretext and other times citing more abstracted Islamic rationalizations.

Among the plans that were discussed and discarded, there was the bombing of a dozen "Jewish" locations in New York and the kidnapping of Richard Nixon and Henry Kissinger (whose policies Nosair and Siddig obscurely blamed for the troubles in Bosnia). Siddig consulted Omar Abdel Rahman at various stages in these discussions. The blind sheikh was not troubled by the idea of a terrorist campaign but suggested that he hit military, rather than civilian, targets.[52]

"Siddig was like a one-man jihad machine," recalled the JTTF's Corrigan. "He'd be driving a taxi cab, and he would think about, here's an airport, if a plane came in here, you'd be able to shoot it. This is a building that has an open front in order to meet."

In late 1992 and early 1993, Siddig began to finalize his list of targets and select a team, which included Abdullah Rashid, some of the Pennsylvania trainees, and various other people he knew, including Victor Alvarez, a Latino American who had converted to Islam after dabbling in Santeria, as well as three Sudanese immigrants who had not yet attained citizenship.

The scope of the plan was staggering. Siddig and his team would drive cars and trucks laden with bombs into the Lincoln and Holland tunnels, set the detonators on timers, then flee. There would be other simultaneous attacks—car bombings in underground parking garages below the United Nations and the FBI's New York field office.

"Siddig Ali was buoyed by the fact that a successful plot had taken place, but the competitor aspect of his nature was that he wanted to outdo the other guys," recalled former FBI agent Chris Voss, who also served on the JTTF. "And he felt bad that he had been left out, so he wanted to create a plot that was bigger and better, he had to outdo them."

In order to upstage the World Trade Center plotters, Siddig Ali had decided to kill thousands of New Yorkers in a single "Day of Terror." All he had to do was avoid getting caught.

THE FINAL ACT

While Siddig was narrowing his focus to the home front, Abdullah Rashid was becoming more and more international.

A typical day at the Third World Relief Agency involved people going in and out of the offices with bags full of cash. At one point, aides to Bosnian president Izetbegovic began to worry that their boss was gay, after he locked himself in an apartment for days on end with Fatih El Hassanein, the charity's titular head. They voiced their concerns to Bosnia's ambassador to the UK, Muhammad Filipovic, who reassured them. "Don't worry about that," he said. "They are counting the money."[53]

Bilal Philips summoned Rashid to Austria to meet with El Hassanein's brother, Sukarno, the number-three man at TWRA, under Hasan Cengic.

Rashid was a typical customer: he left with a lot of cash. He went back to New York with $20,000: $10,000 in his pocket and another $10,000 hidden in his pants, in order to evade the need for a Customs declaration. He made more trips, and so did Abu Ubaidah. Eventually the two brought back between $80,000 and $100,000 in cash for Project Bosnia.[54]

On another occasion, Rashid attempted to travel to Bosnia himself. He was assisted in this task by an American Muslim he had met through Tahir. They made it as far as Zagreb but were turned away at the border.[55]

Although Project Bosnia was still nominally focused on Bosnia, Siddig's Day of Terror was increasingly the fixation of Rashid's battalion of trainees. Siddig broached the idea of bombing the tunnels to selected members of the Pennsylvania team—and to Rashid.

There is some ambiguity about Rashid's response to Siddig's overtures. In conversations taped by the FBI, he seemed to equivocate about hitting American targets. During a May 30, 1993, conversation in which Siddig was asking for detonators and other supplies, Rashid replied,

> If it's not used for jihad, *akie* [brother], so I got, I got blockbusters and mortar rockets and a few others. Your doing it, it has to be for jihad, *akie*. It has to be used for the widows and children (unintelligible words) and in Zagreb and Bosnia and stuff like that.

This exchange took place a few short weeks before the Day of Terror arrests. Later, Rashid specified that he was going to talk to "the head man from Project Bosnia"—Bilal Philips—about getting money, but that Philips was interested only in jihad outside of America.

When pressed by Siddig, Rashid agreed to obtain the detonators, but there is no clear evidence that he followed up with action. Rashid's lawyer, interviewed in 2008, said Rashid was "bullshitting" Siddig in the hopes that this plan, like so many before it, would simply fall by the wayside.[56]

"[Rashid's] passion was jihad, but overseas," recalled Tom Corrigan. "And even in his phone conversations with people, if there were events that occurred over in Bosnia that he was very upset about, he would get almost weepy. He'd get very angry with what was going on over there."[57]

Yet it's also quite clear from the transcript of the conversation that Rashid understood that Siddig was talking about setting off bombs in New York as an act of jihad. Rashid's objections to the plan were pretty mild in comparison to the magnitude of the crime Siddig was planning, and, needless to say, he didn't alert the police about a mass homicide in the making.

However, he did call Bilal Philips. As Philips told the story, Rashid called him and said the trainees were talking about doing jihad in the United States. (Philips blamed an FBI informant, Emad Salem, for inciting the group to violence, but this claim is not supported by surveillance tapes and testimony about the case.) As Philips recalled the conversation:

> When, uh, Doc [short for Doctor Rashid] heard about it, you know, he was quite upset. He wanted to stop it, told them, "Don't do it, this is not good," and so on so on. And Doc called me up, and told me about it and I told him, "Yes, definitely, you know, disband this group and get them out of there. Let them go to some other country or whatever."
>
> You know, I said, send them anywhere there is some other conflict or where Muslims are suffering, if they wanted to go and do something, this is where they should do it, in the areas of conflict not in, you know, in the United States. It was just totally inappropriate. It becomes, some kind of, you know, terrorism really, you know, unleashing violence against civilian population. It's not acceptable.[58]

One front in particular looked promising: the Philippines. In May, Philips and Rashid flew to the Philippines, where Muslim separatists were fighting the government in the south of the country. There, they met with Mohammed Jamal Khalifa, a Saudi businessman and a volunteer with the Muslim World League. Khalifa was also the brother-in-law of Osama bin Laden, and U.S. intelligence later believed he was an al Qaeda financier with connections to Ramzi Yousef.

Philips assumed that Khalifa could use his connections to businesses and Muslim relief efforts in the south to arrange an introduction with the separatists. According to both Philips and Rashid, the meeting didn't take place. The visit was intended to give Rashid a feel for the location, and a subsequent trip was planned to advance the project.[59]

In one respect, at least, the trip was a smashing success. Rashid was enamored of the separatists and thought that the spirit of jihad was alive and well in Mindanao. It didn't hurt that he had met a young Filipino woman whom he began to court as a second wife (to the great annoyance of the wife he already had in Brooklyn).

When Rashid returned to the States, he waxed on about the trip and the worthiness of the separatists' cause. After hearing Rashid's stories, Siddig Ali was moved. He would indeed be interested in relocating his jihad to the Philippines—just as soon as he was finished with his jihad against New York.[60]

In June Siddig finalized the list of targets and began to purchase components for his bombs. Financing came from Mohammed Saleh, a Hamas associate, and not from the Project Bosnia bankroll (although the team's members had been trained on TWRA's dime). Siddig told his coconspirators that they would all escape to the Philippines after the bombs went off.

The team rented a safe house in Queens so that they could start to build the bombs—at which point the plan fell apart.

The JTTF had been watching Siddig and Rashid for months, but after the World Trade Center bombing, the Justice Department decided Corrigan and his team deserved the resources they had been asking for all along. The surveillance was stepped up dramatically, and the investigators were given permission to reactivate Emad Salem, a strong informant whom the FBI had unwisely fired the year before. Salem taped nearly every conversation he had with Siddig. He joined the conspiracy and was given the job of finding a safe house—which the FBI then wired for video.[61]

On June 14 Rashid, Siddig, and Salem met to discuss their plans. Rashid was asked about his perennially delayed efforts to obtain detonators and other supplies Siddig needed to complete his preparations. Rashid assured them that he was working on it and then said he was leaving for the Philippines at the end of the week. On hearing this, the authorities decided to move in.[62]

On the evening of June 24, they burst into the safe house and arrested eight people inside, including Siddig, in the act of building their bombs.

Rashid wasn't at the safe house, but he was arrested at his home the same night. His wife, Alia, was out of town when it came down. She returned to New York and visited Rashid in prison. On the ride back, she found herself in a car with Siddig Ali's wife, Shema. It was the first time the two had met.

"My husband told me if anything happened, there's a righteous brother out there, you know, call him," said Shema.

"What's the brother's name?" Alia asked.

"Rashid."

"Well," Alia replied, "the righteous brother's in jail, so how can you call him?"

A number of people escaped prosecution, for various reasons. Bilal Philips had left the country but was named by prosecutors as an unindicted coconspirator (for which he blames Emad Salem). Today he lives in Qatar, where he works in Islamic education. Some years after the events in New York, he gave his view about the United States during a 2003 interview:

> The United States considers any serious Islamic action as contrary to its cultural principles. I am one of those who believe that the clash of civilizations is a reality. So I say that western culture led by the United States is enemy of Islam, as it seeks to oblige the Islamic culture to accept its secular system.[63]

In a 2010 interview with the author, he did not back down from this view, although he phrased the premise in slightly softer terms:

> [The] secular outlook on life, is completely, completely opposite to the *shariah* perspective, where everything is looked at from the perspective of God and the law of God. [. . .] So that obviously is a foundational clash. It's a clash of concepts. I'm not necessarily saying it has to be a military clash, but it's a clash of concepts, right? And then the issue of democracy, you know, where the fundamental concept of human beings making laws for the whole society, in all aspects, [is] again in conflict with the *shariah* perspective, where that is the role of God.[64]

One person who slipped through the cracks was former marine gunnery sergeant Qaseem Uqdah, the head of the Muslim Military Members organization, who provided Philips and al Qaeda member Tahir with information about Muslim soldiers who could be recruited for the Bosnia project.

During his trial Rashid used a false name when testifying about "the marine sergeant," and JTTF investigators never learned the marine's name. The CIA had spotted Rashid and Philips together. After sneaking a look at documents carried by Philips on an international trip, they pegged him as someone who had an interest in infiltrating the U.S. military, but Uqdah never came to their attention.[65]

Uqdah was subsequently hired by Abdurrahman Alamoudi's American Muslim Council (AMC) to head outreach to Muslims in the military, an operation that later spun off into its own organization, the American Muslim Armed Forces and Veterans Affairs Council (AMAFVAC).

In his capacity with AMC and later with AMAFVAC, Uqdah was responsible for selecting, training, and certifying Muslim chaplains for the U.S. military. The chaplaincy program was created in large part thanks to Philips's success in converting soldiers during the Gulf War. Uqdah continues to be involved with the certification of Muslim military chaplains to this day.[66]

I began trying to reach Uqdah for comment on the Bosnia program in May 2009. I followed up with periodic e-mails through 2010 describing the general nature of my questions and my contacts with Rashid and Philips. While writing this book, I also began trying to reach him by phone. Calls to his office were met with a busy signal; calls to his cell phone went directly to voicemail; calls to his home went unanswered.

Finally, in November 2010, I placed a call to Uqdah from a Washington, D.C., phone number, which I had not provided to him in my e-mails. This time, I got through.

We spoke for about ten minutes. Uqdah informed me he had received my previous messages and that he was dealing with serious health issues. He said he was focused on his family and his health and would not comment on anything for the book or clarify his role in the Bosnia recruitment program.

"Whatever you're going to print, you're going to print," he said. "As long as it's the truth, we're good." He refused to answer any question that related to the program or his actions.

TRANSFERENCE AND THE FAR ENEMY

Aside from its obvious ambition, there are a number of interesting features in the Day of Terror plot and its relation to the war in Bosnia. Without the Bosnian cause to draw the participants together, the plot would likely have failed to gain critical mass. And although I was unable to find evidence that the Third World Relief Agency funded the bombing plot directly, it did finance the activities that brought most of the conspirators together.

The majority of the participants were drawn into the plot on the pretext that they were training to fight on behalf of the Bosnians, whether as trainers, mujahideen fighting abroad, or support workers in the United States. Sometimes this pretext was extraordinarily thin. At other times, it was incredibly intense. But nearly every one of the nine people prosecuted in the Day of Terror attacks (not counting Nosair and Rahman) claimed that they got involved in the plot because of Bosnia.

Of course, most of them also claimed they had not done things they were caught on tape doing. To this day, Abdullah Rashid denies he committed the acts for which he was convicted. In an e-mail sent from prison in 2009, he insisted that the FBI had admitted he was not guilty of the crimes for which he was imprisoned.[67]

Nevertheless, wiretaps and surveillance logs clearly back up the conspirators' universal claim that they originally became involved in the plot because they thought they were doing something on behalf of Bosnia. The leaders of the cell fixated on Bosnia and endlessly discussed what they could do to help the Bosnian Muslims.

From a May 30, 1993, audio recording:

> HAMPTON-EL: All those powers of [infidels] being aided by people like, Mubarak, Hussain, Khomeini, Assad et cetera, et cetera, um. What's happening now, *akie* [Arabic for "brother"], is that here in America, the government story in the news media to justify to their physical attack on Muslims [inaudible]. In fact the people of the world who don't really give a damn what's going on in Bosnia, will say [inaudible] a Muslim [inaudible] because the people in Bosnia—
>
> SIDDIG ALI: Massacred.
>
> HAMPTON-EL: *Hamdillah* [praise Allah], I mean massacred and the world has not cried out with outrage. You know, we'll keep talking. Ah, the Muslims of America, at that time coming [they will] need preparation, very few of them are.

Similarly, Siddig, in a lecture where he appeared after Saffet Catovic, berated the audience for passively sitting by while Muslims were dying.[68]

With their passions inflamed, the participants in the Day of Terror plot took incremental steps in the direction of violence—first buying weapons, then training, then buying more weapons, then stockpiling ammunition, and finally purchasing the components for bombs.

Equally incremental was the change in intent, from waging jihad in Bosnia to waging jihad in New York in the name of Bosnia. In the language of jihadist theology, this change in focus is known as the "near enemy" versus the "far enemy," a concept championed by Al Qaeda's second-in-command, Ayman Al Zawahiri.[69]

Near and far in this context refer to the distance from the offending behavior. For Bosnia, the near enemy was the Serbs; the far enemy was the United States, whose policies (in Siddig's worldview) were enabling the Serbs to carry out their atrocities.

The distinction between fighting the near and far enemies is useful in distinguishing between jihadism and terrorism, at least during this period. Jihadists often tend to work in a gray area of morality, fighting battles that are to some degree justifiable against targets seen as directly persecuting Muslims—in other words, the Serbs. In contrast, terrorists often aim for the symbolic target, those they see as supporters or even just passive enablers. However, the recent wars in Iraq and Afghanistan have blurred the distinction between the two classes of combat, perhaps irretrievably, as terrorist tactics and the intentional targeting of civilians have become part and parcel of the jihadist-insurgent handbook.

It's unlikely that either Siddig or his disciples had a deep-enough grasp on jihadist theology to understand the distinction between near and far. Siddig was parroting themes he had heard from Rahman and Nosair. For instance, in January 1993 Rahman gave an incendiary speech at a conference on "Solidarity with Bosnia-Herzegovina," in which he directly tackled the "far enemy" and specifically erased any distinction between jihadist and terrorist:

> The Western mass media is accusing those who perform jihad for the sake of God of being terrorists. And when we defend ourselves saying "No, we are not terrorists, we are far away from terrorism." As if we are standing in the cage of the accused persons and our enemy is accusing us because we are trying to defend our religion. And we defend ourselves against what we are accused of. And this is a bad way that we are putting ourselves in the cage of the accused persons.
>
> We are defending ourselves and refuting the accusations. No, if those who have the right to have something are terrorists, then we are terrorists. And we welcome being terrorists. And we do not deny this charge to ourselves. . . .

> There are two main enemies. The enemy who is at the foremost of the work against Islam are America and the allies. Who is assisting the Serbs? And who is providing them with weapons and food? Europe and behind it is America, who are providing them with weapons, money and food, in order to completely exterminate the Muslims, and because they declared that they do not want the establishment of an Islamic republic in Europe.[70]

Chris Voss, an FBI agent who worked on the case, feels strongly that Siddig was a terrorist first and a jihadist second, who knowingly used manipulative tactics to win over people whose intentions might have been good in the beginning. His observations are important to understanding the process by which American Muslim terrorists are born.

> Siddig and the others that were recruiting knew that if you could recruit someone to go and fight in Bosnia or any other place in the world, you got an individual to agree to engage in battle. So at that point, it's a much smaller step to simply change the battlefield. And that was Siddig's intention. It might not have been the person that was being recruited, it may have not been their intention when they were starting out, and sort of by definition these people in many ways walked into this very unwilling.
>
> If you're a Muslim and you see Muslims being exterminated in another country, you can't help wanting to do something about it, in some fashion or another. Anybody, if you identify strongly with a religious group or your ethnicity, if they are being exterminated someplace else, if there is massively unjust bloodshed going on, it might be easy to manipulate you into, maybe you donate, maybe you feel strongly enough that you want to go and fight. And if you're willing to train, that might have been your intention all along, but the recruiter is thinking something else, they've got their own agenda.[71]

Beyond the ideological currents and the manipulation lies a simpler, more human dynamic that merits consideration.

At the start, Siddig's jihadist volunteers were pumped up with anger, their heads filled with heroic fantasies of traveling to strange lands to rescue fellow Muslims.

Then the training began, which made the prospect seem more tangible and grounded in the real world. Training could take place only on weekends because they had to work. Wives and families complained about their frequent absences. The training was difficult—even within Project Bosnia's relatively short span, about 75 percent of the recruits washed out.

They found themselves penned in by more and more obstacles: the cost of travel, the language barrier, fear, inertia, sickness, family obligations, and other factors beyond their control. Some—like Rashid—managed to overcome all of these hindrances, only to be stopped at the final stage of a difficult border crossing.

And so their romantic dream failed—but they were still angry. Because every day the news brought reports of yet another massacre, and every Friday, the imam was still talking about Bosnia.

And the "far enemy" began to look like the realistic enemy. The enemy next door.

5
Rebuilding the Network

After the twin disasters of the World Trade Center bombing and the subsequent Day of Terror plot, the Al Kifah Center in New York was, for all intents and purposes, finished. But the jihad was heating up, especially in Bosnia, where Western media reporting meshed with the rhetoric of Muslim speakers to create a sense of urgent and growing outrage.

Omar Abdel Rahman had welded his Islamic Group to the Al Kifah brand, and the combined operation dwarfed the remaining handful of independent jihad recruiters. His spectacular fall left the direction of the entire American movement up in the air. As the hammer of federal law enforcement smashed down on Brooklyn, the movement dispersed to satellite centers around the country.

Al Kifah's office in Boston, established in the early 1990s, emerged from the World Trade Center debacle relatively unscathed. Little more than two weeks after the bombing, the head of the Boston office, Emad Muntasser, changed the name of the Boston office from Al Kifah to CARE International.[1]

Positioning itself as a nonpolitical charity (at least as far as non-Muslims were concerned), CARE applied for and received a tax exemption from the IRS, but its operations continued as before—supporting jihad overseas with money and men.[2]

Al Kifah's Boston operation was leaner and more focused than the Brooklyn office had been. Largely absent were the power struggles and the intrigues, and absent, too, were the angry young men hatching plots to kill Americans on American soil. Jihadists passing through Boston were more likely to be focused on conflicts overseas.

One example was Layth Abu Al Layth, a Moroccan who had moved to the United States in 1990. While working at a Dunkin' Donuts in the Boston area, he met other local jihadists who inspired him to join the Afghan mujahideen in 1991. Given the timing, that likely meant training with al Qaeda. Abu Layth trained at the camps, then entered combat to "purify" Afghanistan of any lingering non-Islamic influences. In February 1993 he was killed in battle when he stepped on a land mine.[3]

The main recruiting tool for the Boston office was a newsletter called *Al Hussam*, which translated as "The Sword." Published in both English and Arabic, the newsletter was stuffed with short, informative news items from various fronts in the global jihad. Bosnia, the most active theater, took up most of the ink, but updates also flowed in from Chechnya, Afghanistan, Algeria, Egypt, and elsewhere. The authors tried, with less success, to whip up support for Islamic revolts in Saudi Arabia and Libya.

The issues were filled out with short articles written by local jihad supporters and the occasional reprint of classic tracts by Abdullah Azzam and other jihadist luminaries. The articles urged Americans, in no uncertain terms, to take up the banner of jihad.

Al Hussam's publication was the next rung in an evolution of tone from the early days of American jihadists. Although the newsletter still occasionally celebrated the "miracles" that Abdullah Azzam had leveraged so effectively, the thrust was more abstractly religious than some of its predecessors, quoting chapter and verse from the Koran and *hadith* (stories of the life of Mohammed) and waxing on about the need for Islamic solidarity and its attendant religious obligations.[4]

In part, this was a function of the end of the Soviet war, which was a clearer case of enemy aggression, where the lure of adventure often made complex ideological concepts unnecessary. The end of the Soviet occupation had not ended the need for jihad, the newsletter explained. "There are still many solutions to problems in the hands of those who are not playing the roles they should."[5] Jihad was not just a boy's adventure anymore. It was, the newsletter trumpeted, an absolute imperative and an individual obligation for every Muslim.

> It is no longer a secret to Muslims on earth that they are struck repeatedly everywhere: their scholars are crushed and dispersed, their morals are tram-

> pled. Wherever the Muslims show military force or action, the infidels move and antagonistic camps are set up against Muslims warning and threatening, promising and pledging, foaming and frothing, then striking and destroying.[6]

The newsletter was sometimes frighteningly reductive in its view of the primacy of jihad over any other imaginable activity. One article, citing accounts of the Prophet's companions, argued,

> [Y]ou find that the first thing mentioned is "He took part in all of the attacks." It does not say "He gave a hundred speeches" or that "he wrote such and such a book," or "he had a lot of money." It says "He took part in all of the attacks." This is the greatest virtue, excellence, or merit of the friends of the Messenger. The value of someone in Islam is measured by the "number of battles he took part in."
>
> Today when they write about our dead, what do they say? Do they mention how many attacks they took part in? No. If they are truthful they will write "This famous scientist, this matchless preacher did not shoot one bullet for Allah's cause in all of his life."[7]

The authors of *Al Hussam* fired back at Muslim critics in the United States who were under increasing pressure to renounce jihad, which in the minds of most Americans had now become inextricably linked to terrorism. During the mid-1990s, a movement began among more mainstream American Muslim leaders to redefine jihad, at least for non-Muslim audiences.

The greatest jihad, they argued, was resisting temptation within oneself. These gestures toward moderation were a growing problem for *Al Hussam*; mosques were starting to ban the newsletter because of its extremist views.[8] One of *Al Hussam*'s leading voices, a writer using the pen name Abu Zubair, had little use for such semantics.

> Some are amazed when they hear that self-jihad is less than other jihads, or that jihad for the sake of Allah is less than other jihads or obedience. Yet, if we look at those people's lives, inquire about their history, and ask about the secret of the discrepancy we will find that the explanation of their stand is easy.

> When you follow the lives of those who belittle jihad and instead of fighting and martyrdom they give university lectures, write in magazines or give speeches about fighting and martyrdom in conferences; you will find a common denominator which combines them by reason and unites them in sickness. The common denominator among the discouraging and the refusing—those who have those opinions and theories—is that they did not take part in jihad. There were no opportunities for them, and they were not as lucky to join the military camps of the mujahideen. At those camps luxuries are not available, necessities are few, and they feel the difference between a day in the camp and the day in the university, with air-conditioned classes, restaurants, and playfields.
>
> They did not enter the battle fronts nor did they join the war arenas. One battle which the person takes part in would correct all notions. In few hours, a soldier could see what would turn him gray in bombs and shrapnel, snatching the souls of his best friends, those who traveled with him, trained with him, and went to jihad with him. Those with missiles and explosives detonate over them and they see with their own eyes from down below: hands, feet, and stomachs flying. Then those members with sound, symmetrical bodies end up one-eyed, one legged, one armed or paralyzed. This is the secret of doubt and the abode of sickness. In just few hours or days the Mujahid sees what others will not see in decades: hardship, difficulty, and pain. Those who see these hardships of jihad find it impossible to compare personal jihad to other peaceful calls. So those who enter the issue of jihad, or who want to tell others to quit fighting, should join a camp at least as a janitor, or take part in a battle at least as a cook, and then we will see if the pen is equal to the Kalashnikov for him.[9]

Even though it ventured into deeper intellectual waters at times, *Al Hussam* played all of the classic cards of jihadist incitement, including lurid tales of atrocities and rape. One mailing suggested that readers tell their children tales of the slaughter of Albanian Muslims as a bedtime story—"The evil people killed many Muslim youths, and harassed many women. Even domesticated animals did not escape their savagery." Children who were too young to fight could donate part of their allowance to jihad, the newsletter suggested.[10]

A favorite ploy of *Al Hussam*'s editors was to publish letters purportedly written by jihadists in between battles abroad. These letters combined appreciation for the meaningful nature of jihad with accounts of offenses against Muslims and repudiations of those who did not choose to fight. One letter from a mujahid to his mother (a popular subgenre of jihadist literature) was especially colorful:

> Dear Mother: Remember me with every fragment which the enemies of Allah rip out of the body of this ummah. Remember me with every resounding scream uttered by a pure Muslim woman in the land of Jerusalem, or Chechnya. Remember me with every whip which cracks down on the back of a monotheist in the prisons of the oppressors and tyrants. And, remember me with every victory the Islamic revival achieves, and with every cry of "Allahu Akbar" which is given to shake the earth beneath the feet of the oppressors.[11]

Other articles told the tale of American jihadists in the third person:

> He was seared by the horrifying pictures reaching us from all over. Sleep was driven out of his eyes by the reports of Muslim women's chastity being violated at the hands of the Crusader criminals. His heart was rent by the sight of a Bosnian child slaughtered before his parents, while the whole world looked on apathetically. [He realized] that there could not be a life in this country, for his life could only be lived in the land of jihad. [. . .]
>
> Thus, he packed his suitcases and left, never to return, at a time when the world was starting to turn toward him—he was receiving job offers and marriage proposals from all over. He was well-known for having great respect for his mother, but the call to jihad was stronger, and the screams of the Muslim women were louder to his ears than the words of all seeking to hold him back.[12]

The absolutism of the newsletter belied battles behind the scenes. As in New York, the Boston leadership—about thirty people who had a greater or lesser voice in the office's direction—was divided about the course of jihad in the wake of the Soviet defeat. The argument continued long after the dust of the last departing Soviet tank had settled.

As in Brooklyn and Afghanistan, the question on the table was whether to continue building an Islamic state in Afghanistan or to take jihad to the rest of the world. The top leadership of the Boston office had sworn loyalty to Gulbuddin Hekmatyar, an Afghan warlord who was now working closely with Osama bin Laden. The leaders had reservations about bin Laden, but more and more of them wanted to take the fight to new fronts.[13]

The outbreak of the war in Bosnia helped edge the undecided toward global jihad. The highly visible atrocities provided an easy hook for recruiting and fund-raising—in some ways even easier than Afghanistan, although the secular proclivities of Bosnian Muslims blunted some of the enthusiasm of the hard-core Islamists. Propaganda videos explained that the mujahideen had to "correct" the Bosnian practice of Islam before fighting could begin. E-mails from CARE's allies complained that "large sums of money were being sent from various 'Jihad' funds to Bosnian, wine-drinking, womanizing, communist 'Mujahideen.'"[14]

The sums were indeed large. Checks flowed into CARE International from individual donors, sometimes only $10 or $50, with the words "mujahideen of Bosnia" or "martyr's family" scrawled in the memo line. Sometimes individual donations ran into the thousands.[15]

Once deposited with CARE, the money was often laundered through other fraudulent charities, including the Benevolence International Foundation and the Global Relief Foundation, both in Chicago, and to front organizations in Bosnia and Chechnya. In total, hundreds of thousands of dollars passed through CARE for distribution to jihadists and jihad-support organizations overseas.[16]

CARE was wired into a national network that included jihadist organizations in Texas, New Jersey, Florida, Louisiana, Michigan, and Illinois. Working individually and sometimes in concert, this more diffuse conglomeration of groups continued the work of the original Al Kifah but also helped it evolve into new forms.

Most of the new breed positioned themselves as nonprofit charities, rather than political organizations, which would eventually provide the basis for prosecuting them after September 11. CARE was ultimately brought down on tax charges rather than for its promotion of jihad, as Aloke Chakravarty, the federal prosecutor who handled the case, explained to me:

> It's not the U.S. government's role to ever persecute somebody for what they believe. Our case really has been a testament to the fact that it's not what you

> believe or what you say that should ever result in some kind of culpability. This is all about freedom of expression. However, in our case, you don't have a right to be subsidized to engage in your beliefs. And in our case, CARE International is one of many similar types of organizations that had obtained a tax exemption, so that U.S. taxpayers were actually funding them.[17]

One of CARE's closest alliances was with the American Islamic Group (AIG), the official U.S. chapter of Omar Abdel Rahman's Gamaat Islamiyyah. AIG was founded by Mohammed Zaki, the red-headed Egyptian who had saved the leg of Brooklyn mujahid Abdullah Rashid after he stepped on a land mine in Afghanistan.

Zaki inspired fierce loyalty in those he met. One of his comrades described him as "a man whose like is rare nowadays," telling a colleague that "you will be amazed by him."[18]

After relocating from Brooklyn to San Diego, Zaki created AIG, along with a number of so-called charities that actually helped finance and supply the mujahideen in Bosnia and Chechnya, including the Islamic Information Center of the Americans and American World Wide Relief, also known as Save Bosnia Now. The first organization focused on fund-raising and propaganda; the latter helped fly mujahideen—including al Qaeda operative and naturalized American citizen Hisham Diab—from the United States to Bosnia so they could take part in fighting.[19]

Zaki traveled back and forth to Boston to take part in Al Kifah events and fire up crowds with his charisma and tough talk. At one point, Muntasser asked him to fly to Boston "because we are looking for a brother who knows about matters [in Bosnia] to give an inciting speech."[20]

But unlike some of his peers, Zaki wasn't only talk. In 1993 and 1994 Zaki traveled to Bosnia, where he fought alongside the mujahideen, becoming well-known as "Abu Umar the American." He also made videotapes of the mujahideen camps, which he took back to the United States to use for fund-raising. In early 1995 he departed for Chechnya, telling a friend, "I hope that I will be granted martyrdom this time."[21]

That wish was granted in May 1995. According to his comrades, Zaki was discussing the Koran with his fellow fighters when the class was shelled by the

Russians. Zaki was the only casualty. Struck by shrapnel, he lingered briefly before dying. On his deathbed, he said that he had seen the virgins of paradise promised to jihadist martyrs, and "they told me I would follow them." His supporters back in the United States took up collections for his family, a wife and four children left behind in San Diego.[22]

ISA AND ISMAIL: A STUDY IN CONTRASTS

Despite the best efforts of *Al Hussam* to drum up interest in Chechnya, relatively few Americans joined Zaki on the Russian front. Many more were attracted to Bosnia, where a significant number of Americans joined the jihad.

In many cases, details are sketchy. A Caucasian American named Abu Mansour was sighted by a few Bosnian mujahideen, one of whom said that he hailed from the Virginia area. Two African Americans named Abu Khalid and Abu Aysha were also seen. The former was killed fighting the Serbs; the latter came late to the conflict and didn't stay long. An American named Abu Musa had come to Bosnia as part of Bilal Philips's recruitment program and stayed until at least 1993, taking part in raids in Serbian territory.[23]

One who stayed was an African American named Clevin Holt, who became a bit of a legend in intelligence circles. In 2010 Holt was spotlighted in *American Jihadist*, a riveting documentary by journalists Mark Claywell and Jody Jenkins, who spent years researching Holt's story and captured hours of interviews with the fighter himself.

Raised in a Washington, D.C., household tense with chaos and abuse, Holt joined the U.S. Army as an underage teenager to fight in Vietnam but was eventually forced out after becoming involved in a race riot on an army base; his true age was revealed during the investigation.

Full of anger and despair, Holt returned to Washington. He considered going on a killing spree, then turned his gun on himself, he told Claywell and Jenkins. Yet before he could pull the trigger, Holt said, he saw a vision of an angel, which caught him up short. Three days later he met an African American Muslim convert who introduced him to Islam. Holt converted, changing his name to Isa Abdullah Ali; he aligned himself with Shi'a Islam and joined an American Islamic group sponsored by the Iranian intelligence service. As he related the change in *American Jihadist*,

> I was greatly influenced by the words of Ayatollah Khomeini. A lot of what he said in the past, matched everything that I ever thought, ever felt, and even some of the things I would verbalize. In my learning experience through Islam, the answers started becoming more and more clear.[24]

Although his angel had stopped him from embarking on a campaign of indiscriminate killing, Ali felt that his military training was all that he had in the world. He left to fight in Afghanistan for one month in 1980, making him one of the very first true American jihadists—Ali arrived on the scene before virtually any other foreign fighters, let alone Americans.[25]

Soon after that, he joined the Shi'ite Amal Militia in Lebanon, where he fought during the civil war, earning another rare distinction—American mujahideen have almost never fought Israelis directly. He came to Lebanon strapped for war and packing ordinance, including military-grade explosives. In Lebanon he trained Hezbollah and Amal fighters (even women) and took part in combat, killing at least nine Israelis by his own account.[26]

"When advice is needed, I give it. When it's not, I'm a sniper," Ali told the *Washington Post* in 1982. During the same interview, he described his wish to see death in battle:

> I'm quite sure that sooner or later I'm going to get killed. Where the end is only my God knows. When the Iranians reach [Jerusalem], I ask my God to give me martyrdom. Once Palestine is free, I have no desire to stay in this life any longer.[27]

Ali considered himself a "professional soldier of Islam" who was trying to achieve martyrdom, but he was too good at the former to accomplish the latter. In *American Jihadist*, he remembered:

> I started talking to the angel of death. And I told him, straight up, look, you need to get inside of me. You know, and take all these human characteristics away from me . . . I actually stopped counting in 1981. I stopped counting the number of the persons I had killed. I had stopped at that time at 173. There are countless numbers that I don't even know, to this day.

"He was special. He had high training skills," said Hamzah akl Hamieh, a military leader of the Amal Militia at the time. "He put makeup on his face for an undercover operation. All of this attracted the guys. He was that violent phenomena for them. And he trained a lot of them."[28]

In 1983, Ali was spotted outside a U.S. Marines barracks in Beirut, not long before the installation was bombed by militants believed to be connected to Hezbollah. At 6'3" and 250 pounds, with a shaved head and decked out in full combat gear, he was hard to miss. Yet he was never charged or directly accused in the attack. Soon afterward, dismayed by the growing presence of terrorist tactics in Lebanon's Shi'ite factions, Ali broke with the groups, which resulted in an assassination attempt that he barely survived.

He returned to the United States but found little satisfaction in ordinary life. In the mid-1990s, he was taken by media reports about atrocities against Muslims in Bosnia.

> I heard a television interview with [Karadzic], a Bosnian Serb political official. And the thing was that he made a statement that during the time of war here that he was doing Europe a favor by ridding Europe of the Islamic presence. As a result of that, I began to think, OK, here I am sitting in Washington, D.C., and this man is making that statement. And I said, well, I'm going to be fortunate that I can be sitting here. And had I been sitting in Bosnia at this moment probably more likely I would be one amongst many who would suffer these various types of problems in Islam.[29]

In Bosnia, he joined the 7th Muslim Corps, a unit of mujahideen, bringing a host of military hardware and his long experience as a soldier to the conflict. After the war, he married a Bosnian woman who had served in the regular Bosnian army.

When asked to explain his motives for taking part in jihadist causes, Ali sounded like many other jihadists of the 1980s and 1990s. He said he was motivated by a desire to help other Muslims who were being oppressed and victimized.

> In Islam, there's a saying. We are like one body. And when one part of the body hurts, the rest of the body's going to feel the pain. So that's what happened to me. I felt the pain. [. . .]

> The highest level of faith is when you see a wrong being committed, that you stop it with your presence, with your hands. The second level is to speak out against it with your words. The lowest degree of faith is to hate it in your heart and continue about your way. [. . .]
>
> I kill only when it's necessary. And the rest of the world is standing by, you know, giving lip service and no action, and I see that it is necessary for me to commit myself to such a time and a place, I'll go and help those people, whoever they may be.[30]

Ali's story was, in many ways, atypical. Relatively few Americans came to jihad through Shi'a Islam. Ali had joined the fight long before most Americans and even before many Arabs. On the face of it, his justifications were compelling. On Bosnia, for instance, he insisted,

> I'm not a terrorist, I'm not an aggressor, I'm not a war junkie. I didn't think I was coming here like the savior of the world. I just wanted to be part of what was taking place here, and to show that they were not alone. And for them to know that they weren't forgotten.[31]

In other comments, however, it seemed as if his inner demons may ultimately have driven him more than ideology. Ali's account of a sniper attack in Lebanon was chilling:

> I saw this guy coming down the road. And first I sighted in on him. And I'm looking at him, and I can see on his epaulet that he's an officer. So then I followed this guy, and then suddenly I just started think, I said, wow, this guy looks like he's a family man. And I'm sure he has a mother and a father. Wife and children. And then I said, they're gonna miss him. And I just said, "fuck it," and I put that lead on him, and pow, that was it. I didn't feel anything except the recoil from my rifle.[32]

Watching Ali speak in *American Jihadist*, one gets the impression that he sees himself fundamentally as a killer and that Islam provided a framework for him to indulge that impulse in a way that he viewed as morally acceptable. "I felt like I was part of death," he said at one point. "It was a serious drug. It was a serious 'get high' situation."

Despite his jihadist path, Ali did not adopt the typical life of a strict Islamic fundamentalist. He is a Muslim in the Bosnian mold: he smokes, curses, and dresses like an American. Unlike Mohammed Zaki, who longed for the maidens of paradise as he lay dying, Ali speaks of leaving this life in weary, nihilistic terms. During the assassination attempt in Lebanon, he was clinically dead at the hospital before medical workers revived him.

> That was like a really beautiful, peaceful moment. Being between this life and that life, and then you're seeing into eternity, and that was like one of the most peaceful moments I have ever seen. There, all the madness, all the insanity of what I had seen over the years and even before [going to Lebanon], I knew that I was going to be free from this life. But that wasn't the plan of the creator. . . . As far as death, or anything is concerned, I welcome that. Because this life is shit. To me. Maybe not to everybody else, but to me it is.[33]

For many reasons Isa Ali was an exceptional case, but his stated justifications fell in line with what other American jihadists were feeling. Whether he was driven by his own experience and a personal rage, in jihad he found a hook on which to hang his darker impulses, perhaps even to redeem them. Ali now lives in Bosnia with his family and travels freely back to the land of his birth. American authorities have no apparent interest in prosecuting him.

As with Afghanistan in the 1980s, the plight of Bosnian Muslims had received a sympathetic hearing from the U.S. media and political establishment. This opened up the pool of recruits to a much wider range of American Muslims, some of whom did not share the rabid anti-Americanism of ideologues such as Omar Abdel Rahman. They saw no conflict between being an American and helping Bosnian Muslims.

One of these relatively mainstream combatants was a young Caucasian convert named Ismail Royer. Born Randy Royer, his American experience couldn't have been more different than that of Isa Ali's, yet Royer too found his way to Bosnia as a combatant and eventually as a resident.

Royer grew up in a stable, loving family. His father was a photographer, his mother a former Roman Catholic nun turned public school teacher. They lived in

St. Louis, where, encouraged by his parents, young Randy grew up with a keen sense of compassion and social awareness. He and his father sometimes volunteered together in homeless shelters.[34]

Randy was a voracious reader whose intense ability to focus seemed to evaporate when it came to schoolwork. "He was very intelligent, very smart," his father Ray recalled. "And unfortunately, he thought he knew more than the teachers. Which is true, he did."[35]

By the time Randy reached college, he had straightened up, majoring in political science and producing a string of As. He especially enjoyed philosophy and music.

After reading the *Autobiography of Malcolm X*, Royer became interested in Islam. He was moved in part by Islam's commitment to social justice and its diversity, which stood in stark contrast to rising racial tensions in the United States at the time. A deciding moment came when he visited a mosque shortly after race riots in Los Angeles (provoked by the beating of Rodney King) grabbed headlines.

> It was me and this guy, who was white, and a guy who was black. And then an Arab and a Pakistani guy came, and we were all there talking. And I was like, "This is amazing. We're all talking. There are no barriers between us." It was really amazing to me how that could be. I just felt something.[36]

Royer began to explore the religion with Muslim friends. He remembered one conversation in a park, where a bird was singing, that marked a turning point in his acceptance of Islam.

> I said, "Wow, that's a very beautiful bird." And he said, "In Islam, that bird is Muslim, because the bird follows God's laws and can do nothing but follow God's laws. And if you see how beautiful and peaceful that bird is, that's the kind of peace that human beings can achieve if they follow God's laws."[37]

At age nineteen he converted, taking the name Ismail, just as the war in Bosnia was beginning. Royer's local mosque was helping resettle refugees from the war, and Ismail volunteered to help. His work with the refugees led him to start following the news coverage. "I was struck by footage of emaciated civilians in Serbian concentration camps and news of rape camps and massacres," Royer recalled.[38]

Information flowing in from both mainstream media reports and Muslim sources also touched on familiar themes that had led many others before him to the fields of jihad—atrocities against Muslims in general and Muslim women in particular.

> I just kept seeing on the news about women in rape camps and pregnant women having their children carved out of their womb and it was really disturbing to me, and I saw that no one was really helping them anywhere in the world.[39]

Stirred to action, he decided he had to act. He told his father he was going to Bosnia.

"I said, 'There's a war going on, Randy. Don't you understand there's a war going on?' And at that point, I thought I better sit down, and relax a bit," his father recalled in a 2008 interview. "And, I figured well, he's old enough to determine what he wanted to do in life."[40]

Although Royer told his father he was going to work with a relief organization, he instead signed up with a unit of mujahideen and spent six weeks in combat. "I engaged in firefights to help repel Serbian forces from villages full of innocent women and children whom they sought to ethnically cleanse," Royer wrote later.[41]

After his stint with the mujahideen, he worked in Sarajevo for a while, where he witnessed an infamous marketplace massacre in February 1994 that was one of the worst atrocities in the war up to that point.[42] It reinforced his commitment to the cause. Royer traveled back and forth to Bosnia several times during and immediately after the war. Like Isa Ali, he eventually married a Bosnian woman before moving back to the United States in the late 1990s.

If Isa Ali is a nihilist, Ismail Royer is a idealist. Yet both cite the same general principles in support of jihadist intervention. In 2002 Royer wrote,

> The only difference between a "political" event and a "personal" event is the difference in scale and geographic proximity to the event. Thus I never understood why if my neighbor or relative is raped, God forbid, it's considered

> a "personal" event, but if many women are raped in Bosnia or Indonesia in the course of a war, it's a "political" event, and therefore I should somehow not be as concerned. Only someone lacking in humanity would make a distinction between two equivalent events that differ only in location.[43]

Yet Royer also presents a far more sanitized version of the jihadist experience. Consider his account of his time with the mujahideen, which depicts the fighters as noble warriors following a strict code of conduct:

> I never witnessed or heard tell of any deliberate killings of civilians by my unit or anyone else in the Bosnian army. In fact, the parent brigade of my unit issued a field manual laying down the rules and ethics of warfare in Islam as provided for in the Koran and words of the Prophet: no harming civilians or clergymen, no targeting of houses of worship, no harming animals or even cutting down trees and crops.
>
> Those I encountered seemed to understand that the only legitimate reason for warfare in Islam is self-defense or removal of oppression. [. . .] Unlike extremists, at no time was I ever motivated by a desire to impose my religion on others, to "kill the infidel," or to battle America or "the West," nor did I hear any such sentiments from my compatriots or superiors in Bosnia.

Royer's account of the Bosnian mujahideen stands in stark contrast to the evidence, including videos and photos produced by the mujahideen themselves during the war. One video shows mujahideen fighters playing soccer with the decapitated head of an executed captive. Photographs show Bosnian members of the mujahideen standing with their boots on a bucket full of decapitated heads, among which was at least one noncombatant. Civilians were also tortured and killed for nonmilitary offenses, such as a Serb who was tortured to death in public for the transgression of marrying a Muslim woman. Royer may not have personally witnessed these events, but it's hard to believe he was totally oblivious to them.[44]

There is also the question of al Qaeda's role in Bosnia. Royer denied in a letter to the author and in other forums that al Qaeda played any role in the war or with the mujahideen—at least, as far as his direct knowledge.

The evidence again stands in contrast. U.S. intelligence and phone calls intercepted by the Bosnian government show communication between the Bosnian mujahideen and al Qaeda commanders, and several individual mujahideen were connected to al Qaeda.[45] In addition, Osama bin Laden sent resources and financially interacted with the Bosnian mujahideen.[46]

Royer has a tendency to dismiss views that conflict with his as uninformed, superficial, dishonest, or a combination of all three. His denials may simply be self-serving, but it is also possible that he did not have direct contact with anyone he knew to be part of al Qaeda.[47]

AL QAEDA IN BOSNIA

The connections between the Bosnian mujahideen and al Qaeda were not widely known at the foot-soldier level, even to insiders with both groups. One former fighter, who was involved with both al Qaeda and the Bosnian mujahideen at different times, told me that "not a single member of al Qaeda at that time joined the fight," although he said that many Bosnian volunteers became affiliated with al Qaeda after the war.[48]

Nevertheless, in addition to Tahir, the American al Qaeda member described in Chapter 4, the record shows that a few active members of al Qaeda did take part in the war.

One of them was Christopher Paul, an African American who converted to Islam, changing his name to "Abdul Malek Kenyatta." Around the end of 1990, Kenyatta traveled to Pakistan seeking to sign up for jihad. He ended up in an al Qaeda guesthouse in Peshawar. He met several members of al Qaeda and eventually attended a training camp in Afghanistan, where he learned to use assault rifles and rocket-propelled grenades and mastered other military techniques. A few months later, he was selected for advanced training in military tactics and the construction of improvised explosives.

As al Qaeda began the process of moving to Sudan in the early 1990s, Kenyatta bristled at the prospect that his time in combat might be coming to an end. After a brief return to the United States, where he trained aspiring Ohio jihadists in martial arts, he flew to Europe and made his way into Bosnia, where he took part in combat. After Bosnia, he continued to work for al Qaeda, training would-be terrorists in Ohio and Germany in bomb making, with the aim of killing Americans at home and abroad. That eventually formed the basis for his prosecution in 2008, which ended with a guilty plea and a twenty-year prison sentence.[49]

Al Qaeda also had financial ties to the war in Bosnia, many of which ran through the United States and involved American citizens. One of the most significant charities providing support to the Bosnian mujahideen was the Benevolence International Foundation.

Spawned from a Pakistan-based organization active at the end of the Soviet jihad, a substantial part of the Benevolence operation was moved to the United States in the early 1990s by Enaam Arnaout, a Syrian who had fought alongside Osama bin Laden and later oversaw logistics for some of al Qaeda's early camps in Afghanistan. Arnaout was joined there by Loay Bayazid, the Kansas City mujahid who had been present at the founding of al Qaeda.[50]

Benevolence had operations in major conflict zones around the world, with a strong focus on Bosnia and Chechnya. Like many charitable organizations linked to terrorism, it really did perform charity work, but a substantial sum of money was reserved for the mujahideen. Benevolence bought uniforms and equipment for fighters in both Bosnia and Chechnya and produced propaganda videos on their behalf.

More important, the charity made travel possible for jihadists, helping at least nine people move from Afghanistan to Bosnia, including senior al Qaeda leaders. Sometimes Benevolence's leadership knew the people and their purpose in traveling, but it wasn't always formal. If someone was known to the charity or came with an introduction, this person would get help, no questions asked, usually in the form of papers stating that the traveler worked for Benevolence, which could then be used to obtain a work visa at the desired destination.[51]

Overseas, Benevolence served as an intelligence hub for al Qaeda, in addition to its other functions. The Benevolence office in Sarajevo archived and digitized a massive collection of al Qaeda documents, including records of the organization's founding and personnel. It also created detailed reports on the activities of the mujahideen and their relationships with one another and with suspected American intelligence agents.[52]

The Sarajevo office's greatest intelligence coup, however, was the cultivation of a high-level mole in the Bosnian government who funneled hundreds of pages of classified documents to al Qaeda through the Benevolence staff. It was a devastating counterintelligence success, collecting detailed logs of phone conversations intercepted by the Bosnian government, reports on the activities of the mujahideen, and even highly classified CIA cables.

One such cable was particularly sensitive: a request from the CIA to Bosnian intelligence for the detention of Anwar Shaban, the commander of the foreign mujahideen who was a senior leader in Omar Abdel Rahman's Islamic Group and had extensive ties to Osama bin Laden and al Qaeda. Shortly after the request was sent, Shaban was mysteriously assassinated.[53]

The Benevolence network was part of the fabric of the American jihadist movement. The CARE International office in Boston used Benevolence to distribute its funds in many cases, along with another Chicago-based charity called the Global Relief Foundation. And both CARE and Benevolence were intertwined with Mohammed Zaki's American Islamic Group.[54]

Zaki's second-in-command was an influential jihadist propagandist named Kifah Jayyousi, a Jordanian of Palestinian descent with an unfortunate tendency to giggle at inappropriate moments. Jayyousi immigrated to the United States in 1979 and became a naturalized American citizen.[55]

Through Jayyousi, the American Islamic Group maintained close ties with CARE in Boston. CARE's directors sponsored speaking tours by Jayyousi to raise funds and recruit fighters for Bosnia and Chechnya. During speeches at Boston University and MIT in 1996, Jayyousi regaled audiences with tales of Russian atrocities against Muslims and showed videotaped battles of the Chechen mujahideen. Tapes of Jayyousi's lectures were also distributed by Muslim Students Association branches around the country.[56]

Like CARE, AIG focused on recruitment and fund-raising for mujahideen overseas. Jayyousi personally recruited fighters in addition to leveraging his speeches, taped lectures, and AIG publications in the service of jihad. The cell also moved thousands of dollars among various other charities that supported the mujahideen, including a Hamas front known as the Holy Land Foundation and mujahideen support organizations functioning in Bosnia, Kosovo, Chechnya, Azerbaijan, Libya, Egypt, and Somalia.

Pretty much any front was all right, one member of the organization commented during a meeting with Zaki and Jayyousi. "As long as there is slaughtering, we're with them. If there's no slaughtering, [. . .] that's it, buzz off."[57]

This bloodthirstiness was typical of AIG, especially after Zaki's death. Unlike CARE, which was more narrowly focused on the guerrilla combat of military jihad, AIG was at times unabashedly supportive of terrorism. Jayyousi published a newsletter known as the *Islam Report*, which was initially filled with details of the terrorism trial of Omar Abdel Rahman. Jayyousi also helped Rahman—now in prison—stay in contact with members of his Egyptian jihadist network overseas. One issue of *Islam Report* described convicted World Trade Center bomber Mahmud Abouhalima as "A Good Citizen and a Muslim Hero."[58]

At one point, Jayyousi reached out to CARE officer Samir Al Monla to ask for financial help to move Abouhalima's family out of the United States. Al Monla, suspicious that his calls were under surveillance, asked Jayyousi to use a false name when referring to Abouhalima, which prompted one of Jayyousi's trademark nervous giggles. Al Monla finally agreed to provide $1,000 toward airfare for Abouhalima's wife and four children and to try to raise funds for the remainder. However, he added, they should tell people that the money was "for helping the poor, or the needy or an orphan [. . .] without mentioning any names at all."[59]

One of Jayyousi's top deputies was an outspoken Palestinian activist named Adham Hassoun. A computer programmer who had moved to the United States in 1989 and illegally overstayed a student visa, Hassoun headed up an early office of the Benevolence Foundation. Soon after, he began to work closely with both CARE in Boston and AIG in San Diego from his home base in the South Florida town of Sunrise.[60]

Hassoun was a prolific jihadist recruiter, constantly working the phones and roaming the community in search of bodies and dollars to support the cause. Like Jayyousi, his definition of jihad was widely inclusive of terrorism and the killing of civilians. When talking to Jayyousi and other members of his jihadist network, Hassoun used simple codes to communicate, assuming (correctly, as it turned out) that the FBI might be listening in. "Terrorism" became "tourism," and military jihad became "football" or "soccer."[61]

Hassoun and Jayyousi helped move thousands of dollars and perhaps dozens of men to jihad fronts in Bosnia and Chechnya. They also worked to establish and financially support an active cell of jihadists in Somalia and neighboring Ethiopia.[62]

Some of their recruits ended up in al Qaeda, which was gearing up to begin its assault against the United States in earnest. The terror network was actively seeking U.S. citizens who were willing to go beyond the concept of defensive jihad and embrace an all-out war against a much broader array of enemies.

JOSE PADILLA

Born Roman Catholic, Jose Padilla grew up on tough streets in Chicago. As a young teenager of Puerto Rican descent, he became involved with a gang known as the Latin Disciples and soon wound up in prison after the kids he was running with pulled off a brutal murder. Worried about his downward trajectory, Padilla's family moved to the Fort Lauderdale area to get away from the gangs, but Padilla's temperament continued to sour, culminating in a 1991 incident in which he pulled a gun on a cop during a routine traffic stop.[63]

That got him ten months in a Florida prison, where he was impressed with Muslim prisoners who were serving time at the same facility. One prisoner in particular, a member of the Nation of Islam, debated with Padilla about Islam. Padilla later described this as the "turning point" of his life. After being put in solitary confinement for fighting, Padilla said he had a vision of himself floating in the air, wearing a black hood and a blue robe. The vision inspired him to learn more about Islam.[64]

After his release, he voraciously pursued information about Islam while working at a Taco Bell in Davie, Florida, near Fort Lauderdale. His inquiries led him to Adham Hassoun.

Padilla soon converted and eventually changed his name to Abdullah Al Muhajir. Although by no means a bright student, he applied himself industriously to studying Islam and learning Arabic. He married a Jamaican immigrant, who also converted, and it seemed—all too briefly—that he had turned his life around. But Padilla embraced his new religion with a passion that frightened those closest to him. His mother told a neighbor that she feared he had joined a cult.[65]

Padilla began to adopt Arab garb and a conservative posture, which stood out as unusual even at the Koran studies classes he took in 1995 and 1996. Going deeper still into his religion, he decided that he wanted to become an imam and arranged to travel to Egypt for further study. The trip was encouraged and financially sponsored by Adham Hassoun, who also helped "psychologically prepare" Padilla for the journey he was about to undertake. Not the journey into Egypt—but the journey to al Qaeda.[66]

Padilla spent a couple of years in Egypt, supposedly honing his language skills but finding time to run errands as a cash courier for Hassoun. While there, he married a second wife, after abandoning his first but before divorcing her.

He soon left his now-pregnant second wife as well. In 2000 he made the hajj pilgrimage to Saudi Arabia, where he met a Yemeni al Qaeda recruiter and was invited to take the history-laden path first to Pakistan, from there into Afghanistan, and finally into the heart of darkness. On July 24, 2000, he filled out an application form to join al Qaeda's Al Farooq training camp in Afghanistan, where he studied religion, surveillance, improvised explosives, and communications.[67]

Padilla and others were assigned to come up with a terrorist attack on U.S. soil by al Qaeda's military commander Mohammed Atef. Padilla approached the job with zeal, discussing various improvised explosive schemes and pie-in-the-sky ideas like spraying cyanide on people at nightclubs.[68]

His enthusiasm often outstripped his ability. At one point, Padilla approached Mohammed with instructions on how to build a nuclear bomb, which he had found on the Internet. The webside was a parody, but Padilla had taken it seriously. Undeterred, he returned to his computer and soon came back with an idea for building a dirty bomb: a conventional bomb combined with radioactive material designed to contaminate the target area.[69]

Finally, in June 2001 Atef decided on a mission. Padilla and his team would rent apartments in high-rises that used natural gas for heat. They would breach the building's gas lines and ignite the fumes to bring the buildings down. Padilla's partner in this assignment was another American al Qaeda member—someone Padilla already knew.[70]

ADNAN SHUKRIJUMAH

Adnan Shukrijumah was born in Saudi Arabia in 1975 and moved to the United States with his family during the 1990s. The clan landed in Brooklyn. His father, Gulshair Shukrijumah, was a Saudi-sponsored imam who spent time at the Al Farook Mosque on Atlantic Avenue, which had been attached to the Al Kifah Center.[71]

The elder Shukrijumah served as a translator for the blind sheikh, Omar Abdel Rahman, and was friends with Abdullah Rashid, the African American mujahid who had lost his leg in Afghanistan. Shukrijumah testified on Rashid's behalf as a character witness.[72]

Padilla had blundered through his American life, cutting a broad swathe for journalists and investigators to navigate. Adnan Shukrijumah was more circumspect, leaving few clues in his wake. The family moved from New York to the suburbs of Fort Lauderdale in 1995.

Working as a used car salesman, Shukrijumah paid his way through Broward Community College, majoring in computer science and chemistry. Although he left little trace of his views, Shukrijumah's mother said he became disgusted by American society, including the use of drugs and alcohol and what he saw as sexual promiscuity, all the while growing angry over U.S. foreign policy in the Muslim world.[73]

Toward the end of the 1990s, while watching events in Bosnia and Chechnya, he became obsessed with the idea that he should be taking part in jihad. He became known at local mosques as a radical. At one point, a local immigrant with more ambition than ability tried to assemble a terrorist cell of area Muslims, inspired by Osama bin Laden. Shukrijumah appears to have been unimpressed with the poser. Instead of signing up for the local scheme (which had already been infiltrated by the FBI), Shukrijumah left in search of the real deal. Investigators later concluded that he had sniffed out the informant.[74]

He made his way to Afghanistan and the training camps of al Qaeda, where he started as a dishwasher, worked his way up the ranks, and eventually received advanced training in weapons, battle tactics, camouflage, and surveillance. He was gifted and was soon given more responsibility. Shukrijumah traveled around the world on still-mysterious al Qaeda business, with sightings in the Middle East, Trinidad, South America, and other locations.

In 2001 Shukrijumah returned to the United States for the last time and took a cross-country trip by train. For an ordinary young American man, such a trip might have been a coming-of-age story. For Shukrijumah, it was reconnaissance.[75]

6
War on America

In 1991, Special Agent John Zent of the FBI's San Francisco field office had what is known in intelligence circles as a walk-in: an area Muslim was volunteering his services as an informant. The field office was interested in investigating a radical Palestinian mosque in nearby Santa Clara, and Zent thought the man might be useful.

He was wrong. The informant instead alerted the subjects of the investigation that the FBI was interested in them. Nevertheless, Zent kept the channel open.[1]

During one conversation in 1993, the would-be informant began to talk more freely. He knew a man named Osama bin Laden, who was building an army under the aegis of an organization called al Qaeda. From his home base in Sudan, bin Laden was thinking about mounting a revolution in Saudi Arabia. The informant said that he had worked for al Qaeda, training Osama bin Laden's men in intelligence tactics and "anti" hijacking techniques.[2]

John Zent had just joined a very exclusive club—American government employees who knew what al Qaeda was, courtesy of Ali Mohamed, Osama bin Laden's master spy, who had recently finished his assignment as a U.S. soldier serving at Fort Bragg. Mohamed had picked the San Francisco field office as the target for his latest effort to infiltrate the FBI. Mohamed's modus operandi was to play both sides of the field, offering real intelligence value in exchange for access. It was a risky play.

A handful of people in the military had heard the phrase "al Qaeda" as early as 1991.[3] The CIA had picked up the name in 1993 in connection with a hotel bombing in Aden, Yemen.[4] But no one was putting the information together yet, and no one would for some years to come.

Al Qaeda, however, had already set its sights on America. Starting in 1991, Osama bin Laden had begun to preach against the United States at the camps in Afghanistan. After the invasion of Iraq, the U.S. military had established a small permanent base in Saudi Arabia. Bin Laden and his deputies started saying that the United States should get out of the Persian Gulf altogether.[5]

Bin Laden said the United States was "the head of the snake," which had to be cut off. Fatwas were issued toward the end of 1992, and the wheels of war were set into motion. The first World Trade Center bombing was arguably the opening shot.

Mohamed was the advance scout. In 1989 he had trained the men who would bomb the World Trade Center. In 1991 he had helped al Qaeda relocate its base of operations from Afghanistan to Sudan. Mohamed had trained al Qaeda's operatives in Afghanistan, and he continued training them in Sudan, overseeing a specialized course for Osama bin Laden's bodyguards.[6]

He wasn't done yet. Mohamed and Wadih El Hage, the American Muslim from Tucson, were the senior American Al Qaeda members with an ongoing presence in the country. Together, they managed a loose network of al Qaeda members and the occasional freelance employee in the United States.

Now based in Sudan, al Qaeda was enjoying the best operating conditions it would ever know. Al Qaeda in the mid-1990s was a corporation. It owned subsidiaries, occupied an office building, and maintained a regular payroll with benefits for its employees.[7]

El Hage served as the company's paymaster and as Osama bin Laden's executive assistant on a day-to-day basis. Al Qaeda owned a number of semi-legitimate businesses in Sudan and elsewhere, including a honey farm, a tannery, and construction and shipping companies.

El Hage managed some of these companies. Traveling around Africa and Europe using his U.S. passport, he also helped al Qaeda members with transportation and lodging, procuring forged passports and providing other assistance. Working with Ali Mohamed, El Hage helped convert some of al Qaeda's assets into diamonds and other precious stones. He also recruited other Americans for a transaction that was particularly important to bin Laden—the purchase of an airplane.[8]

Essam Al Ridi was an Egyptian national who became a U.S. citizen in 1994 after more than a decade of living in the United States. In the early 1980s, he was one of the first Americans to follow Abdullah Azzam's call, fighting in Afghanistan and later working in Pakistan. He met bin Laden and El Hage in Peshawar.

After the war against the Soviets ended, Al Ridi was dismayed by the influx of young Muslims spoiling for a fight—any fight—and decided to leave. When he heard that Azzam had been killed, he recalled, "the Afghan chapter and jihad were closed for me."

Al Ridi didn't join al Qaeda but remained friendly with El Hage, who called him in 1992 with a business proposition. Bin Laden wanted to buy a large jet that could carry cargo, in order to transport Stinger missiles from his armory in Afghanistan to his new base in Sudan.[9]

Al Ridi, who had trained as a pilot, found a U.S. military surplus plane in Arizona for about $200,000 and agreed to fly it to Khartoum. A few years later, bin Laden asked him to move the plane, but the brakes failed on landing. Al Ridi expertly crashed it into a sand dune, avoiding any injuries, but the plane was a total loss.[10]

Al Ridi's copilot on the doomed flight was Ihab Ali, another naturalized American citizen who had moved to Orlando, Florida, with his family as a teenager. Ali did not assimilate well, and during the 1980s, he heard Azzam's siren call. Ali worked for the Muslim World League in Peshawar during Azzam's tenure there, then joined al Qaeda soon after its founding.[11]

He was trained in terrorist techniques by Ali Mohamed, who kept tabs on him back in the United States, where Ihab Ali studied flying at an obscure institution called the Airman Flight School in Norman, Oklahoma. A few short years later, 9/11 hijackers Mohammed Atta and Marwan Al Shehhi would visit the Airman school seeking flight lessons. Al Qaeda operative Zacarias Moussaoui would attend the same flight school in 2001.[12]

Mohamed himself was constantly on the move but returned frequently to California, where his partner, Khalid Abu El Dahab, was running a communications hub on behalf of al Qaeda. Among other responsibilities, Dahab would patch calls from Egypt to Afghanistan and Sudan, in order to foil intelligence surveillance.

Dahab and Mohamed were also responsible for recruiting Americans into al Qaeda, under orders from bin Laden himself. According to Dahab, they found ten naturalized Americans from the Middle East who were willing to join. To support all of these efforts, Dahab worked as a car salesman, but it was difficult to hold down both professions at once, and he soon dropped the more mundane job.[13]

Ali Mohamed was prolific during these years, balancing multiple assignments and overseeing projects on three continents. In the United States, he smuggled al Qaeda operatives into the country, on one occasion even using his FBI contacts to get one of his trainees released after he was detained by Canadian customs. At bin Laden's behest, he set up meetings and joint training sessions between al Qaeda and Hezbollah. And in Africa, he played a key role training bin Laden's men and advancing bin Laden's secret war on America.[14]

In 1993 bin Laden dispatched Mohamed to Somalia, where a civil war was raging. The United States had deployed to Somalia for Operation Restore Hope, an effort to impose some kind of stability on the country and support United Nations relief efforts. Bin Laden was enraged at what he saw as a broader plan to establish American hegemony in Africa, starting with Somalia and then (he imagined) expanding to Islamic Sudan.[15]

Al Qaeda provided training to Somali tribes who were fighting UN and U.S. forces, and Mohamed took part in this effort. More significantly, he was in the country during the U.S. intervention. In October 1993 Somali forces trained by al Qaeda— most likely including Mohamed—shot down a U.S. helicopter in the notorious "Black Hawk Down" incident that left eighteen Americans dead.

Bin Laden wasn't done punishing the United States for having the temerity to try to save lives in Somalia. He asked Mohamed to start casing targets for another African attack. The former U.S. soldier dutifully surveilled a dozen locations in Nairobi, Kenya, taking pictures, drawing maps, and writing up reports on the security of each installation. He took his reports back to Khartoum. Bin Laden zeroed in on the photos Mohamed had taken of the U.S. embassy, pointing out where a truck bomb could be most effectively deployed. A second team selected the U.S. embassy in Dar Es Salaam, Tanzania, for a simultaneous attack. After the targets were chosen, Mohamed took teams back to Kenya to conduct advanced surveillance. They took their time—it would be nearly five years from surveillance to attack.[16]

As part of its covert war on the United States, al Qaeda wanted to obtain weapons of mass destruction. Bin Laden especially coveted a nuclear bomb.

Another trusted American was dispatched to handle this effort: Mohamed Loay Bayazid, the American citizen jihadist from Kansas City who had been present at al Qaeda's founding. It should be noted that Bayazid, who declined to be interviewed for this book, has denied all of what follows.[17]

In late 1993 or early 1994, Jamal Al Fadl, one of Al Qaeda's earliest members who had been recruited by the Al Kifah Center in Brooklyn (see chapter 3), got a call from the head of al Qaeda's financial committee. Someone in Khartoum had uranium to sell, and the asking price was $1.5 million. Al Fadl was sent to check it out and set up a meeting.

Bayazid was brought in to oversee the proposed transaction. Al Fadl and Bayazid went to meet the seller, switching cars along the way to foil any possible surveillance. At the meeting place, the seller brought out a cylinder two or three feet tall, engraved with technical details about the supposed contents. Bayazid carefully checked the information against the requirements to build a working nuclear bomb. It was a match. After the meeting, Bayazid arranged for a machine to be shipped from Kenya to test the material itself.

Al Fadl said that he was praised for his work and sent on his way. He never heard whether the material checked out or whether the purchase had been completed. Bayazid subsequently returned to the United States, where he became involved with the Benevolence International Foundation in Chicago, a charity that provided money and logistical assistance to al Qaeda.[18]

Al Qaeda needed cash badly. Osama bin Laden had been hemorrhaging money since he arrived in Sudan. Some of it was simply lost due to bad business decisions. More was lost to corruption, which included his own employees stealing from him. And running a global war—even an improvised war—involves substantial costs.[19]

In early 1995 Bin Laden dispatched his second-in-command, Ayman Al Zawahiri, to the United States on a fund-raising trip. Ali Mohamed was responsible for making the trip safe. Zawahiri traveled under an assumed name—Abd-al-Mu'izz—and, using forged documents obtained by Mohamed, toured several mosques in northern California. By one account, he raised as much as $500,000, although most people put the figure considerably lower: $3,000 or less.[20]

Despite his close relationship with both bin Laden and Zawahiri, not everyone in al Qaeda trusted Mohamed. Mohamed Atef, al Qaeda's military commander at the time, told another al Qaeda member, L'Houssaine Kherchtou, not to disclose his travel plans to Mohamed. El Hage explained to Kherchtou that Atef feared Mohamed was working for the U.S. government.[21]

The nature of the dispute was unclear. Dahab thought it had something to do with money, but there may be a simpler explanation. Toward the end of 1994, things were boiling over with the FBI. Mohamed's name had come out during the investigation of the World Trade Center bombing and Siddig Ali's thwarted Day of Terror. While Mohamed was in Kenya, working on the embassy bombings surveillance, he began to get calls from home. The FBI wanted to talk.[22]

Mohamed returned to California to face the music. In December 1994 he sat down with FBI special agent Harlan Bell and Assistant U.S. Attorney Andrew McCarthy, who was preparing to prosecute Omar Abdel Rahman and his followers for the Landmarks bomb plot. McCarthy described the meeting in his 2008 book, *Willful Blindness: A Memoir of the Jihad*:

> [Mohamed] had been pitched to me as an engaging friendly by his handlers: FBI agents in Northern California with whom he was purportedly cooperating, though it quickly became clear who was picking whose pocket. By the time I got to that conference room, though, I already knew better. And if I'd needed any confirmation, it was right there in the steady glare of eyes that didn't smile as he finessed his best cordial greeting, extending a hand that, when I shook it, coolly conveyed his taut, wiry strength. Ali Mohamed was a committed, highly capable, dyed-in-the wool Islamic terrorist. I couldn't prove it yet. But I was sure it was true, and in that moment, I understood that he knew I knew.[23]

The full contents of that meeting remain unknown. McCarthy declined to discuss most of it in his book, citing national security classifications. A 1998 court document revealed that Mohamed claimed he had been working in the scuba-diving business in Kenya.

But he did talk about bin Laden, telling the men that he had helped move the Saudi from Afghanistan to Sudan in 1991 at the request of Mustafa Shalabi, the head of the Al Kifah Center in Brooklyn, not long before Shalabi was murdered.

McCarthy added that Mohamed talked about El Sayyid Nosair and his belief that Islam would "triumph" (McCarthy's word) over the world. Whatever else was said remains under the seal of government secrecy.[24]

Mohamed dutifully reported the incident to al Qaeda, but it only reinforced the opinions of those who distrusted him. Over the course of the next year, al Qaeda began to freeze Mohamed out of its inner circle. His overseas travel ground to a near complete halt, and his assistance on the East African embassy bombings plot was no longer required.[25]

The mistrust was not complete or universal. Significantly, al Qaeda did not change its target in North Africa, which it would have if bin Laden suspected that Mohamed had gone over to the enemy. It's more likely that the al Qaeda leader was influenced to shut Mohamed out by those who genuinely mistrusted him, combined with the obvious fact that the former soldier was now a potential target for U.S. intelligence coverage.

Shunned but not totally out of the loop, Mohamed returned to his efforts to ingratiate himself into U.S. intelligence at various levels, applying for a job as an FBI translator at one point and trying to get work as a security guard for private contractors doing classified work for the government. He stayed in touch by phone and mail with other American al Qaeda members, including Wadih El Hage and Ihab Ali, who were also in contact with each other. In late 1995 El Hage even visited Mohamed in California.[26]

The FBI was slowly closing in on al Qaeda's American cell. In 1996 Jamal Al Fadl walked into a U.S. embassy in Eritrea and surrendered. The United States hadn't been looking for him, but he surrendered anyway. Al Fadl had been caught stealing more than $100,000 from al Qaeda. Osama bin Laden directly confronted him about the theft, seeming more hurt than angry, as Al Fadl remembered it:

> I don't care about the money, [bin Laden said,] but I care about you, because you have been with us from the beginning. You worked hard in Afghanistan; you are one of the best people in al Qaeda. We want to know . . . we give you a salary, we give you everything. When you travel we give you extra money. We pay your medical bills. Why you did that? What did you need the money for? Did someone outside of al Qaeda put you up to it?[27]

Bin Laden told Al Fadl that he would be forgiven if he repaid the money, but Al Fadl had already spent it. So he left Sudan and went searching for refuge. At the embassy in Eritrea, he stood in the visa application line, and when he reached the window, he told the clerk, "I don't want visa, but I have some information for your government and if your government help me, and I have information about people, they want to do something against your government."[28]

Patrick Fitzgerald, a federal prosecutor who had worked on the Day of Terror case, was dispatched to debrief Al Fadl. The Sudanese jihadist had been close to the center of al Qaeda, and he started to provide U.S. investigators with a wealth of information on the terrorist network, including its American operatives.

After the meeting, Fitzgerald called Tom Corrigan, the Joint Terrorism Task Force member who had investigated the Landmarks case. It was the first time Corrigan heard the name al Qaeda.

> [Fitzgerald] called me from overseas and he explained this, what this group was, it made sense. [Al Fadl] was like the Rosetta Stone telling us everything that was going on and what its relationship was to other groups and other events. [. . .] Even Jamal, he was from New York, he lived in Brooklyn for a while. He knew people that were affiliated with our case and affiliated with the Brooklyn and Queens and Jersey City area. He was a person that was overseas and filled in this incredible background but also had information that was pertinent to what we were doing over in the States.[29]

The FBI began to watch the Americans. In mid-1996, soon after Al Fadl started to talk, a phone tap was placed on Wadih El Hage's house in Kenya, and his calls were recorded.[30]

As more and more information came out concerning bin Laden, Sudan grew increasingly inhospitable, partly due to pressure from the United States. Bin Laden had lost a considerable amount of his inheritance by this time and couldn't give his hosts much incentive to stand behind him. In May 1996 bin Laden retreated back to Afghanistan, seething.[31] A few months later, he erupted with a formal declaration of war on America, a fatwa published by an Arabic-language newspaper based in London. Bin Laden wrote,

> It should not be hidden from you that the people of Islam had suffered from aggression, iniquity, and injustice imposed on them by the Zionist-Crusaders alliance and their collaborators; to the extent that the Muslims blood became the cheapest and their wealth as loot in the hands of the enemies. Their blood was spilled in Palestine and Iraq. The horrifying pictures of the massacre of Qana in Lebanon are still fresh in our memory. Massacres in Tajikstan, Burma, Kashmir, Assam, [the] Philippine[s], Fatani, Ogaden, Somalia, Eritrea, Chechnya and in Bosnia-Herzegovina took place, massacres that send shivers in the body and shake the conscience. [. . .]
>
> Terrorizing you, while you are carrying arms on our land, is a legitimate and morally demanded duty. It is a legitimate right well known to all humans and other creatures. Your example and our example is like a snake which entered into a house of a man and got killed by him.[32]

The CIA secretly put together a plan to kidnap bin Laden, but it foundered amid political infighting with the FBI and the National Security Council. Nevertheless, Ihab Ali, now living in Orlando and working as a cab driver, wrote to El Hage in Kenya, warning him to "be cautious" because the "enemies" in the United States wanted to "grab" bin Laden.[33]

Around the time the letter was written, El Hage went to Afghanistan for a meeting with bin Laden, where the order was given: step up operations in Africa, especially in Somalia. El Hage transmitted the order to several al Qaeda members who had been working on the embassy bombings preparations. At every stage, he reported back to bin Laden, often traveling to Afghanistan to do so in person.[34]

Then the world came crashing down around him. While El Hage was in Afghanistan meeting with bin Laden in 1997, FBI agents came knocking on the door of his family's home in Nairobi. With the cooperation of Kenyan authorities, they were there to search the house.

El Hage's American wife, April; her mother; and the couple's six children watched as the FBI combed through the house, taking the Macintosh computer, papers, business cards, address books, and anything else that might provide clues. Some of the FBI agents suggested that it might not be safe to stay in Nairobi.[35]

An FBI agent left his notebook at the house during the search. El Hage politely returned it after he got home a day or two later. Within a month, the family sold all their possessions and returned to the United States—just as the FBI had intended.

The raid was meant to disrupt the al Qaeda cell in Nairobi, which is not to say that the FBI agents weren't interested in what they found during the search: phone numbers for bin Laden, Ali Mohamed, Ihab Ali, and more. Soon after the family returned to the United States, settling in Arlington, Texas, El Hage was summoned to New York to appear before a grand jury investigating bin Laden.[36]

El Hage may not have been prepared for what was awaiting him. The FBI was finally up to speed on his long history. They had questions about the murder of Rashad Khalifa, the murder of Mustafa Shalabi, that time he sold a gun to World Trade Center bomber Mahmoud Abouhalima, his relationships with Ihab Ali and Ali Mohamed . . . and, of course, Osama bin Laden.

El Hage did his duty—he lied and evaded. But it was too late. Al Qaeda put him on the shelf, like Ali Mohamed before him.[37]

It was Mohamed's turn next. The FBI called him in for another chat. As before, Mohamed appeared disarmingly frank, although in reality he was keeping plenty of secrets in reserve. He admitted he had trained bin Laden's bodyguards. He admitted he had been in Somalia while the United States was there, and he acknowledged that al Qaeda was responsible for the deaths of U.S. soldiers.

Mohamed talked about his assistance in moving bin Laden from Afghanistan to Sudan back in 1991. According to an FBI report on the interrogation, "he did this because he loved bin Laden and believed in him." He explained that a fatwa to attack the United States was unnecessary because it was "obvious" that America was the enemy of Islam. He admitted he had trained people in "war zones" and ominously added that "war zones can be anywhere."[38]

After the interview he walked out a free man. Yet again.

In early 1998 Ihab Ali wrote a letter to Ali Mohamed. The letter indicated that although the American cell might have been pushed to the side, its operatives were still in touch with al Qaeda in Afghanistan. Ali wrote,

> At any rate please give my best regards to your friend O'Sam and his copartner and tell him—Sam—that I apologize that I couldn't finish what he requested of me, due to some personal problems. As far as Mr. Wadeeh [Wadih El Hage], he's presently staying in Texas. I had (illegible) him prior

> to traveling and he filled me in on his social/business life. He told me that after having met with and finishing a business deal with Mr. Sam and while returning home he was contacted by one of the opposition company called Food and Beverage Industry based in the U.S. He was given an extensive interview.[39]

Federal prosecutors later said "O'Sam" was likely a coded reference to "Osama," and Food and Beverage Industry meant FBI. The letter showed that all three American al Qaeda members were still in play, even if they had been placed in strategic retreat.[40]

Less than two months later, "O'Sam" upped the stakes, issuing a fatwa that expanded his earlier declaration of war against the United States. Bin Laden wrote,

> The ruling to kill the Americans and their allies—civilians and military—is an individual duty for every Muslim who can do it in any country in which it is possible to do it. [. . .] This is in accordance with the words of Almighty Allah, "and fight the pagans all together as they fight you all together," and "fight them until there is no more tumult or oppression, and there prevail justice and faith in Allah."[41]

In May 1998 bin Laden granted an interview to John Miller of *ABC News*:

> We say to the Americans as people and to American mothers, if they cherish their lives and if they cherish their sons, they must elect an American patriotic government that caters to their interests not the interests of the Jews. If the present injustice continues with the wave of national consciousness, it will inevitably move the battle to American soil, just as Ramzi Yousef and others have done.[42]

It would be the final warning. On August 7, 1998, the embassy bombings plot—so long in the making—finally came to fruition. Within four minutes of each other, two al Qaeda teams bombed the U.S. embassies in Nairobi, Kenya, and in Dar Es Salaam, Tanzania. More than two hundred people were killed in Nairobi—the operation Ali Mohamed had planned—and eleven died in Dar Es

Salaam. The bomb in Kenya was a suicide bomber, and the bomb in Tanzania was meant to be—but the driver panicked and fled before it went off.[43]

Bin Laden's declaration of war had become a reality.

Not long after the blast, Ali Mohamed's phone rang. He told the FBI agents on the line that he had heard something years ago about a planned attack on the embassy in Nairobi, but that he had discouraged the plotters from carrying it out. He knew who the bombers were, but he had no intention of naming names.[44]

The FBI also showed up on Wadih El Hage's doorstep. He too lied, telling them he had quit working for bin Laden back in 1994 and hadn't seen him since. El Hage said he wasn't aware of anyone working for bin Laden in Kenya or Tanzania. At any rate, bin Laden couldn't be behind the attacks because he was a "humanitarian," besides which he would have done the bombing at a time of day to minimize harm to innocent bystanders.[45]

Despite such humanitarian leanings, El Hage was able to explain to the FBI why bin Laden hated America so much. According to FBI agent Robert Miranda,

> He said that any true believing Muslim, it was the duty of any true believing Muslim to drive out the US from the Saudi Peninsula because the Koran had reserved the Saudi peninsula only for Muslims. He also said that the US government unfairly supported Israel, and by that he described his statement by saying that the US was quick to come to the aid of Israel if something happened to it but that if Israel did something illegal that the US was slow to act.
>
> And then he also said that Israel was expanding to take control of the entire Middle East. And finally in response to that questioning, he said that many people wanted to make the world live according to the Koran, but that they don't have the resources, but Bin Laden has the resources to make the world live according to the Koran.[46]

A few days later, FBI agents searched the California home of Ali Mohamed. They discovered a shocking collection of documents that showed just how sophisticated al Qaeda was: manuals describing surveillance techniques and tactics used by government intelligence agencies, instructions for creating improvised explosives, codebooks, coded letters, al Qaeda intelligence reports (including one written by Wadih El Hage), and reports on the activities of U.S. law enforcement.[47]

Mohamed was dragged before a grand jury investigating the embassy bombings, and he lied again. This time, he could feel the walls closing in, although the prosecutors had not yet decided whether he was connected to the bombings. FBI agents accompanied him under guard back to his hotel. Mohamed excused himself to go to the bathroom and, with the door closed, began ripping pages out of his personal address book and flushing them down the toilet. When he came out of the room, he was arrested. Later Mohamed admitted that if he hadn't been arrested, he would have been on the next flight to Afghanistan.[48]

Days later El Hage was arrested. Khalid Abu El Dahab, Mohamed's California crony, was captured in Egypt. Ihab Ali, Mohamed's trainee and the would-be pilot, was picked up in 1999.[49] Loay Bayazid, the Kansas City mujahid who had helped found al Qaeda, retired from the group and stayed in Sudan.[50]

The FBI had rounded up some of the most dangerous and experienced al Qaeda members in the United States, albeit belatedly. Unfortunately, there would be more where they came from. Some had already started their journey to al Qaeda.

7
The Rise of Anwar Awlaki

Las Cruces, New Mexico, is an old pioneer town turned small city, where the sun shines 350 days out of the year. It began life as an armed encampment to protect settlers from Apache raids. Legend holds that the town was named after the cross-shaped grave markers littering the valley in the wake of those attacks.[1]

In more recent times, the city was home to Dr. Nasser Al Awlaki, an agronomist studying at New Mexico State University. In 1971 his wife gave birth to a son, Anwar Nasser Awlaki.[2]

The Awlakis lived in the United States until young Anwar was seven, when they returned to their homeland, Yemen. The family was influential, and the elder Awlaki became the country's agriculture minister during Anwar's formative years.[3]

His son was raised on a diet of tales from the front lines in Afghanistan. "There was constant talk of the heroes who were leaving Yemen to join the fight and become martyrs and go to paradise," one of his Yemeni neighbors remembered. Around the neighborhood, mujahideen videotapes were treated like a cross between family entertainment and the evening news.[4]

Awlaki was an intelligent boy, speaking flawless, unaccented English with an equally impressive command of Arabic. He consumed American popular culture voraciously and returned to the United States in 1991 to study engineering at Colorado State University—on a U.S. government scholarship awarded to foreign students. He lied about his citizenship in order to qualify.[5]

In 1993 Awlaki took a trip to Afghanistan, but documentation is sparse. At the time the country was being ripped apart by an internecine war among factions that had managed to unite only long enough to drive the Soviets out. A college friend said in 2010 that Awlaki had spent one summer training with the mujahideen in Afghanistan, but there is no other information about the trip.[6]

When Awlaki returned to Colorado, he was no longer interested in engineering. Instead he started to volunteer as a lecturer at the Denver Islamic Society. During the 1990s Awlaki immersed himself in Islamic studies through correspondence courses and by studying with various mentors. One of the more notable figures who tutored Awlaki in the ways of Islam was Hassan Al Ahdal, a Yemeni sheikh who spent several years writing and editing for the Muslim World League's English-language magazine. Al Ahdal's writings tended toward militancy and anti-Semitism.[7]

Awlaki's facility with the English language, combined with his encyclopedic religious knowledge and credible Arabic, made for a powerful cocktail of skills. He was remembered as a gifted speaker who was capable of moving men to action. He soon moved from volunteer status to a paid position.

"He could talk to people directly—looking them in the eye. He had this magic," one member of the mosque remembered.[8]

Even at this early stage in his career, he was a study in contradictions. To some who heard him speak, he was the voice of moderation, representing the most uplifting elements of Islam. Yet others perceived a dark side.

Awlaki consistently preached that Muslims around the world were under constant attack and that these attacks justified an armed response, themes that would continue throughout his career. He was so persuasive that he convinced one Saudi student attending college in the area to abandon his studies and join the jihad in Bosnia. The student was later killed while fighting in Chechnya.[9]

Awlaki soon moved on to bigger things, landing in the San Diego area, where he became the imam of the Ar-Ribat Al-Islami mosque in La Mesa. Ribat was a modest building in a residential neighborhood, flanked by palm trees. It looked more like a Presbyterian church than a mosque. Awlaki lived in a house on the property. He enjoyed going fishing and would sometimes share his day's catch with the neighbors.[10]

Yet the affable imam's dark side was never far from the surface. Even as religious devotion became the defining characteristic of his career, Awlaki's personal choices reflected an inner conflict—he was twice arrested for soliciting prostitutes and once for "hanging around a school."[11]

A rare recording from Awlaki's San Diego period discusses the practice of *takfir*: declaring Muslims with whom one disagrees to be apostates or infidels, outcasts from Islam who may be killed under Islamic law. During a Friday *khutba* (sermon), Awlaki told listeners that the practice was dangerous and wrong, basing his argument on a story from the *hadith* (non-Koranic traditions about the sayings and actions of Mohammed) in which the Prophet showed mercy to a Muslim who was suspected of insincerity.

> [If] you tell your brother that he is [an apostate], if he is not, it will come back on you. [. . .] We do not know what is in the hearts of people. [If we think] this man is saying with his tongue what he doesn't mean in his heart, [the *hadith*] tells us we are not ordered to open up and seek what is in the hearts of people. He is not ordered clearly [. . .] I am not told by Allah to seek what's in the hearts of people. Meaning that we call people to Islam, but we are not judges over them. We do not judge the people. We leave the judgment to Allah, [glory to him].[12]

At the same time, however, Awlaki rattled off a number of occasions under which *takfir* was acceptable—if someone publicly says he or she is not a Muslim or clearly states belief in something that is incompatible with belief in Allah. Other qualifying offenses include "giving the attributes of Allah to a human being" (an offense known as *shirk*) or insulting the prophets of Islam.[13]

Another lecture made some time during his residence in the United States showed an early interest in the concept of jihad.

> And if you look at the wars, not only the fights between individuals, but even wars between nations and states, most of the time, it's over wealth. It's over *dunya* [earthly or material concerns]. What are they fighting for? Over oil, over land, over natural resources. That is why wars happen.
>
> Therefore, the only justified war, the only justified war is jihad. Because that is the only fight that is happening for the sake of Allah [the glorious]. Everything else is happening for the sake of *dunya* [the material world]. They attack jihad in Islam, as if their wars are justified. What are they fighting for?[14]

Awlaki had a remarkable ability to bridge the American experience with the tenets of Islam. His speeches were peppered with humor and references to American popular culture.

> Isaac Asimov, in an interview with him, a few months before he died, he was asked the question, "What do you think will happen to you after you die?" This is one of the most prominent science fiction writers that the world has seen. He said, "Nothing. Nothing. Nothing will happen to me after I die. I will turn into dirt." His knowledge, and the books that he wrote, and all of that intelligence, and all of that fame and wealth doesn't make him any different from the most ignorant and illiterate non-believer in Mecca 1400 years ago the ones who rejected resurrection.[15]
>
> Thomas Friedman, he is a famous writer in the U.S., he writes for the *New York Times*. He says the hidden hand of the market cannot survive without the hidden fist. McDonald's will never flourish without McDonnell Douglas—the designer of F15s. In other words, we are not really dealing with a global culture that is benign or compassionate. This is a culture that gives you no choice. Either accept McDonald's, otherwise McDonnell Douglas will send their F15s above your head.[16]

In 1998 the Yemeni-American imam took a job as vice president of a Yemeni charity called the Charitable Society of Social Welfare (CSSW). The charity was controlled by a Yemeni sheikh named Abdel Majid Al Zindani, under whom Awlaki also claimed to have studied Islam.[17] (Zindani has denied that Awlaki was his student.)[18]

Zindani was linked to both the Muslim Brotherhood and the MWL.[19] He was renowned as a scholar and a warrior, having cut his teeth in battle alongside Osama bin Laden during the Afghan jihad and in the Afghan civil war that followed. In the postwar era, he became known as a recruiter for the war in Bosnia and later for al Qaeda. His nephew, Abdul Wali Zindani, ran the Al Kifah Center in Brooklyn after the murder of Mustafa Shalabi during the 1990s.[20]

If Awlaki was looking for a mentor in extremism, he couldn't have found a better man. The Charitable Society for Social Welfare was Zindani's vehicle in the United States during the 1990s, with offices in several locations, including Brooklyn and San Diego.[21]

CSSW was the subject of an al Qaeda financing investigation code-named "Black Bear," but the charity was never formally designated a terrorist financier. Although it subsequently shuttered its American operations, the charity nevertheless received millions of U.S. taxpayer dollars as recently as 2010 as part of a partnership to fight child labor overseas.[22]

Around the same time, Awlaki was approached by an al Qaeda facilitator named Ziyad Khaleel. Khaleel was, in the words of one acquaintance, "obnoxious." He had been vice president of Awlaki's Denver Islamic Society some years earlier, when the men probably first met. Now he was a fund-raiser for the Islamic American Relief Agency, which was linked to CSSW. IARA was later named by the U.S. government as an al Qaeda financing vehicle. In his spare time, Khaleel helped acquire and maintain a satellite phone account for Osama bin Laden.[23]

In light of these suspicious connections, the FBI opened a file on Awlaki. The investigation began some months after he took the job with CSSW and ended in March 2000. The agent who closed the case wrote that Awlaki had been "fully identified and does not meet the criterion for [further] investigation."[24] It was an evaluation he or she would live to regret.

At the mosque Awlaki was beginning to attract devotees. His followers numbered roughly two hundred to three hundred and were—according to Awlaki—"very religious and simple."[25]

Omar Al Bayoumi, a Saudi national who had moved to the United States in 1994 to learn English and attend college, was one of Awlaki's admirers. Bayoumi earned an MBA in 1997 and went on to study accounting in graduate school, but the subject bored him, and he dropped out.[26] His education was financed by his employer, a Saudi government agency responsible for overseeing aviation in the kingdom. Despite his employer's generosity—his salary topped out at more than $6,000 per month—he performed no clearly identifiable work related to aviation during his time in America.

When he wasn't attending his children's football games, Bayoumi was very involved with local mosques, including a Kurdish mosque in the San Diego area, where he helped arrange financing to acquire a building. Although he claimed that he held no formal position with the mosque, Bayoumi maintained an office on the premises and helped settle disputes.[27]

Bayoumi enjoyed talking about religion, and one of his discussion partners was Anwar Awlaki. Beyond their direct contacts, Bayoumi befriended some of

Awlaki's most fervent disciples. Among them was a young Saudi named Omer Bakarbashat, who lived in an apartment complex in a cul-de-sac around the corner from the Ribat mosque and worked at a local Texaco station that had become a hangout for Arabic-speaking Muslims in the neighborhood.

Bakarbashat was shy but not too shy to pursue one of his female coworkers, even proposing marriage to her at one point. (She declined.) He viewed Awlaki as "almost a god."[28] According to Bayoumi, Bakarbashat was fat and delusional, allegedly believing himself to be possessed by demons.[29]

One day in 2000 Bakarbashat met two Saudis, friends of Bayoumi who had come to Ar-Ribat to attend one of Awlaki's services. Their names were Nawaf Al Hazmi and Khalid Al Mihdhar. Both men were members of al Qaeda—and both would take part in the hijacking of American Airlines Flight 77 and its subsequent crash into the Pentagon on September 11. Bakarbashat tutored Hazmi in English. Mihdhar also asked for lessons but quickly lost interest.[30]

In early 2000 Bayoumi and an American friend had driven to the Saudi consulate in L.A. They met the pair in a restaurant, and Hazmi and Mihdhar later showed up in San Diego looking for Bayoumi. They asked for help finding a place to stay in the area. Bayoumi set them up in the San Diego apartment building where he lived. He helped them open bank accounts and paid for various expenses. Hazmi told an acquaintance that he considered Awlaki to be "a great man" and the pair's "spiritual leader."[31]

The web of associations grew thicker. Another member of Awlaki's flock at Ribat—and a friend of Bayoumi's—was Mohdar Abdullah, a Yemeni college student who was, like Awlaki, fluent in both English and Arabic.[32]

Abdullah was charismatic and well liked, although the FBI considered him a slick liar. He lived in an apartment complex around the corner from Awlaki's mosque, in the same building as Bakarbashat. Abdullah's computer was stuffed with anti-American sentiments, including e-mails proposing extravagant terrorist plots and references to martyrs and grenade launchers.[33]

In the late spring or early summer of 2000, Omar Bayoumi introduced Abdullah to Hazmi and Mihdhar. Abdullah became friends with the two hijackers, acting as both a translator and a chauffeur, driving them around the area and even to Los Angeles. He helped them get driver's licenses—and fill out applications to flight schools.[34]

A third man, Jordanian immigrant Osama Awadallah, for a time shared an apartment with Bakarbashat at the complex around the corner from Ar-Ribat.[35] Awadallah's home was filled with photographs, videotapes, and news articles featuring Osama bin Laden, as well as flyers containing bin Laden's fatwas.

Hazmi had a piece of paper with Adawallah's phone number in the car he used to drive to the Washington Dulles International Airport on September 11. Four days after the attack, Adawallah, a student, scribbled in one of his notebooks, "One of the quietest people I have met is Nawaf. Another one, his name is Khalid."[36]

Awadallah and Mohdar Abdullah both worked at the same gas station as Bakarbashat. In time, so would Hazmi. The al Qaeda man told his coworkers that he would be famous some day. Shortly before the two hijackers left San Diego for good in late 2000, Hazmi brought a third hijacker, Hani Hanjour, to meet his coworkers. Before they drove off, Hazmi told his San Diego friends that they were going to take flying lessons.[37]

Awlaki's followers were not the only ones going out of their way to offer hospitality to the future September 11 killers. Awlaki himself knew both of the hijackers and Bayoumi. The 9/11 Commission speculated that he may have met them as soon as their first day in San Diego—nearly two months before the FBI closed its investigation of the imam.[38] Four calls were made to Awlaki using Bayoumi's cell phone during February 2000, the same month the hijackers arrived in the area. One FBI agent later said he was "98 percent certain" that the calls were made by the hijackers.[39]

Awlaki met with Hazmi several times, often behind closed doors. Like Awadallah, Awlaki found the al Qaeda operative to be soft spoken and slow to open up. Hazmi didn't come off as particularly religious; he didn't wear a beard and didn't pray five times a day. Or at least that was what Awlaki told the FBI later.[40]

In late summer of 2000, Awlaki stepped down from his position at Ar-Ribat and embarked on travel overseas to what he would describe to reporters only as "various countries." Awlaki told a neighbor that he was going to Yemen. Mihdhar had left San Diego for Yemen just weeks before to visit his pregnant wife. During the period that Awlaki was out of the United States, Ramzi Binalshibh, an al Qaeda facilitator supervising a different team of hijackers, also traveled to Yemen in an effort to obtain a U.S. visa. [41]

By now, word was beginning to spread about Awlaki's oratorical skills. He was a much-sought-after commodity in Muslim religious circles—knowledgeable and fluent in English, with a flair for captivating young audiences. Recordings of his lectures on CD became brisk sellers, including a series on the Prophets of Islam and another on the Companions of the Prophet.

One American Muslim told me he was especially moved by Awlaki's fifteen-hour series on Abu Bakr Al Siddiq, a companion of Mohammed and the first caliph of the Muslim world. Awlaki, quoting *hadith* (traditional stories about the Prophet Muhammad's life), described Abu Bakr as the most devout and pure of the Prophet's companions.

> [The Prophet Muhammad] was once sitting in the *masjid*, and he asked the Sahabah, "Who's fasting this day?" Abu Bakr Al Siddiq said, "I am."
>
> "Who has visited an ill person?" Abu Bakr Al Siddiq said, "I did."
>
> "Who has [attended a funeral]?" Abu Bakr Al Siddiq said, "I did."
>
> "Who on this day has given [something extra to charity]?" Abu Bakr Al Siddiq said, "I did."
>
> And everybody else in the *masjid* was looking around, and the only hand that is going up is the hand of Abu Bakr. [. . .] He would always come out the first.
>
> And the amazing thing is that it didn't seem as if Abu Bakr Al Siddiq [. . .] wasn't doing it to compete with anyone. It came natural. See, what the others, they were trying to compete with him. Abu Bakr [. . .] was trying to compete with Abu Bakr.[42]

Awlaki was hired at Dar Al Hijrah in Falls Church, Virginia, one of the nation's most prominent mosques. Dar Al Hijrah had been founded in the 1980s and grew to a respectable size during the early 1990s, when it became associated with members of the American Muslim Brotherhood. Members of Hamas were also known to attend the mosque.[43]

Johari Abdul-Malik, the mosque's current imam, explained to the press how Awlaki came to be hired:

> Our community needed an imam who could speak English, not like many *masjid*, who have an imam who is from the old guard, he—he speaks broken

> English, if he speaks English at all, but someone who could convey that message with the full force of faith. He was that person. And he delivered that message dutifully.[44]

As he had in San Diego, Awlaki began to attract devotees at Dar Al Hijrah. His talks during this period were positioned as moderate, but flashes of darkness surfaced from time to time. During a 2001 lecture on tolerance, he explained that Muslims were the most tolerant people in history, then qualified that statement to exclude a call for tolerance in modern times.

> Now, is there [. . .] a problem among the Muslim community of intolerance towards other faiths? Well, to some extent there is. To some extent there is.
>
> However, when one is dealing with the issue of tolerance, usually the party that is asked to be tolerant is the party that is in power, the party that is in control. However, when a people are suffering, and oppressed, it is not easy, or it's not, doesn't even make a lot of sense to bring up the issue of tolerance.[45]

Awlaki was highly critical of U.S. foreign policy, and his attraction to the phenomenon of jihad continued, though often carefully framed. One undated lecture was an eight-hour dissertation on a classic book about jihad, which Awlaki attempted to disarm with a prefatory disclaimer:

> Now I want to state in the beginning and make it *very clear* that our study of this book is not an exhortation or invitation to violence or promotion of violence against an individual or a society or a state. This is purely an academic study. We are studying a book that is 600 years old.[46]

One of the regulars who attended his sermons was an army psychiatrist named Nidal Hasan. Hasan, whose father had died two years earlier, had coped with his grief by turning more fervently to religion. Hasan's eyes would light up when he talked about Awlaki's teachings.[47]

There were also familiar faces. The FBI and the 9/11 Commission determined that at least two and as many as four of the September 11 hijackers attended the imam's services at Dar Al Hijrah, including Hani Hanjour and Awlaki's San Diego disciple Nawaf Al Hazmi.[48]

As in San Diego, a handful of people from Awlaki's flock stepped forward to help the hijackers accomplish small tasks on the road to September 11. Jordanian Eyad al Rababah offered to help Hazmi and Hanjour find an apartment and ended up helping them get driver's licenses (illegally) before escorting them around the East Coast on a trip he described as "sightseeing." The apartment he eventually found for them was in New Jersey. As in San Diego, FBI agents suspected, Awlaki had tasked Rababah to assist the hijackers. In early 2001 Rababah had asked Awlaki for help finding a job; he started to assist the hijackers immediately thereafter.[49]

The relationships among Awlaki, Omar Bayoumi, and the hijackers and the helpers remain ambiguous to this day, even among those who were in a position to know. FBI agents working the case wanted badly to arrest Awlaki but couldn't come up with the hard evidence.

The 9/11 Commission left its section on Awlaki open-ended but clearly opinionated; the final report found Awlaki's role suspicious enough to explicitly mention but said the commission was "unable to learn enough about Awlaki's relationship with Hazmi and Mihdhar to reach a conclusion."[50]

On the topic of Omar Bayoumi, the commission was similarly conflicted. The final report of the commission described him as "devout," "obliging," and "gregarious," and investigators "find him to be an unlikely candidate for clandestine involvement with Islamist extremists." On the other hand, the commission conceded that it could not be sure whether Bayoumi's initial "chance meeting" with the hijackers "occurred by chance or design."[51]

The nature of Bayoumi's job is extremely unclear. He was known in the local community as someone who actively sought out new Muslims in town and helped them get settled. Many people assumed he performed this role on behalf of the Saudi government, which tends to be very activist about taking care of its citizens abroad. Although his interactions with the hijackers may simply have fallen within that mandate, questions linger.[52]

The placement of the hijackers within Awlaki's social circle raises significant questions. Bayoumi first met the hijackers in L.A., where he had connections with both the Saudi embassy and the Saudi-financed King Fahd Mosque. In San Diego he held a position of some importance at a Kurdish mosque not far from Alwaki's Ar-Ribat mosque, where he could easily have arranged assistance with housing, transportation, and English lessons. Perhaps he felt the Saudis would be more comfortable at Ribat, which had a strong Saudi-Salafist orientation.[53]

Or perhaps there is another explanation. In the immediate wake of September 11, many journalists probed into Bayoumi's role with the hijackers without success. Questions were raised but never answered about the possibility that Bayoumi might have been a "handler" for the hijackers, working on behalf of someone in Saudi Arabia. A congressional probe into 9/11 found that Bayoumi had "tasked" San Diego Muslims to assist the hijackers.[54]

Yet after Bayoumi's initial contact with Hazmi and Mihdhar, most of the people who provided assistance to the hijackers were as close to Awlaki as they were to Bayoumi, if not closer. An FBI agent, whose name was redacted from released records, told the 9/11 Commission that "if anyone had knowledge of the plot, it was Awlaki."[55]

For most of the helpers, Awlaki was not only a friend or an acquaintance but an authority figure who inspired fervent devotion. Yet perhaps the most damning indicator of Awlaki's involvement with the hijackers came several months after San Diego—when Awlaki's followers performed the same helper function on the opposite coast, a social transaction with no apparent link to Bayoumi.

Finally, there is Awlaki's connection to Ramzi Binalshibh, the al Qaeda facilitator who provided logistical assistance to several of the September 11 hijackers—but not Hazmi and Mihdhar, who were being helped by Awlaki's followers on both coasts. Binalshibh was in Yemen during the summer of 2000, around the same time Awlaki said he would be there. More significantly, when investigators searched Binalshibh's apartment after September 11, they found the phone number of Awlaki's mosque in Virginia, Dar Al Hijrah.[56]

If Awlaki was helping the hijackers, the final question then becomes this: what did he know?

Did he know they were extremists? Terrorists? Al Qaeda? Did he know they were planning to kill on U.S. soil? Did he know exactly what they were going to do? Awlaki has notably declined to address these questions. Even after he fully committed to terrorism (see chapter 9), he never raised the issue of September 11.

Unless Awlaki is arrested and charged in a U.S. courtroom, these questions may never be answered. But Awlaki's neighbor in San Diego, Lincoln Higgie, remembered an ominous pronouncement the imam made when he left San Diego for Virginia:

> He said, "I'm going back to Virginia, and shortly after that, I'll be going to Yemen." And I said, "Well, I do hope you'll be coming back to San Diego soon." And he says, "No, I won't be coming back. And in a little while, you'll understand why."[57]

Whatever Awlaki knew or didn't know before September 11, his meetings with the hijackers were not destined to be his last contact with al Qaeda.

8
Scenes from September 11

It defies preconceptions, but on a per capita basis, Arizona may have hosted more al Qaeda members than any other state in America.

Tucson residents included some of Osama bin Laden's closest associates, such as early al Qaeda financier Wael Julaidan, the American citizen jihadist Wadih El Hage, and the American citizen Loay Bayazid, who was present at the founding of al Qaeda (see chapter 2).[1] An Islamic newspaper based in Tucson issued an ID card to World Trade Center bombing mastermind Ramzi Yousef in 1992.[2]

A branch of the Al Kifah Center was located in the city during the 1980s, recruiting Americans to fight the Soviets in Afghanistan.[3] There was so much jihadist activity, over so many years, that U.S. intelligence officially labeled Arizona a "long term nexus for Islamic extremists."[4]

Then there were the pilots. Essam Al Ridi, Osama bin Laden's personal pilot, traveled to Arizona during the 1990s. Suspected Islamic extremists from all over the world—Saudi Arabia, Kenya, Jordan, and Pakistan—were spotted by the FBI at Embry-Riddle Aeronautical University in Prescott, Arizona, a few hours away. One of them flat-out told FBI agents that the United States was a "legitimate military target" for Muslims and that al Qaeda's murderous attacks on U.S. embassies in Kenya and Tanzania were justified.

In July 2001 the FBI's Phoenix field office proposed a full-scale investigation to headquarters, citing its belief that the would-be pilots were linked to Osama bin Laden, but its plea fell on deaf ears, and the investigation foundered.[5]

Hani Hanjour had first visited Tucson some ten years prior. A devout Muslim and an experienced jihadist who fought in Afghanistan, he came as a student to learn English, left, then returned to the United States in 1996 to train as a pilot. First, he qualified for a private pilot's license. Later, he succeeded in being certified as a commercial pilot.[6]

Hanjour spent about five years in the United States, much of it of Arizona, often in the company of al Qaeda–linked extremists who had been noticed by the FBI.

On the morning of September 11, 2001, Hanjour was seated in the cockpit of a commercial jet, American Airlines Flight 77, just as he had trained for in the heat of an American desert. Under his steady hand, the plane screamed down out of the sky and slammed into the side of the Pentagon, disintegrating in a fiery explosion and killing 189 people, including himself.[7]

ANWAR AWLAKI

On the morning of September 11, Anwar Awlaki was also sitting in an airplane bound for Washington.

The Yemeni-American imam was returning home from a conference in San Diego, the city where he had first befriended two of the men who were even now helping Hanjour complete his suicide mission. A third hijacker on Flight 77 had also met Awlaki, later, at the Dar Al Hijrah Mosque near Washington, where the imam now worked.

Awlaki was landing at Reagan National Airport around the time that the hijackers were boarding their flight at the nearby Washington Dulles International Airport. The timing was extraordinarily tight. Awlaki heard news of the hijackings during his cab ride home.

Awlaki rushed to the mosque. After a consultation, the facility's leaders decided to close the facility for the rest of the day, citing security concerns, and issued a press release condemning the attacks. That night, they called the police after someone drove up to the mosque and started shouting at the people huddled inside.

ABDULLAH RASHID

The African American mujahid from Brooklyn was a long way from his glory days in Afghanistan. For the last eight years, Abdullah Rashid had been living in a series of prisons. Since 1999 his home had been the federal penitentiary at Terre Haute, Indiana.[8]

Not long after the planes hit, Rashid was taken out of his cell and moved to death row.

"They said it was the safest point in the prison," his wife, Alia, recalled. "I said, 'That's bull.'"

Alia believed that they wanted to "get him outta their face. [. . .] He was gettin' on their nerves real bad, and they fixed him."[9]

Rashid remained on death row for more than a year. After that, it was on to another prison.

JOHN WALKER LINDH

On a morning when the rest of America was waking up to the reality of war, John Walker Lindh was already there—in a foxhole in Afghanistan, fighting on behalf of the Taliban.

It had been a long, unlikely path that brought him to this point. He had spent his adolescence in Marin County, the heart of American liberalism. Lindh had been named after John Lennon. He was called quiet and sweet, a sickly child, homeschooled for a time, then educated at a progressive California school.[10]

Lindh had converted to Islam as a teenager, drawn to the religion after watching Spike Lee's film about Malcolm X. One year later he traveled to Yemen to study the Arabic language. He landed at the Al Iman University in Sanaa, headed by Abdel Majid Al Zindani, a close ally of al Qaeda and mentor to Anwar Awlaki.[11]

From Yemen, he went to Pakistan, where he enrolled in a madrassa with the intention of memorizing the Koran. There he was exposed to the Taliban, and in the spring of 2001, he traveled to Afghanistan to fight on their behalf against the Northern Alliance, an anti-Taliban militia and an enemy of al Qaeda.[12]

In June 2001 he trained for combat at al Qaeda's Al Farooq camp, where he heard rumors about suicide attacks in the works against the United States. He even met Osama bin Laden, who thanked him for taking part in jihad.[13]

Lindh was fighting with a foreign fighter unit on behalf of the Taliban on September 11. News of the attack traveled quickly, even in this remote, rugged terrain. Word came down that al Qaeda personnel were being deployed to face the inevitable U.S. response. Lindh stayed with his unit.

In November Lindh's unit was captured by the Northern Alliance, which was now fighting the Taliban and allied with the United States. The detainees staged an escape, during which a CIA agent was killed.

Lindh was quickly recaptured. He was hiding in a tunnel with other Taliban when it was flooded by U.S. forces. He emerged, muddy and tattered. Photos of his capture would be splashed over every newspaper and television broadcast in the world under the words "American Taliban."[14]

ADNAN SHUKRIJUMAH

From Pakistan, near the border, Adnan Shukrijumah called his mother in Florida.

"Did you hear what happened?" he asked her. "They're putting it on the Muslims."

She told him not to come home. They were arresting all of the Muslims, she said.

"'No, I didn't do nothing," he replied. "I will come, don't worry about this."

But he never came.[15]

ISMAIL ROYER

He had fought and trained as a jihadist in Bosnia and Kashmir, and now Ismail Royer was the civil rights coordinator for the Council on American-Islamic Relations. Royer had arrived at his office just before 9 a.m. when he heard coworkers calling from the conference room. They were huddled around the TV, staring at the gaping hole in the first tower of the World Trade Center.

"I hope Muslims didn't do this," he said.

Within hours of the hijackings, Royer had written and issued a press release condemning the attack and urging Muslims to report harassment. The phones were now ringing off the hooks, and it was his job to answer them. Many of the calls were reporting hate crimes and harassment.[16]

Yet after he left the office—near midnight—Ismail Royer's mind was elsewhere. A message had been passed through his circle of friends, half a dozen men he had spent hours training with outside the office. Everyone in the group who owned a gun was to assemble for a meeting.[17]

That meeting took place four days after September 11, at the behest of an American-born cleric, Ali Al Timimi. Timimi told Royer and the other gathered jihadists that the Muslims of Afghanistan now needed their help, far more than the Kashmiri Muslims on whose plight the group had previously focused. The Muslims of Afghanistan had a new enemy, and that enemy was the United States.

Armageddon was at hand, Timimi told his rapt audience. September 11 was a sign of the impending apocalypse, and everyone in the room had a part to play.[18]

ALI MOHAMED

Al Qaeda's most accomplished spy, the American citizen Ali Mohamed, had been living in the witness protection wing of a federal prison for the past few months. Mohamed had cut a plea deal and agreed to provide information about al Qaeda in the hope of winning a reduced sentence.

That hope went out the window on the morning of September 11, when he was abruptly hustled out of his cell and moved to solitary confinement. No contact with other prisoners and especially no news of the world—no television, radio, or newspapers.

A few days later, the questions began. "How did they do it?"

Calmly, Mohamed laid it all out. This is where you sit to hijack a plane; this is how you get a blade through security. He had taught these tricks to his fellows at al Qaeda. Mohamed had obtained a copy of the FAA's security procedures manual and given it to al Qaeda. One of his trainees, Ihab Ali, had attended the Airman Flight School in Norman, Oklahoma, which Mohammad Atta had contacted to ask about flight training.[19]

Ali Mohamed may not have known that the September 11 attack specifically was in the works, but he knew an awful lot about how it *could* be done.

Mohamed must have known that day that he would not be receiving a reduced sentence. In fact, he would never be sentenced at all. While other prisoners would become hot topics among civil libertarians, Mohamed just faded away without a fuss. After September 11, his plea deal was little more than a joke. Ali Mohamed was too dangerous to ever walk the streets again.

9
The Descent of Anwar Awlaki

In the days after September 11, Anwar Awlaki spoke to the press over and over again, one of many Muslim leaders stepping forward to give the community's response to the attacks.

Although his statements were mostly conciliatory, there was an unmistakable edge. Awlaki was eager to blame the United States for inciting the terrorist attack through its "anti-Muslim" foreign policy.

"Our hearts bleed for the attacks that targeted the World Trade Center as well as other institutions in the United States, despite our strong opposition to the American biased policy toward Israel," Awlaki said during the first Friday *khutba* following the attacks.[1]

A week later he continued to drum the message home, using language that seemed to justify the attack. "We were told this was an attack on American civilization. We were told this was an attack on American freedom, on the American way of life. This wasn't an attack on any of this. This was an attack on U.S. foreign policy."[2]

Awlaki then turned the focus toward the alleged victimization of Muslims in the United States due to bigotries stirred by the 9/11 attack.

"Most of the questions are, 'How should we react?' Our answers are, especially for our sisters who are more visible because of [wearing a head scarf]: Stay home until things calm down."[3] Yet Awlaki was unable to produce any victims of hate crimes, such as the woman he claimed was beaten with a baseball bat.[4]

Behind the scenes, Awlaki was having other conversations—with the FBI, which had quickly identified him as a point of contact for the hijackers.[5] Awlaki's story shifted, depending on the day and the person to whom he was speaking. The FBI called him in for at least four interviews in the weeks following September 11.[6]

On September 17 Awlaki admitted to the FBI that he had known Nawaf Al Hazmi in San Diego—well enough to describe his appearance and personality in some detail.[7] Scant days later, he told an Associated Press reporter tracking the investigation that he didn't know any of the hijackers. Instead he sought to turn scrutiny back on the FBI. "Our people won't listen to us when they see this is how the FBI is treating them," he said. "It strengthens our belief that we are a community under siege, whose civil rights are being violated."[8]

The imam was under pressure because of his relationship to the hijackers, and his worldview turned ever darker. Under the watchful eyes of FBI surveillance, he turned back to an old vice, visiting prostitutes in the D.C. area, at least one of whom was underage.[9]

His sermons also darkened, taking an increasingly combative tone. Awlaki had always been an advocate of the view that Muslims were victims of discrimination and violent persecution around the world, parroting the Saudi-influenced scholars who had come before him. Now, by his account, that persecution had come squarely to America.

Rather than focus on the perpetrators of 9/11—whom he had, wittingly or unwittingly, assisted in their suicide mission—Awlaki pointed, with increasing stridency, at the U.S. government. As the days stretched into weeks, Awlaki's condemnations of terrorism became ever more equivocal and convoluted. In an October *khutba*, Awlaki delivered a speech that blamed terrorists for their violent acts while blaming the United States exponentially.

> The fact that the US has administered the homicide of one million Iraqi civilians, and supported the murder of thousands of Palestinians does not justify the killing of one civilian in NY or Washington DC. And the killing of six thousand American civilians does not justify the killing of one innocent Afghani. Two wrongs don't make a right.[10]

Awlaki's peers didn't see anything particularly radical about the imam from San Diego. "We could have all been duped," said Johari Abdul-Malik after Awlaki had come out of the jihadist closet in 2009, echoing the view of others in the community. "But I think something happened to him, and he changed his views."[11]

Shaker El Sayed, another imam who served at Dar Al Hijrah, echoed this view, dismissing the idea that Awlaki's contact with the September 11 hijackers should have been scrutinized.

> Well, he was an imam when he left and he was an imam at the Islamic center in San Diego. And being an imam myself, I get in touch with lots of people, but does this necessarily mean that I agree with what they are doing behind my back? Of course not.
>
> So the government, in the case of Muslims, they did not look for the serious scrutiny; they spread a broad dragnet of suspicion around Muslims, in general, and the Islamic centers in particular.[12]

Awlaki's sermons continued to spiral into radicalism. At times, he blamed the Jews for the plight of American Muslims, saying that they controlled the media and the government and citing recordings of Richard Nixon in the White House as evidence.[13] Awlaki also fixated on Muslim prisoners in the United States, a topic to which he would return again and again. He seemed to be projecting his own personal worries into these lectures, but his *khutbas* also reflected concerns being expressed across a broad spectrum of the Muslim community. The difference was the tone: Awlaki tended toward unabashed fearmongering and wasted little effort trying to put a mainstream gloss on his point.

It's also useful to look at the lectures in the context of his personal history. Awlaki's earlier lectures had been delivered in a clear, steady voice. As the content became more and more hysterical, so too did Awlaki's voice. His lectures came faster and at a higher pitch and volume. His voice at times wavered as he sought to generalize the actions of law enforcement into a broad alarm for American Muslims.

When the FBI raided several Islamic institutions in Virginia as part of a terrorism-financing investigation in early 2002, Awlaki made the stakes as plain as could be during a *khutba* delivered at Dar Al Hijra:

> So this is not now a war on terrorism. We need to all be clear about this. This is a war against Muslims. It is a war against Muslims and Islam. Not only

> is it happening worldwide but it's happening right here in America, that is claiming to be fighting this war for the sake of freedom, while it's infringing on the freedom of its own citizens just because they're Muslims. *For no other reason.*
>
> And as Muslims, if we allow this to continue, if we do not stop it, it ain't gonna stop! It's not gonna stop. [. . .] Maybe the next day the Congress will pass a bill that Islam is illegal in America. Don't think this is a strange thing to happen. Anything is probable in the world of today because there are no rights unless there's a struggle for those rights.[14]

In March 2002, shortly after giving this speech, Awlaki left the country and his post at Dar Al Hijrah for London. In August he gave a speech before the annual conference of an Islamic charity known as JIMAS (Jamiat Ihyaa Minhaaj Al Sunnah). The topic was the role of Muslims living in the West.

After a largely unremarkable hour of speaking, Awlaki suddenly turned apocalyptic—literally—with a digression into his own belief, based on Muslim traditions, about what will happen at the end of time during the Islamic version of Armageddon:

> *Dawah* [the invitation to Islam] will flourish in the West, and many Westerners will become Muslim. And they will be with the Muslims. [. . .] However, the majority won't, and the majority who won't become Muslim are going to be the spearhead in the effort to fight Islam. [. . .] The Romans are going to approach all of the Arabs who are living in their midst, and every Arab man and woman and child will be killed. They will all be exterminated. A holocaust.

Awlaki's speech was cut short by the organizers, purportedly due to his exceeding his allotted time. He seemed to realize he had gone too far. Poignantly, he groped for an upbeat conclusion.

> I have to take few more minutes. I don't want to close on this pessimistic tone. We have to have a better ending. [. . .] Islam will flourish all over the world. [. . .] Our *Dawah* in the West is a peaceful *Dawah*. We are not al-

> lowed to commit aggression, to take up arms. It is a *Dawah* of patience and subtlety. [. . .] We do not fight back. We do not strike back.[15]

In the United States, the FBI was engaged in a heated internal debate about the imam's status. The Joint Terrorism Task Force in San Diego, having scrutinized Awlaki's contacts with the hijackers, was eager to press a case against the imam.

The consensus was that the evidence didn't yet justify charging the cleric in relation to 9/11. The task force had other options. In Awlaki's traffic with prostitutes in Washington, D.C., he had transported some of the women across state lines, which opened the possibility of federal charges, although it would be clear to everyone that this was only a pretext to get him into custody, with an eye toward additional charges later.

Awlaki had also lied on his passport application in the 1990s, claiming he had been born in Yemen in order to obtain a U.S. government–funded scholarship. An immigration charge looked better, and it was a standard tactic for making a pretextual arrest. Because the passport fraud had taken place in Colorado, the charges were filed there, and a judge issued an arrest warrant. All they had to do now was wait and hope that Awlaki came back to the United States.[16]

The trap was set. After appearing at several conferences in the UK, Awlaki began to travel, reportedly visiting Yemen and Saudi Arabia during mid-2002. Finally, he walked into the net. On October 10, 2002, Awlaki and his family returned to the United States on a flight from Riyadh to New York. Customs and immigration officials had been alerted to detain him, and the family was escorted to a secondary screening area.

Once Awlaki had been secured, however, something went wrong. When customs officials contacted the FBI, they discovered that the arrest warrant had been revoked—one day earlier. After fewer than four hours in custody, he received an apology and was permitted to connect with a flight to Washington, D.C.[17]

The decision to revoke the warrant was made by an assistant U.S. attorney in Denver, David Gaouette, who said in 2009 that his office "couldn't prove the case beyond a reasonable doubt and we asked the court to withdraw the complaint," adding that he couldn't prosecute someone for a "bad reputation." The decision did not go over well with his colleagues in the Justice Department and the State Department's investigative service, who were infuriated at the cancellation of the warrant.[18]

The writing was on the wall. Awlaki left the United States for good and returned to London, where he continued to lecture prolifically at the Masjid At-Tahwid mosque and various forums and conferences. After his departure from the United States, he took his long-held narrative about the victimization of Muslims further than ever before. In December 2003 he gave the Friday *khutba* at the East London Mosque.

> You have over 520 Muslims who are locked up in jail and are left to rot in there, and there's no crime. They have not committed anything. There are no charges brought against them. And they are left there for months at end to just rot in those prison cells. What have you done for them? [. . .]
>
> [Allah] will revenge for himself. [Allah] does not need us. But the thing is, we cannot allow such things to happen and we watch. We just sit there watching, doing nothing. Thinking by ducking down and by being quiet, we'll be safe. If you don't stop it now, it's gonna happen to you, it might happen to your wife, it might happen to your own daughter. You need to stop it in its tracks before it grows.[19]

As if a foreboding had gripped him, Awlaki was becoming increasingly obsessed with prison and the horrors that might be visited on a Muslim who had been detained. His speeches were colored, perhaps, by his own sexual demons.

> The Jews and the Christians will not be pleased until you become like them. How can you have trust in the leaders of *kufr* [the infidels], when today, right now, right now, there are Muslim brothers who are in jail? Every sinister method of interrogation is used against them. They would use against them homosexuals to rape them. They would bring their mothers and sisters and wives, and they would rape them in front of these brothers. The United Nations knows about it. Amnesty International knows about it, and they are doing nothing. In fact, sometimes they are encouraging it.[20]

Awlaki traveled to a number of mosques and Islamic centers in the UK, sponsored by the Muslim Association of Britain, where he spoke more and more openly about jihad, "the most beloved deed to Allah."

He left dozens, perhaps hundreds, of radicalized disciples in his wake, such as University of London students Roshonara Choudhry and Omar Farouq Abdulmutallab. The former tried to assassinate an English parliament member for supporting the Iraq war, and the latter tried to bomb a U.S.-bound airliner on Christmas Day 2009 but succeeded only in setting his underwear on fire.

In 2004 Awlaki returned to his ancestral home in Yemen. He began to lecture at Sanaa University, where he continued his attacks on U.S. foreign policy. Soon he moved to Iman University, also in Sanaa, which was run by his old mentor and al Qaeda associate Abdul Majid Zindani. The university was known for fostering radicalism. One of its former students was John Walker Lindh, the American Taliban.[21]

When the *9/11 Commission Report* was released in July 2004, it outlined the commission's suspicions about Awlaki. At that time, few in the mainstream media showed interest in exploring Awlaki's role further, let alone his current activities.[22] Yet by now, terrorism investigators in several countries were taking notice.

Awlaki was an emerging player in the radicalization of English-speaking Westerners. Members of a terrorist cell known as the Fort Dix Six, which was planning to attack U.S. military personnel in New Jersey, listened to Awlaki's lectures during training. His recordings were also linked to a group of Somali Americans in Minnesota who had traveled to fight jihad in Somalia.[23] In case after case, investigators fighting terrorism found copies of Awlaki's lectures on the computers of their suspects.

Part of his wide appeal was attributed to the use of the Internet to spread his message. Awlaki maintained a Facebook page with thousands of followers and a widely read blog. He was accessible; his followers could e-mail him and receive a personal response. Awlaki was far from the only Islamic preacher using the Web to reach an audience, but he was particularly successful because of the moderate gloss he put on a message that could be rotated just a few degrees for a dramatically different effect. Large numbers of mainstream Muslims had been drawn to him for his inspirational works. A small but significant minority continued with him down the road to jihad.

In Yemen Awlaki fell in with a rough crowd, and trouble soon followed. In 2006 he and five others were arrested on charges of kidnapping a teenager for ransom. They were also planning to kidnap an American military official stationed in

Yemen. The five men took care of the violence; Awlaki provided a fatwa purporting to offer an Islamic justification for their criminal activity.[24]

The imam's nightmare of imprisonment had finally become a reality. But Awlaki's account of his time in jail provided a stark contrast to his earlier tales of rape or torture. His prison cell was clean and empty. He was kept in solitary confinement for most of the time he was detained. He was not allowed to have pen, paper, or outdoor recreation. Toward the end, some of these restrictions were loosened. If he had been subjected to rapes, he did not speak of them.

He was subjected to interrogations, however. According to Awlaki, the FBI came to see him, again. They asked about September 11, again. And they left with nothing . . . again.[25]

When Awlaki emerged from prison in December 2007, he was different. Although his account of life in prison seemed a far cry from his worst imaginings, the experience led him even further down a dark path.

Before his arrest, Awlaki had been careful, always skirting the edges of the debate. His lectures were popular among aspiring radicals but not because they openly called for violence. Rather, they provided justifications and rationalizations. He called for action but did not say what that action should be. Now he was edging closer and closer to a true, unambiguous call to violence.

Awlaki's blog offered justifications for suicide bombings and prayers for the destruction of America—but not a specific instruction to act on that prayer.[26] He began to talk in increasingly glowing terms about jihad but still refrained from directly exhorting violence, as in this August 2008 blog entry:[27]

> Because confusion usually surrounds what is meant by Jihad whether it is the Jihad al Nafs [struggle with oneself] or Jihad of the sword I do not exclusively mean one or the other and I do not exclude one or the other. What I mean by Jihad here is not just picking up a gun and fighting. Jihad is broader than that. What is meant by Jihad in this context is a total effort by the Ummah to fight and defeat its enemy.[28]

In 2008 he posted an entry praising Al Shabab, an extreme jihadist movement fighting in Somalia (see chapter 10).

> Al Shabab not only have succeeded in expanding the areas that fall under their rule but they have succeeded in implementing the sharia and giving us a living example of how we as Muslims should proceed to change our situation. The ballot has failed us but the bullet has not.[29]

The invocation of the bullet over the ballot was a distortion of a turn of phrase most famously deployed by Malcolm X. In recent years, it has come to be used as a jihadist slogan.

Even having gone this far, Awlaki was still holding back. At the time he issued the message, Shabab was still fighting a primarily military conflict in a contained geographical zone. It wasn't quite the same as endorsing al Qaeda. And Awlaki couldn't help but end the message with a suggestion that Shabab—known as an extraordinarily violent movement—practice kindness toward the Somalis it sought to conquer.

> I would like to take this opportunity to advise my brothers to be kind and soft with the masses; to excuse them for centuries of ignorance and false beliefs; to teach first and hold responsible last. I would advise you to go by certainty and to leave doubts; to prefer forgiveness over revenge. The masses of the people are suffering from the illnesses of tribalism, ignorance, and a campaign of defamation of *Sharia*. Therefore you need to win the hearts and minds of the people and take them back to their [true nature].[30]

The dreaded prison cell had taken Awlaki ever closer to joining the ranks of violent jihadists, yet he still held back. It would take a fellow American to strip away all pretensions and push him firmly into the camp of terrorism.

THE FORT HOOD SHOOTINGS

On November 5, 2009, Maj. Nidal Malik Hasan walked into a medical processing center in Fort Hood and opened fire on unarmed soldiers who were between deployments. He discharged his weapon more than a hundred times, killing thirteen and wounding at least twenty-nine more.[31]

Within the first few hours, the media covered the story as a mass shooting consistent with such lone gunman cases as the 2007 Virginia Tech massacre, where a schizophrenic college student went on a shooting spree that left thirty-two people dead. But reports soon began to filter out that during his spree, Hasan had been shouting "Allahu Akbar!"—a Muslim superlative exclamation meaning "God is great" that has been appropriated by jihadists to celebrate attacks.[32]

An American born in Virginia in 1970 to Palestinian immigrants, Hasan worked for the family business before attending Virginia Tech, where he majored in biochemistry. In 1997 he enlisted in the U.S. Army and enrolled in medical school, his tuition paid in full by the U.S. government. He specialized in psychiatry—according to an uncle, he chose the specialty after fainting at the sight of childbirth during medical school. In exchange for his tuition, he agreed to an extended tour of duty—he was committed to the army through at least 2010.

Hasan was a lonely man, religious to begin with and even more religious after the death of his mother in May 2001 (his father had died a few years earlier). He worshipped at the Dar Al Hijra mosque in Falls Church, Virginia, where he became captivated by the imam, Anwar Awlaki. During the same period, Hasan could count at least two of the September 11 hijackers among his fellow worshippers.[33]

Desperate to marry, he nevertheless rejected the few women he managed to meet for failing to meet his standards.[34] To be his wife, a woman would have to be a virgin, an Arab, and young. She had to cover her head and pray five times a day and live according to the Koran and Sunnah. He considered dozens of women, but no one was right.[35]

At the Walter Reed Army Medical Center, where Hasan was stationed as a psychiatrist after his graduation, things weren't going much better. After September 11 Hasan told friends he had been harassed by fellow soldiers. He told his psychiatric patients to look for healing in Islam, and he was prone to lecture random colleagues who crossed his path about the Koran. He told his fellow soldiers he was deeply opposed to the war in Iraq and tried to get out of the army, but he was not released from his obligation.[36]

In June 2007 the then captain Hasan gave a PowerPoint presentation to a room full of medical colleagues as part of his residency. His topic was not medical, however; it was religious: *The Koranic [sic] World View as It Relates to Muslims in the U.S. Military*.

The presentation aimed to provide tools for military officers to "identify Muslim soldiers that may be having religious conflicts with the current wars in

Iraq and Afghanistan." Hasan could hardly have offered a better diagnostic tool than the presentation itself.

Much of the PowerPoint was pure proselytization—slide after slide of quotes from the Koran, along with basic concepts and generalizations about Islam. But it didn't take long for Hasan to show where his real interests lay. One slide defined an "Islamist" as one who "advocates rule by Gods [sic] law." Jihad was "a Muslim holy war or spiritual struggle against infidels." He derided American Muslim clerics' fatwas on America's wars as "vague and ambiguous" and suggested that they were made "under duress."

Muslims who killed other Muslims were condemned to hell by the Koran, Hasan continued. This conflict could lead to "adverse events," such as the 2003 murder of two U.S. soldiers by Sergeant Hasan Akbar, who threw a grenade into three tents at a base in Kuwait. Hasan delved into complex justifications for defensive jihad, at times grasping for the language of Islamic scholarship.

He went further still, outlining arguments for offensive jihad—the concept that Muslims are obligated to take political control of the world—and quoting the notorious jihadist slogan, "We love death more than you love life."

Under "Conclusions," Hasan laid out a view of Islam that should have raised red flags among his fellow officers. "Muslims may be seen as moderate (compromising), but God is not," the slide read. "Fighting to establish an Islamic State to please God, even by force, is condoned by the [sic] Islam." Finally, "Muslim Soldiers should not serve in any capacity that renders them at risk to hurting/killing believers unjustly."[37]

Hasan's colleagues were stunned, but no action was taken to evaluate the captain's suitability for the military. Some chalked the speech up to religious zeal. Others noted that complaining about a fellow soldier's religious views was a good way to end the complainer's career. Ironically, Hasan would later receive the Global War on Terrorism Service Medal.[38]

Having faced no consequences for his presentation, Hasan decided to revisit the topic when he was required to give another talk. This time, he decided that he needed to do more research, so he e-mailed his former imam—Awlaki, who had only just been released from a Yemeni prison.[39]

The example of Hasan Akbar and his "adverse event" lingered in Hasan's mind. The men's worldviews had similarities. One month prior to his attack, Akbar had written in his diary, "I will have to decide to kill my Muslim brothers fighting for Saddam Hussein or my battle buddies. [. . .] I may not have killed any Muslims, but being in the Army is the same thing. I may have to make a choice very soon on who to kill."[40]

When Hasan wrote to Awlaki, he asked whether Akbar would have been considered a martyr. At least eighteen e-mails were exchanged between the two men, most of them from Hasan to Awlaki. The e-mails followed the same lines as the PowerPoint and two subsequent presentations Hasan gave to colleagues on the same topic.

The army wasn't the only institution that failed to respond to the warning signs; the FBI intercepted Hasan's e-mails to Awlaki but didn't investigate. Awlaki was, by most accounts, cautious about the missives from a U.S. military man he had barely met years earlier. He did not advocate violence, officials said, and Hasan did not volunteer that he was planning an attack.[41]

Yet there were clues. At one point Hasan wrote, "I can't wait to join you [in the afterlife]." He asked for guidance about when jihad was justified and whether it was Islamically permissible for innocents to be killed in suicide attacks. Elements of these discussions surfaced in his later presentations at Walter Reed, in which he praised suicide bombers and characterized the war on terrorism as a war on Islam.[42]

The e-mails continued through June 2009. In July Hasan was assigned to Fort Hood, Texas. His initial assignment was to evaluate soldiers headed for the front lines; then he too would be deployed to a combat zone. In Texas he lived life as a man who cared little for it, renting a rundown unit in a bad part of town near the base. He had few friends.[43]

Like the 9/11 hijackers (also students of Awlaki), Hasan frequented a strip club in the final days before he carried out his mission, paying $50 for private lap dances from fully naked women.

The strip club was next door to the gun shop where Hasan armed himself for the attack. Two days before his killing spree, Hasan took an extended round of target practice at a local range. The night before the attack, he stayed up all night. That morning he gave his perishable groceries to his neighbors.[44]

The evidence of premeditation and planning is overwhelming. The evidence of Hasan's involvement with jihadist ideology is overwhelming as well. He may also have been mentally ill; certainly he was lonely, frustrated, and socially inept.

But his expressions of jihadist ideology and his patterns of reinforcement closely track with other American jihadist cases in which mental fitness is not an issue. A Mafia enforcer might be a stone-cold psychotic, but he is still a member of the Mafia. Mentally ill individuals can and do join street gangs and crime cartels—or, for that matter, the armed forces and the police. Acknowledging mental illness does not erase affiliations.

There is no evidence Hasan was delusional. He sought out and embraced an established ideology outside the mainstream of American Islam but certainly well within the mainstream of jihadist thought. He voiced his belief in the same worldview that has justified acts of murder by many other people around the world. His actions cannot be lightly dismissed as an act of random insanity. They must be placed within the jihadist/terrorist context.

OUT OF THE CLOSET

The Fort Hood shootings thrust Awlaki into the spotlight at long last. Two days after the shooting, news reports began to connect Awlaki to Hasan. Two days after that, Awlaki took to his blog with his most aggressive public statement to date. Not only did he justify the attacks, he damned American Muslims who had condemned the attacks.

> Nidal Hassan [sic] is a hero. He is a man of conscience who could not bear living the contradiction of being a Muslim and serving in an army that is fighting against his own people. This is a contradiction that many Muslims brush aside and just pretend that it doesn't exist. Any decent Muslim cannot live, understanding properly his duties towards his Creator and his fellow Muslims, and yet serve as a US soldier. The US is leading the war against terrorism which in reality is a war against Islam. Its army is directly invading two Muslim countries and indirectly occupying the rest through its stooges.
>
> Nidal opened fire on soldiers who were on their way to be deployed to Iraq and Afghanistan. How can there be any dispute about the virtue of what he has done? In fact the only way a Muslim could Islamically justify serving as a soldier in the US army is if his intention is to follow the footsteps of men like Nidal. [. . .] The American Muslims who condemned his actions have committed treason against the Muslim Ummah and have fallen into hypocrisy.[45]

Yet once again, at the very edge of the precipice, Awlaki pulled back, as he always had. Rather than call on all American Muslims to take up arms and follow Hasan's example, he instead suggested they leave the United States.

> The inconsistency of being a Muslim today and living in America and the West in general reveals the wisdom behind the opinions that call for migration from the West. It is becoming more and more difficult to hold on to Islam in an environment that is becoming more hostile towards Muslims.[46]

In an interview soon after, Awlaki admitted exchanging e-mails with Hasan but still denied encouraging him to commit violence.[47]

Awlaki's peculiar lack of commitment in his public discourse might have been born out of his morbid obsession with imprisonment. He seemed to lack the courage of his convictions, at least when he was in the public eye, but his wall of evasion was crumbling fast.

A few months earlier, a young Nigerian Muslim named Omar Abdulmutallab had made his way to Yemen and joined a training camp run by the local terrorist franchise al Qaeda in the Arabian Peninsula (AQAP). Mutallab was trained for a suicide operation: the detonation of a bomb smuggled onto a U.S bound airliner. He made his attempt on December 25, 2009—Christmas Day—but failed when the bomb, which he had hidden in his underwear, merely caught fire, severely burning his genitals. One of his trainers, he told the FBI after his arrest, was Anwar Awlaki, who had explicitly directed him to carry out the attack.[48]

Fueled by the two attacks in close proximity, coverage of Awlaki exploded. A Nexis search showed seven stories mentioning Anwar Awlaki in major newspapers during 2007. In 2008 there were five stories. In 2009 there were 651 stories, almost all of which were published in November and December. In the first six months of 2010, there were 948, in addition to countless television and Internet stories.

The coverage took on an increasingly hysterical tone. Dozens of reports characterized Awlaki as "the next Osama bin Laden" and one of the most serious threats to the United States in years.[49] In late 2009 the Obama administration put Awlaki on a list of high-value targets, authorizing U.S. covert operations to capture or kill the American citizen.[50]

In March 2010, perhaps realizing he had nothing left to lose, Awlaki finally pulled the trigger. An audio message released to jihadist Internet forums positioned him squarely on the side of terrorism—while he continued to deny his connection to any previous attack. The speech was masterful and remarkably attuned to an American audience, invoking an almost Reaganesque sense of nostalgia before lowering the boom.

> To the American people I say: Do you remember the good old days, when Americans were enjoying the blessings of security and peace? When the word "terrorism" was rarely invoked? And when you were oblivious to any threats?
>
> I remember a time when you could purchase an airline ticket from the classified section of your local or college newspaper, and use it, even though it was issued to a different name, because no one would bother asking you for an ID before boarding a plane. No long lines, no elaborate searches, no body scans, no sniffing dogs, no taking off your shoes and emptying your pockets. You were a nation at ease.
>
> But America thought that it could threaten the lives of others, kill and invade, occupy and plunder, and conspire, without bearing the consequences of its actions. 9/11 was the answer of the millions of people who suffer from American aggression. And since then, America has not been safe.[51]

Awlaki mocked America's inability to defeat the "mujahideen" of al Qaeda and celebrated Nidal Hasan and Omar Abdulmutallab, characterizing the latter's failure to accomplish his mission as a success because he almost succeeded. Awlaki laid out a "defensive" rationale for the actions of al Qaeda as a response to U.S. "aggression," citing Guantanamo Bay and the abuse of captives by U.S. soldiers at Iraq's Abu Ghraib prison. He stated that al Qaeda's goal was to establish Islam "over all other" religions. Finally, he pointed the way forward.

> I for one, was born in the US, I lived in the US for twenty-one years. America was my home. I was a preacher for Islam, involved in non-violent Islamic activism. However, with the American invasion of Iraq, and continued US aggression against Muslims, I could not reconcile between living in the

> US and being a Muslim, and I eventually came to the conclusion that Jihad against America is binding upon myself, just as it is binding on every other able Muslim. [. . .]
>
> The Muslim community in America has been witnessing a gradual erosion and decline in core Islamic principles, so today many of your scholars and Islamic organizations are openly approving of Muslims serving in the US Army, to kill Muslims, joining the FBI, to spy against Muslims, and are standing between you and your duty of Jihad.

Soon afterward, Awlaki was interviewed in a video published online by al Qaeda in the Arabian Peninsula (AQAP), the first time he ever publicly associated with a terrorist organization.[52] In July AQAP began publishing an English-language magazine for aspiring jihadists, which Awlaki was said to oversee (see chapter 11).

In November 2010 Awlaki went further still, releasing a video in Arabic that unequivocally called for killing Americans. "Do not consult anyone in killing the Americans," he said. "Fighting Satan does not require a [religious ruling]. It does not require consulting. It does not need a prayer for the cause. They are the party of Satan."[53]

Anwar Awlaki was no longer struggling to balance his inner darkness against the light. He had formally and finally embraced the role of terrorist.

THE MEASURE OF THE MAN

Awlaki's status is nothing if not a moving target. When the Western media discovered him in late 2009, he was far more successful and influential among Muslims who are fluent in English or for whom English is a first language than he has with the Arabic-speaking Muslims who dominate the leadership of terrorist networks. His lectures and writings, beloved in the English zone, were rarely posted to the leading jihadist websites. Among hardcore jihadist ideologues and networked terrorists, he barely registered a blip.

Even as the U.S. media was throwing Awlaki a coronation, his terrorist protégés had mostly turned out to be embarrassing failures. (That is likely to change sooner or later, perhaps even during the space between this sentence being written and this book being published.)

His status began to change in April 2010, when U.S. officials revealed that Awlaki had been approved for targeted killing by the CIA. No American citizen had ever been added to the CIA's target list, even though several other Americans held very important positions with al Qaeda's central operation in Afghanistan and Pakistan. No rationale for Awlaki's unique status was offered to the public. [54]

AQAP soon fired back with a statement in Arabic vowing to protect Awlaki from any U.S. attempt to capture or kill him.[55] The interview followed quickly, and Awlaki began issuing statements in Arabic, which were enthusiastically received by the Arabic-speaking jihadist community. New fans began seeking out his older material, which was widely available from download sites and on both the Arabic- and English-language versions of YouTube.

At the end of October, AQAP planted two bombs in parcels and shipped them to the United States. The bombs were intercepted and defused before they reached their targets. Twenty days later AQAP published another issue of its English-language magazine detailing the attack and its goals. One article, printed under the byline "Head of Foreign Operations," was believed by some analysts to have been penned by Awlaki, suggesting he had settled into a formal role within the organization as a fully operational terrorist.[56]

But is Awlaki the next Osama bin Laden?

It's extremely important to understand Anwar Awlaki in context. There is no question that he is an important and dangerous figure who presents the United States with a serious and significant challenge. He has been directly involved in planning and executing terrorist attacks, and he has inspired a large number of would-be terrorists in the Western world.

Comparing him to bin Laden is dangerous, however, because it elevates Awlaki's status based on a fundamental misunderstanding of each man's role and capacity.

It's certainly possible Awlaki was working for the core al Qaeda organization before September 11, and it's virtually certain he was working with al Qaeda in the Arabian Peninsula before the relationship was officially announced. Yet there's very little evidence that he held a position of significant authority in either group before 2010.

No evidence has emerged as of this writing to suggest that Awlaki has ever pointed a gun at a human being and pulled the trigger. His terrorist operations have been underwhelming at best, embarrassing at worst. They can still cause chaos, of course, especially when the West is willing to mobilize thousands of people and millions of dollars in response to every new terrorist strategy it sees. But overall, Awlaki's successes have owed more to Western failures than operational brilliance.

Now consider Osama bin Laden. Bin Laden is far more influential than Awlaki simply as far as his preaching and ability to inspire. All of Awlaki's jihadist adherents are also adherents of bin Laden, but the reverse does not necessarily apply, even with Awlaki's recent gains.

Bin Laden doesn't stop at getting people fired up. The Saudi kingpin of terror cut his teeth in combat against the Soviets during the Afghan jihad. His supporters may have wildly exaggerated his accomplishments during that conflict, but no one disputes that he is experienced in matters of war.

He's even more experienced and proficient at managing terrorist operations. Osama bin Laden studies his enemy, looks for vulnerabilities, and uses that information to select a target. He spends years on surveillance and planning, and when that is done, he sends multiple teams of highly trained terrorists to carry out his plans. Bin Laden is detail oriented. During the East African embassy bombings, he pointed out where the truck bomb should be placed in Nairobi for maximum casualties.

In contrast, Awlaki attracts lunatics, points them at America, and pushes.

It's absolutely appropriate to treat Awlaki as a serious threat. One 2010 intelligence report estimated that as many as three hundred Americans had trained with al Qaeda in the Arabian Peninsula.[57] If the estimate is accurate, it would represent an unprecedented migration of Americans into the ranks of jihadists, and Awlaki was almost certainly driving that recruitment.

But the rush to anoint him as the next bin Laden may also be fueling his recent success. Awlaki's writings and lectures were not heavily promoted on the most important terrorist forums until after AQAP publicly accepted him, and that didn't happen until months after the media push began and then only after the United States announced he had been targeted for death.

There is no question that Awlaki's status among terrorists was greatly enhanced by the media's estimation of his importance. Even with that helpful push, however, it's hard to imagine that Awlaki could ever fill the shoes of Osama bin Laden. But the end of Awlaki's story has yet to be written, and the American imam has proved himself to be full of surprises.

10
A Diverse Threat

In the wake of September 11, more than one thousand Muslim Americans and Muslim immigrants were detained in the United States, often without charge. There were indisputable abuses.

In some cases people were arrested simply because their names came up during the investigation of the attack.[1] In other cases, innocent employees of terrorist-linked charities were detained merely because of where they worked. In 2009 a court of appeals described the detention of Muslims after 9/11 as "repugnant to the Constitution and a painful reminder of some of the most ignominious chapters of our national history."[2]

Yet some of the detentions were legitimate. Few Americans realized the extent of al Qaeda's presence in the United States or the history of American involvement in jihadist activity, some of which was closely linked to terrorism. Neither the CIA nor the FBI had the slightest idea how many Americans had trained in al Qaeda's camps in Afghanistan.[3]

It soon appeared that the most dangerous American members of al Qaeda proper had already been taken off the streets by the embassy bombings investigation. In the weeks and months that followed, the FBI's reach would become more precise and less sweeping.

Much of al Qaeda's infrastructure in the United States remained intact on September 12, 2001. The most significant operation was the Benevolence International Foundation in Chicago, which had financed al Qaeda, as well as jihadists in Chechnya and Bosnia. The deceptive charity was shut down and its director,

Enaam Arnaout, arrested. He eventually pleaded guilty to defrauding donors by spending Benevolence funds to support mujahideen fighters in Bosnia and Chechnya.[4]

The directors of CARE International—the former Al Kifah office in Boston—were arrested, tried, and convicted of tax fraud for redirecting charitable contributions to jihad.[5] The Holy Land Foundation, a Hamas financier in Texas, was also shuttered and its directors convicted.[6]

A few small cells with direct links to al Qaeda were uncovered. In Lackawanna, New York, six American citizens of Yemeni descent were arrested for having trained at an al Qaeda camp prior to September 11. A seventh American member of the cell was killed by a CIA drone strike in Yemen. Although all were Americans, they lived in a highly insular, ethnic Yemeni community.[7]

Abdurrahman Alamoudi, the head of the mainstream American Muslim Council, was arrested in 2003 for helping Libya try to assassinate Saudi crown prince Abdullah.[8]

In Portland a group of seven Americans who had been training for jihad prior to September 11 made a series of attempts to reach Afghanistan and fight in the service of al Qaeda and the Taliban. Four were arrested in Portland, another in Dearborn, Michigan. A sixth was captured in Malaysia, and the last succeeded in reaching al Qaeda and was killed in battle.[9]

American-born Muslim convert James Ujaama, a Seattle resident, tried to set up a terrorist training camp in rural Bly, Oregon, under the guidance of radical London-based cleric Abu Hamza Al Masri. Ujaama was arrested as a material witness and later charged with offering material support to the Taliban. He cut a plea, skipped out on his parole, and eventually ended up back in prison.[10]

There were more—many more. Between September 11, 2001, and August 2010, scores of U.S. citizens were indicted for terrorism-related offenses. A relative few were arrested for assisting Hezbollah and Hamas. Most of these were financing and weapons cases; the vast majority of violent offenders—or would-be violent offenders—were connected to al Qaeda and an increasingly diffuse group of related Sunni terrorist organizations outside of Israel.

AL QAEDA

In the post–September 11 area, Adam Gadahn emerged as one of al Qaeda's most important American recruits. He started life on a goat farm in rural Winchester,

California, a little more than an hour's drive north of San Diego. His father, a Christian convert of Jewish descent, sold *halal* meat (the Islamic equivalent of kosher) to the local Arab community.

Although Gadahn was raised in an informally Christian environment, he found the concept of the Christian trinity illogical (a rift cited by many Muslim converts) and turned away from the religion. He went through a typically difficult teenage phase, listening to heavy metal music and fighting with his parents. One night he was listening to a fiery, radical Christian radio preacher rant about the "Islamic threat." The rebellious teen figured that if this guy hated Islam, there must be something to it, and he began to investigate the religion through discussions with Muslims in online chatrooms.[11]

> I discovered that the beliefs and practices of this religion fit my personal theology and intellect as well as basic human logic. Islam presents God not as an anthropomorphic being but as an entity beyond human comprehension, transcendent of man, independant [sic] and undivided. Islam has a holy book that is comprehensible to a layman, and there is no papacy or priesthood that is considered infallible in matters of interpretation: all Muslims are free to reflect and interpret the book given a sufficient education.

This idea that understanding Islam is an individual prerogative that does not require context or schooling creates a wide-open door for radicalization. Combined with Islam's lack of a central religious authority to decide doctrinal issues, new converts are particularly susceptible to the first person who comes along to explain the religion to them.[12]

For Gadahn, those people were worshippers at the Islamic Society of Orange County, where he formally converted to Islam. The imam at the mosque was Muzammil Siddiqui, a former employee of the Muslim World League. In 1992 Omar Abdel Rahman had visited to give a sermon promoting jihad. In the years since, the Islamic Society had moved more toward the mainstream, but there remained a group of vocal, highly visible militants who were constantly agitating to move the congregation to a stricter posture.[13]

The newly converted Gadahn was drawn to this group and particularly to two members: Hisham Diab and Khalil Deek, the heads of an organization called

Charity Without Borders. Both men were believed to be mujahideen veterans of the Bosnia war.[14]

The older men drilled the impressionable teenager with religious ideology, pushing him to dress in Arab style and grow a beard. They warned him of the dangers of associating with *kaffirs* (infidels) and angrily condemned people at the mosque who took part in interfaith outreach. Their condemnations of the Islamic Society's chairman inspired Gadahn to assault the man.[15] In 1997 Gadahn left the United States for Pakistan, his trip paid for by Charity Without Borders. Except for a brief visit home in 1998, he was finished with America.

Deek moved to Pakistan soon after, and the two men lived in Peshawar.[16] Reports on Gadahn's early involvement with al Qaeda are sketchy. He worked for a while on low-level tasks, handling communications and translations for al Qaeda and other militant groups in the Pakistani city. At some point, he crossed over into Afghanistan and became a part of al Qaeda. For a few years, he labored in obscurity.[17]

Gadahn resurfaced in dramatic style in 2004, when he starred in an al Qaeda videotape. He appeared with his face covered, identified only as "Azzam the American." In an interview with an unnamed questioner, Azzam answered a series of short questions with a series of lengthy diatribes, outlining al Qaeda's case against the United States.

Although he delved into Islamic history and ideology, the core of his anger was reserved for his home country. Speaking in English with an affected or acquired Arabic accent, Azzam the American blasted both the United States and the Muslims who live there peacefully:

> My country of origin, like many extinct, forgotten nations before it, is at war with the truth and wants to replace the genuine teachings of Islam, the genuine teachings of the religion, with a tame, nonthreatening version of Islam, made up somewhere in the greater Washington, D.C., area. My country of origin is making war on Muslims, killing and displacing thousands of them, occupying their homelands and holy places, and plundering and depleting their resources. My country of origin is spreading immorality, economic instability, environmental destruction, and many other afflictions throughout the Muslim world. Throughout the entire world, in fact.[18]

In 2005 Azzam's role became clearer. On the anniversary of September 11, he appeared in a second video, threatening new attacks in the United States (specifically in Los Angeles, a threat that was never realized). A few days later, al Qaeda released a video filmed in the style of a Western news program and titled *Voice of the Caliphate*.[19] Gadahn's voice was clearly recognizable in the video, speaking in Arabic.

It became increasingly clear that Gadahn was not only the front man on these productions; he was involved in their production. al Qaeda's video production unit during the 1990s had been truly professional, producing slick, polished propaganda such as *The State of Ummah*, a two-hour documentary featuring iconic images of al Qaeda's training camps and a long critique of U.S. policies toward the Muslim world.[20]

After 9/11 the media operation had descended into chaos, although audio and video communiqués from top Al Qaeda leaders continued to trickle out. Starting in 2005, that changed. A stream of new productions was released by al Qaeda's media branch, As-Sahab (meaning "the clouds"). Gadahn was believed to be heavily involved in the production of these videos, narrating an English-language Al Qaeda documentary on the September 11 attacks, among other contributions.[21]

He also began to issue more formal communiqués in the style of Osama bin Laden and Ayman Al Zawahiri. *An Invitation to Islam* professed to offer Americans a chance to avoid certain destruction by converting. The video was introduced by Zawahiri, firmly establishing Gadahn's credentials. Subsequent videos warned again and again about imminent and devastating attacks that never seemed to happen.[22]

Over time Gadahn ceased to be a novelty, and his messages became less effective with American audiences, due to a combination of increasing U.S. and Pakistani military pressure on his position and his growing immersion in the culture of al Qaeda.

He was, in many ways, an object lesson in the limitations of American jihadists in communications and more generally. Many of al Qaeda's American recruits become enamored of Arab and Muslim culture early in the radicalization process. They eventually stop talking like Americans and start talking like Arabs. Often, the longer they are involved with terrorism, the less effective they are at reaching U.S. audiences.

Nevertheless, "Azzam the American" continued to be a significant figure in al Qaeda's stream of propaganda communication. In 2009 he appeared in a video titled *The Mujahideen Don't Target Muslims*, which tried to refute the growing (and accurate) perception that al Qaeda's terrorist attacks were killing far more Muslims than "Crusaders," particularly in Pakistan. Gadahn argued that the media had wrongly attributed recent attacks to al Qaeda, part of a frame-up by the governments of Pakistan and the United States.[23]

As of this writing, Gadahn is believed to be in hiding, somewhere along the border between Pakistan and Afghanistan.

Al Qaeda has often exploited its Western members for communications and publicity, but the original goal of recruiting Americans was always to use their passports and their ability to blend in while preparing terrorist attacks. That strategy became front-page headlines when jihadist Jose Padilla returned at long last to U.S. soil.

Padilla had spent September 2001 at the house of al Qaeda's military commander, Mohammed Atef. When an American air strike killed Atef in November, it narrowly missed taking out Padilla as well. The Latino American had been training in explosives when the strike took place. He returned to find the house in ruins and helped dig Atef's body out of the wreckage.[24]

Padilla and Adnan Shukrijumah, his compatriot from Florida, had been ordered to blow up apartment buildings back in the United States, but the two could not get along. Shukrijumah, ruthlessly competent and pragmatic, was intellectually a cut above Padilla, whose ambitions outstripped his ability by a wide margin. Shukrijumah bailed out of the apartments plot, and Padilla was assigned another partner, an Ethiopian named Binyamin Mohamed.

The two men went to Khalid Shaikh Mohammed—al Qaeda's chief of terrorist operations and the mastermind of 9/11—to discuss the plan. Padilla continued to lobby for some kind of nuclear attack, but Mohammed was skeptical. Exasperated, he finally sent the two men to America with money in their pockets and a promise that instructions would follow.

Padilla was arrested the moment he stepped off the plane in Chicago. Binyamin didn't even make it out of Pakistan before getting nabbed by authorities there.[25]

Attorney General John Ashcroft announced Padilla's arrest in dramatic fashion, hyping the dirty bomb threat and labeling him an enemy combatant, which led to the al Qaeda member being incarcerated in a military prison without due process for more than three years. Finally, Padilla was moved back into the legal system, amid questions about whether he was ever all that dangerous and whether an American detained on U.S. soil could be denied his right to a lawyer and a trial.

The surviving leaders of the American Islamic Group—including Adham Hassoun and Kifah Al Jayyousi—had also been arrested and were facing indictment in Florida. Because Padilla had first been radicalized and sent overseas by Hassoun, they were tried together. All were convicted of conspiracy to murder, maim, and kidnap people abroad and sentenced to life in prison.[26]

Things were going better for al Qaeda's other Floridian. Far from being cannon fodder, Adnan Shukrijumah was rising through the ranks.

Starting in 2003 U.S. authorities began to issue a series of increasingly frantic-sounding alerts about Shukrijumah but offered few details about why he was so important. Sightings poured in from around the world: Guyana, Canada, Trinidad, and Tampa, Florida. He had even purportedly cased the Panama Canal for a possible al Qaeda attack.[27]

Some of the leads were solid, but most were sketchy, and the intelligence never included a clear explanation of what Shukrijumah was doing.[28] Rumor had it that his nickname was "Jaffar the Pilot" and that he was training to be the next Mohammed Atta, but no conclusive evidence ever surfaced suggesting that Shukrijumah knew how to fly.[29]

But more credible traces of his activities eventually emerged. In 2009 the FBI broke up a small cell of U.S. citizens and immigrants led by Najibullah Zazi, a naturalized American citizen born in Afghanistan who had moved to Queens as a teenager. Zazi was, as one relative put it, "a dumb kid." He worked a coffee stand in Manhattan before moving to Denver and driving a shuttle bus. In 2006 Zazi flew to Pakistan to find a wife. He married a nineteen-year-old cousin who stayed in Pakistan while he returned to the United States. During his time away, Zazi had become more religious. He grew a beard and started to give a cold shoulder to the non-Muslims he encountered on the job.[30]

In 2008 Zazi went to Afghanistan and visited an al Qaeda training camp, where he received training in weapons and improvised explosives.[31] Drawing on the latter, he returned to the United States with a grocery list of bomb ingredients. He began shopping.

After the invasion of Afghanistan, al Qaeda's training apparatus had been rendered into a permanent state of chaos. During the 1990s the training experience was thorough, long term, and rigorous. Post-9/11, the training regimen for most recruits became haphazard and much shorter, sometimes cramming months' worth of information into just a few days. Like many of al Qaeda's new brigade of volunteers, the "dumb kid" didn't learn his lessons very well. When he was arrested shortly before the anniversary of September 11, he was in a panic, having just called overseas for advice on how to complete the job.[32]

When the FBI questioned Zazi and his accomplices, they discovered that the man who had ordered the former coffee vendor to bomb his adopted home was none other than Adnan Shukrijumah.[33]

In August 2010 the FBI issued yet another alarming alert with precious few details attached. The new media blitz claimed that Shukrijumah had taken over the job of his old boss, Khalid Shaikh Mohammed, and was now the head of al Qaeda's external operations.[34]

The ramifications of this development were unclear, as was the source. The FBI refused to discuss Shukrijumah for this book.

Clearly, an American would theoretically be well equipped to plan attacks on the United States, but being the "new" Khalid Shaikh Mohammed was a very different thing in 2010 than being the "old" KSM.

In 2001 Mohammed had the ability to travel with relative freedom, stable facilities to work from, a significant budget to work with, and a small army of professional operatives to make his plans a reality. Shukrijumah, in contrast, had a fraction of the money, no stable geographical base, and a small brigade of enthusiastic but inept amateurs such as Zazi and his friends.

AMATEUR HOUR CONTINUES: THE TIMES SQUARE BOMBING

Faisal Shahzad was born in Pakistan and moved to the United States as a college student, where he majored in computer science and engineering at the University of Bridgeport, Connecticut. For more than a decade, he lived in the United States without attracting much notice. Shahzad made a good living in the United States and seemed to be comfortable in his new home, if not fully at ease.

He maintained strong ties in Pakistan, even after marrying an American Muslim from the Denver area. His wife covered her hair, and he often dressed in

Pakistani-style clothing, but they didn't stand out as being unassimilated. Firmly ensconced in the upper middle class, the Shahzads were, by most accounts, relaxed and unremarkable. He became an American citizen in 2009.[35]

Yet behind closed doors, Faisal Shahzad was discontented, and that discontent was growing. In the years following September 11, he became enamored of jihadist propaganda and began to segregate himself from non-Muslims, at least internally.[36]

In many ways, it was a classic jihadist turn, focused on the victimization of Muslims abroad, especially the rape of Muslim women. Unlike earlier American-born converts, however, Shahzad steeped himself in theological arguments before turning toward action.[37]

After the U.S. invasion of Iraq, he began to believe that America was working to harm Muslims. That perception was reinforced by the words of English-language jihadist ideologues such as Abdullah Al Faisal and Anwar Awlaki. He began posting to jihadist message boards and railing to his friends about U.S. foreign policy.[38] In 2006 he wrote to a friend,

> We all know that most of our *Ummah* is ignorant of Islam or illiterate of Koran and *Sunnah* [practices of the Prophet Mohammed]. Koran and *Sunnah* is our very base and purpose of creation in this world. Most of us get confused with current wars when we try to make logic with our worldly knowledge. Have you every try to look at [it] with Allah's prospective [sic], do you try to read and understand Koran? Except for just clinging to one excuse that Islam does not allow innocent killings? Not saying that it is right, but we are not sure of who does that either? It might be U.S.A fighter who gives his life to Allah can never disobey His commands. [. . .] We don't know the realities on ground as to what the Mujahideen goes through but you would have to agree to the fact that there is a force out there that is fighting the west and is defeating them.[39]

During trips back to Pakistan, Shahzad increasingly immersed himself in radical company. He worshipped at the Red Mosque in Islamabad, a notoriously radical institution known for catering to worshippers and students from Pakistan's Northwest Frontier Province, an al Qaeda and Taliban stronghold.[40] In 2007 militants at the mosque began to kidnap people they deemed immoral, including police officers and local brothel workers. Pakistan's security forces stormed the mosque in July 2007, killing dozens of people.[41]

Shahzad was in America at the time, gripped by news reports of the violence. Investigators would later conclude that the siege was the "triggering event" that pushed the Connecticut computer expert over the edge from talk into action. His outrage was further stoked by apparent civilian casualties from U.S. drone strikes in Pakistan's tribal areas, where key al Qaeda leaders were suspected of hiding. Shahzad's family had roots in the region, and the tribal connection put an exclamation point on his rage.

In early 2008 Shahzad returned to Pakistan with a sense of purpose. Through contacts in Islamabad, he sought out the Pakistani Taliban. Initially the Taliban suspected he was a spy and kept him at arm's length. Yet over time and with the help of friends in the country, he won the group's confidence, even meeting with its leader, Hakimullah Mehsud, one of Pakistan's most wanted militants.

By 2009 Shahzad was ready to pack in his American life and moved his family abroad soon after taking his oath of U.S. citizenship. He returned to Pakistan with the intent of creating a life there, but the Taliban had other plans for him.

Before September 11 an al Qaeda operative who was intended for an attack on the United States would receive months of expert training before being sent on a mission. But the Taliban was not al Qaeda—the strike, if successful, would have been the group's first attack abroad. And the luxury of time had been deeply disrupted by the U.S. invasion of Afghanistan and the corresponding Pakistani crackdown along the border.[42] Shahzad was shuttled into a training camp in the border region of Waziristan, where he went through a few short weeks of general training followed by only five days of instruction on the art of bomb making.[43]

The utter failure of Shazad's training was on full display when he returned to the United States to make his move. During the course of a few months, he gathered bits and pieces of flammable and explosive materials, any two or three of which would have been enough to create a fairly dangerous bomb, and then he proceeded to mash them together in the back of his Nissan Pathfinder SUV. He stuffed fireworks, propane, gasoline, and fertilizer into the vehicle and wired it up with a bizarre combination of timers and fuses, all purchased with thousands of dollars of Taliban money.

Despite the demented design, dumb luck might have ignited the improvised bomb into a significant fireball. Fortunately, Shahzad was poised at the nexus between competent and incompetent. If he had been a little better at his job, it would have worked. If he had been a little less ambitious with his design, it would have worked. He fell perfectly in the middle.

Shahzad drove the SUV to Times Square on the evening of May 1, 2010, and left it parked on the side of a crowded street. The detonator mechanism created so much smoke that it choked off the oxygen supply that would have ignited the flammable components. The fertilizer he chose for its supposed explosive power turned out to be inert. He forgot to arm a key component of the bomb—and he left his car and apartment keys in the Pathfinder.[44]

The attack was a disaster, just not the disaster that Shahzad had intended. As he fled back to his apartment in Connecticut, the Taliban e-mailed a triumphant audio to the terrorism news website The Long War Journal, claiming credit for what it described as a "jaw-breaking blow" against the United States.[45] Shahzad was captured while trying to flee the country.

After cooperating with investigators for several weeks, Shahzad appeared in court on June 21, 2010, and entered a defiant guilty plea—"guilty and one hundred times more"—calling himself a "Muslim soldier" and insisting that he acted alone while in the United States. Questioned by the judge about his willingness to kill children in Times Square, Shahzad was unrepentant.

> Well, the drone hits in Afghanistan and Iraq, they don't see children, they don't see anybody. They kill women, children, they kill everybody. It's a war, and in war, they kill people. They're killing all Muslims. [. . .] I am part of the answer to the U.S. terrorizing the Muslim nations and the Muslim people. And, on behalf of that, I'm avenging the attack. Living in the United States, Americans only care about their own people, but they don't care about the people elsewhere in the world when they die.

LASHKAR-E-TAYYIBA

Al Qaeda and the Taliban are not the only organizations recruiting Americans for violent jihad. There are a host of enemies, stretching from West Africa through the Middle East, Asia, South Asia, and on into Southeast Asia: al Qaeda in the

Islamic Maghreb, the Libyan Islamic Fighting Group, Lashkar-e-Jhangvi, Fatah Al Islam, Hamas, Tawhid and Jihad, the Abu Sayyaf Group, and a score more of various sizes and shapes.

Most are concerned primarily with local issues, but they also accept foreigners in their ranks. Some aspire to play on a broader stage.

In Pakistan, not far from the Taliban's domain, a cold war has been threatening to go hot for more than twenty years. The border between Pakistan and India is disputed. The conflict has played out in the Indian state of Jammu and Kashmir, a Muslim-majority area known for its great natural beauty.

India and Pakistan have been fighting over the region to a greater or lesser extent since 1947. The dispute was settled in favor of India, but an insurgency has festered since 1989, fueled by mujahideen fighters and terrorists from Pakistan and abroad, with significant covert support from Pakistan's intelligence service. In addition to the two nation-states tussling over the region, a move for Kashmiri independence was also roiling internally.[46]

As the twentieth century wound to a close, Randall Royer, the white kid from Virginia who had joined the Bosnian mujahideen, was growing restless. He moved in heady circles during his day job with the Council for American-Islamic Relations, rubbing shoulders with top State Department officials (including its counterterrorism coordinator) and even attending White House functions. At one, he had his picture taken with President Clinton.[47]

It was a job that seemed to fit his disposition, but in time he found his attention drawn once more to the fields of jihad. With a group of friends—up to a dozen American-born citizens and immigrants from the Washington, D.C., area—Royer began to train with firearms for jihad in Chechnya, where an Islamist insurgency had been carrying out a campaign of guerrilla war and terrorism against the Russian government.

They practiced for jihad using paintball guns, as well as live weapons, including the weapon of choice for mujahideen around the world, the Russian-made Kalashnikov assault rifle, better known as an AK-47. Three members of the group were U.S. military veterans, and the team practiced at times on military firing ranges.[48] In April 2000 Royer applied for a visa to go to Pakistan, where he met with members of Lashkar-e-Tayyiba (LeT), Urdu for "Army of Righteousness."

LeT was a Pakistani Islamist group formed in 1989 that had attracted a significant number of Afghan war veterans. Royer had arranged an introduction through mujahideen fighters he had met in Bosnia who were now in Pakistan.[49]

According to Royer, he researched the group before going to Kashmir and determined that it had not been designated a terrorist organization.[50] This was technically true (LeT was not formally designated as such until December 2001), but it would have been difficult to research the group without discovering its terrorist activities.[51] By 2000 the organization had been implicated in attacks on Indian civilians and troops in Kashmir. Its members had killed scores of victims in just a few short years.[52]

Royer connected with LeT in Lahore, where he saw what he called an "idyllic" Islamic community. According to Royer, he sought and received assurances that the group was opposed to extremism generally and al Qaeda specifically.

The conflict was different here than in Bosnia, more complex and multifaceted (although, in fairness, the narrative in Bosnia had also been greatly oversimplified by both the press and jihadist ideologues). For Royer it boiled down to a series of indignities against "the oppressed"—meaning the Muslim oppressed, as opposed to the Hindus being terrorized by LeT. Royer went to the Kashmir area and wielded a gun during the visit. He sought to minimize the incident as firing "a few rounds over the front line in the general direction of an Indian military bunker."[53]

Royer returned to the United States and made arrangements for other members of his group to travel to Pakistan to train and eventually fight with LeT. Back in the states, the men continued to acquire weapons, military equipment, and ammunition.

Then September 11 happened. Some members of the paintball group were already in Pakistan. Those who remained were told by their spiritual guide, Ali Al Timimi, that an all-out war would soon break out between the United States and Islam and that fighting Americans was a legitimate act of jihad. Everyone in the room should talk to Royer about joining their comrades at the LeT training camps, Timimi said. After the meeting, Royer began working the phones. Four more members of the group flew to Pakistan by the end of the month.

In Pakistan the former paintballers trained in light and heavy weaponry. Royer sent his family to Bosnia, his wife's homeland, and in December 2001 he took a second group of recruits to join LeT.[54]

Several of the LeT trainees, including Royer, eventually made their way back to the United States. Although no evidence was found of a specific terrorist plot in the works, the FBI swept in and arrested most of the group in June 2003. A dozen men were indicted, including Ali Timimi. Three were believed to be at large somewhere abroad.[55] Two of the men cut pleas; the rest were convicted of conspiracy and material support for terrorism. Timimi was sentenced to life in prison for inciting terrorism.[56]

Royer wrote a long letter to the judge before his sentencing, pleading a combination of good intentions, bad judgment, and a level of obliviousness that is difficult to credit in someone of such obvious intelligence.

> I am not bitter about my arrest. I realize that the government has a legitimate interest in protecting the public from terrorism, and that in this post–9/11 environment, it must take all reasonable precautions. I have repeated this often to law enforcement, and I said as much to the FBI agents who arrested me. As I wrote in March of 2003, in these times, "law enforcement should at least keep tabs on those suspected of being responsible for violence overseas." It is also quite clear to me now that I crossed the line and, in my ignorance and phenomenally poor judgment, broke the law. I will live with regret for my actions and their consequences for the rest of my life. Had I known that my conduct—at the core of my plea agreement—was illegal, I would have done many things differently.[57]

Media coverage of the case often focused on contentious discussions around the paintball exercises, which the defendants had sought to portray as innocent fun. Relatively little attention was given to Lashkar-e-Tayyiba. As a participant in a complicated local conflict abroad, the organization seemed as if it presented little threat outside its corner of the world. But another American recruit would soon show how deadly LeT could be.

Daood Syed Gilani was born in Washington, D.C., in 1960. His father was a Pakistani diplomat and a devout Muslim, conservative but with an affinity for music. Gilani spent his first ten years living with the family in Pakistan, then his mother—Serrill Headley, thoroughly American and a feminist—rebelled and returned to her native Philadelphia and her secular roots, leaving him behind with his father. She opened a bar called the Khyber Pass, which she liked to tell people was haunted.[58]

When Gilani turned seventeen, he joined his mother in Philadelphia to attend a local college. He assimilated into his new life with some difficulty. The contrast between his upbringing in Pakistan and his mother's Western ways was stark. Gilani never left Islam, but he became erratic in its practice—avoiding pork but indulging growing weaknesses for drink, drugs, and women. Gilani's prowess in the latter arena was the stuff of local legend. "Girls fell on their faces for him," said one woman who used to tend bar with him.[59]

Gilani's life seemed to swing on a pendulum. He worked first at his mother's bar, which she turned over to him with disastrous results. They sold the bar and started a video store called FliksVideo, which Gilani eventually expanded to several branches in New York City, making a decent living.[60] Yet the darker side of American life drew him in, and he became involved in heroin trafficking through a Pakistani drug ring in New York City, where he eventually developed a drug habit himself.

His uncle William Headley captured the contradictions perfectly in an interview with the *Wall Street Journal*. "I have this image of him. He would have the Koran under one arm and a bottle of Dom Pérignon under the other."[61]

Starting in the late 1980s, Gilani's extralegal activities began to catch up with him. He was arrested and convicted of heroin trafficking, released, then arrested again several years later. Copping a plea in 1997, he worked for a time as an informant for the Drug Enforcement Agency. He traveled to Pakistan on the agency's behalf, where he rediscovered his roots in Islam. During this time, Gilani grew a beard, adopted Pakistani dress and married a Pakistani Muslim woman, with whom he had four children.

In early 2002 he began commuting to Pakistan to attend terrorist training camps, possibly while he was still working for the DEA, and trained at a camp run by Lashkar-e-Tayyiba.

Gilani was ensnared by the legend of veteran jihadist Ilyas Kashmiri and his "supernatural powers and miracles." Kashmiri had taken part in the jihad against the Soviet Union, running a training camp in Waziristan, the lawless region of Pakistan that shared a border with Afghanistan. In later years he took up the cause of Kashmir as a militant and a terrorist, establishing a relationship with al Qaeda and making a name for himself as one of Pakistan's most wanted. Gilani met Kashmiri during his time with LeT and swore *bayat*, an Islamic oath of allegiance, to the senior leader.[62]

In 2002 LeT still operated with relative impunity. Training started with a three-week course that consisted of strictly religious indoctrination. In August Gilani returned for weapons training. The next year he returned again and learned close combat, grenade tactics, and survival skills. The courses continued through 2003—countersurveillance, intelligence, combat, and tactical maneuvers. By the end of 2003, he was a sworn member of LeT with a host of dangerous new skills.[63]

In late 2005 Gilani's training and loyalty were finally rewarded. He was activated in the early stages of what would be a massive terrorist strike on Indian soil. Unlike most terrorist strikes in the post-9/11 era, this program would be meticulously planned.

Gilani was assigned to visit India, using his valuable U.S. passport, and case possible terrorist targets, including public places and government installations. He changed his name from Daood Gilani to David Coleman Headley, taking his mother's American-sounding name in order to ease any prospect of suspicion during border crossings.

His destination was Mumbai. Armed with a video camera, Gilani prowled the city gathering intelligence on prospective terrorist targets. During the course of multiple trips, he narrowed down the targets, gathering more and more specific intelligence on the best targets. Finally, one stood out as the central location: the Taj Mahal, a sumptuous five-star hotel favored by wealthy Western tourists and political luminaries. His contact at LeT told him that the attackers would come in by boat and conduct a suicide commando raid on the hotel and several other landmarks in the vicinity. Gilani picked out a landing site for the squad.[64]

In November 2008 the plan was executed. A team of 10 terrorist commandos, trained by LeT, hijacked a boat and went ashore. Starting late on a Wednesday, they opened fire on civilians in several locations, seized the Taj, and took hostages from among the 450 guests. The killing didn't stop until Saturday morning. More than 160 people were killed, including six Americans. More than 300 were injured.[65]

Gilani was in Pakistan at the time of the attack, somewhere between Kariachi and Lahore, already working on his next terrorist assignment. This time the target was in Copenhagen, Denmark—the offices of a Danish newspaper, *Jyllands Posten*, that had sparked a global firestorm by publishing cartoon images of the Prophet Mohammed. Many Muslims were outraged by the publication, and radical Muslims like Gilani even more so. Just a few weeks before the Mumbai attack, he had e-mailed former high school classmates on the cartoon controversy.

> Everything is not a joke. [. . .] We are not rehearsing a skit on *Saturday Night Live*. Making fun of Islam is making fun of [Mohammed]. Call me old-fashioned but I feel disposed towards violence for the offending parties, be they cartoonists from Denmark or Sherry Jones (Author of *Jewel of Medina*) or Irshad Manji (Liberal Muslim trying to make lesbianism acceptable in Islam, amongst other things). They never started debates with folks who slandered our Prophet, they took violent action. Even if God doesn't give us the opportunity to bring our intentions to fruition, we will claim *ajr* [credit with Allah for good deeds] for it.[66]

In other messages around the same period, Gilani characterized terrorism, suicide bombings, and beheadings as heroic.

> Some of us are saying that "Terrorism" is the weapon of the cowardly. I will say that you may call it barbaric or immoral or cruel, but never cowardly. Courage is, by and large, exclusive to the Muslim nation.[67]

Gilani's disposition toward violence was not mere talk. In a discussion with his LeT handler, he was already laying out the scope of a new attack. Gilani suggested that they target the Danish newspaper's editor and cartoonist. "*All* Danes are responsible," his handler replied.

Gilani returned to the United States and began to plan his reconnaissance mission. He made up business cards and contacted *Jyllands Posten* to ask about placing an ad, the pretext he would use to enter the office. In January 2009 he flew to Copenhagen. As in Mumbai, he took extensive video of the newspaper's buildings and the surrounding area. He also succeeded at getting inside the building.

Returning to Pakistan, he reported on the site, but the attack had to be postponed. LeT was feeling the heat that Mumbai had created. At the direction of

Ilyas Kashmiri, Gilani was instructed to meet with a contact in Europe who would provide non-LeT manpower willing to carry out a suicide attack. Kashmiri told Gilani to make sure the volunteers recorded martyrdom videos before the attack. Unsatisfied with the grisly carnage that LeT had wrought in Mumbai, he also told Gilani that the attackers should decapitate the newspaper's employees and throw their severed heads out of the building's windows. The attack was to take place as soon as possible, Kashmiri told the American terrorist, intimating that the leaders of al Qaeda wanted it that way.

But in July 2009, Gilani's LeT handler switched gears again, postponing the Denmark attack (to Gilani's dismay) and calling him back to Pakistan in order to work on a follow-up attack in India. Gilani was resistant, complaining that his handlers "had rotten guts" and telling an associate that he could complete the project without the organization's assistance.[68]

He had overestimated his chances. In October 2009 Gilani was arrested at the airport while trying to fly from Chicago to Philadelphia, apparently in preparation to connect to Denmark. In his luggage FBI agents found maps of Copenhagen and a memory stick containing video surveillance of the newspaper office and other locations.[69] He cut a deal and pleaded guilty to complicity in the Mumbai attack.[70]

As of this writing, he may also face charges in India.[71] Under interrogation by Indian officials as part of his plea agreement, Gilani was said to be abusive, referring to his interrogators with "the choicest of Hindi expletives" and mocking Indian intelligence.

"The attack was planned and executed in your own backyard. You didn't even get a whiff of it and now you want to question me," Gilani reportedly scoffed.[72]

AL SHABAB

Somalia has known little but violence since the ruling dictatorship collapsed in 1991. The conflict was one of al Qaeda's earliest investments (see chapter 6). In 2004 a fragile agreement was crafted to restore order to the country under the auspices of a transitional government.[73]

Barely two years later, an Islamist movement known as the Islamic Courts Union (ICU) confronted the young government. The ICU, which wanted to establish shariah law, looked like a group of extremists to many observers, and there were rumors of links to al Qaeda. Although much of its activity was directed against the remaining shreds of the Somali government, ICU leaders blamed neighboring Ethiopia, a predominantly Christian nation, for interfering in Somalia's affairs and blamed the United States for supporting the interference.[74]

The ICU's rise didn't last long, and its fall was swift. Pressured by Ethiopia on one side and the Somali government on the other, then hammered by U.S. air strikes, the ICU crumbled and its leaders resigned.[75]

Soon afterward, a second-wave Islamist movement arose—Al Shabab, made up of the most militant members of the ICU, who had split to form their own organization, and a number of foreign mujahideen. The new militia used any means available to undercut the Somali government, including assassinations and suicide bombings. Most of its victims were, and continue to be, Somalis.[76]

Given the intense internal conflict, including Muslim-on-Muslim violence and a deep entanglement with essentially local conflicts of long standing, Somalia bore little resemblance to previous magnets for the global jihad movement.[77] Unlike the Afghans in the 1980s and the Bosnian Muslims in the 1990s, Al Shabab did not possess a clear claim to the moral high ground, and it certainly did not enjoy the support of Western governments and media.

Nevertheless, Al Shabab has attracted an extraordinary number of American jihadists. In 2007 and 2008, at least twenty young men from Minneapolis, Minnesota, left America to study the art of war at Al Shabab's training camps. Several other Americans from all over the country also left for the battlefield. The vast majority of those who joined the conflict were Americans of Somali descent. Many had been born in Somalia, and most had family or tribal ties to the combatants. In 2008 former Minneapolis resident Shirwa Ahmed earned the unhappy distinction of being the first American suicide bomber.[78]

Some fighters were recruited by people directly connected to Al Shabab or al Qaeda. Al Shabab recruiters were able to successfully leverage the involvement of Ethiopian troops working in conjunction with the Somali government to create a narrative of "Crusader" aggression. In this respect, they recreated some of the strengths of the old Soviet jihad recruiting model, in which jihadists lured young men to the battlefield first, then indoctrinated them with radical Islamic ideas in a tightly controlled environment. By the fall of 2010, U.S. intelligence estimated that several American citizens had risen to senior leadership positions in the organization.[79]

The Minneapolis community most heavily targeted by Al Shabab recruiters faced a particularly difficult version of the American experience, living in poverty and violence in and around a housing project called Riverside Plaza. Murders and drug violence were endemic, and random death came to both criminals and innocent bystanders. The desire for an escape was understandable. Although life with Al Shabab was hardly an improvement in security, some recruits found that the chance to die for a cause compared favorably with the very real risk of dying for no reason at all.[80]

While the problem of American ethnic Somalis joining Al Shabab is a serious concern, it's also diagnosable and thus a manageable problem for intelligence and law enforcement (up to a point). But the appeal of Al Shabab didn't stop there. Starting in 2006 and continuing through 2010, an increasingly diverse selection of American Muslims have tried to go to Somalia to take part in jihad.

Jehad Mostafa was an American citizen of Kurdish descent who was raised as a Muslim. He was known as a friendly young man without any particular extremist leanings. A college friend remembered him as an unlikely mujahideen. "I used to tease him that his name was pronounced like 'jihad,' and I'd say you're named after holy war? He'd say Islam is a religion of peace and love." He prayed at the Islamic Center of San Diego, one of the locations visited by the September 11 hijackers. He married a Somali woman in about 2005, left the country shortly thereafter, and eventually made his way to Al Shabab.[81]

There were several others (see chapter 11), but the most significant player was a Muslim named Omar Hammami, who hailed from the small southern town of Daphne, Alabama.[82]

His father was a Syrian Muslim immigrant, and his mother was an American Christian. In high school Hammami had been a gifted student and the class president. Popular and well liked, Hammami showed little interest in his father's religion while growing up, but during his sophomore year, he visited Syria with his father and became enamored of the Muslim culture he saw there. When he returned home, he began a gradual process of conversion.

Hammami eventually adopted the conservative Salafi school of thought. He aggressively pursued *dawah*—calling others to Islam. Not surprisingly, his quest was not well received in small-town Alabama. Eventually, he moved to Toronto with a childhood friend, Bernard Culveyhouse, who had also converted to Islam, thanks to Hammami's influence.

Surrounded by a much more robust and diverse Muslim community, including a significant number of Somali immigrants, Hammami became more attuned to world events. He eventually grew angry and obsessed with America's wars in Iraq and Afghanistan, as well as with conspiracy theories about September 11.

Seeking to educate himself about these issues, he discovered the jihadist Internet and began to take a more militant view of his obligations as a Muslim. Unlike many of his American predecessors, Hammami believed that the only true purpose of jihad was to establish an Islamic state.

Hammami met and married a Somali woman, guiding her from a relatively liberal view of Islam into Salafist conservatism and convincing her to wear an *abaya* and a *niqab*, which in combination form a full-body covering, leaving only the eyes visible.

Hammami and Culveyhouse decided that they wanted to study at Egypt's Al Azhar University. They moved to Alexandria briefly, but their applications were rejected, and Culveyhouse became disenchanted with Hammami's increasingly stringent path. He returned to the United States, leaving his friend behind.

Hammami turned to the Web for reinforcement on his journey. He met a kindred spirit online: Daniel Maldonado, an American citizen also living in Egypt.

The two took a keen interest in Somalia and the activities of the Islamic Courts Union. They were attracted by the ICU's narrative about establishing a pure Islamic state in the war-torn country, the reality of that narrative notwithstanding.[83]

The friends agreed to travel to Somalia and join the jihad. Maldonado's quest ended swiftly and ignominiously (see chapter 11). Hammami had better luck or maybe more commitment. He managed to work his way in with the Shabab fighters, who were now emerging as heirs to the ICU's jihad.

Hammami wasn't the only foreigner impressed with Shabab. Al Qaeda had taken notice of the group as well. Harun Fazul, Osama bin Laden's top deputy in the Horn of Africa, took an interest in Shabab—and in the young American.

Taking the nom de guerre "Abu Mansour Al Amriki," Hammami now became fully engaged in Shabab's jihad against Ethiopia and its corresponding reign of terror over the Somali people. Shabab wasn't only a military operation against the aggressors; it was also establishing a strict shariah code in the country, in the spirit of the worst excesses of the Taliban.

Like al Qaeda, Shabab had established a media division, which was populated largely by Westerners.[84] Abu Mansour appeared in a couple of videos with his face covered. In March 2009 he showed his face for the first time in a video titled *Ambush At Bardal*. The video depicted an operation led by Abu Mansour, apparently in command of a small squad that included Somali American mujahideen from Minnesota. In cinema verité style, the camera caught Hammami speaking in hushed tones as his men prepared for action, his accent still containing traces of Alabama, flavored with an Eastern lilt.

> We met the enemy, *alhumdillilah* [praise God]. So now, we know, we're not seeing enemies. Right at, at this moment, the enemy's very near, and if we hear that the enemy is moving, *inshallah* [God willing], we'll be able to go and meet him. So, the only reason we're staying here, away from our families, away from the cities, away from, you know, ice, candy bars, all these other things, is because we're waiting to meet with the enemy.[85]

The video followed Abu Mansour and his fellow jihadists from preparation to after-action in an ambush on Ethiopian troops. After the attack Abu Mansour reported that two of his men were killed. This, he explained, was a good thing.

> Our main objective, one of the things that we seek for in this life of ours, is to die as martyrs. So the fact that we got two martyrs, is nothing more than a victory in and of itself.[86]

Hammami was also shown offering religious instruction to the mujahideen in English and Arabic. The quality of his theology was simplistic—one day of jihad is worth a month of fasting and prayers. Later in the video, Hammami began to sing and chant, accompanied by a rap song by an unnamed performer. Only someone truly committed to the jihad could bear to listen to his attempts to sing for very long.

Blow by blow, year by year,
I'm keeping these kaffirs living in fear.
Night by night, day by day,
Mujahideen spreading all over the place.
Month by month, year by year,
Keeping them kaffirs living in fear.
Blow by blow, crime by crime,
Only gonna add to my venging rhymes.
Bomb by bomb, blast by blast,
Only gonna bring back the glorious past.[87]

Music is forbidden in Shabab's strict version of Islam, but an exception is made for religiously oriented songs without instrumental accompaniment, called *nasheeds*. Hammami's excruciating singing debut was a big hit with Western jihadists, perhaps due to impaired taste because they were predisposed to be uncomfortable with music. Several follow-up songs were released, featuring other performers speaking, singing, and rapping in American-accented English.

> You must make a choice. Are you gonna live like an honorable man, and die like an honorable man, or are you gonna live like a humiliated coward, and die like one?
>
> *Somalia is the place,*
> *[Emigrants] from every race base come.*
> *Don't delay.*
> *Come before you're bein' judged on Judgment Day.*
> *Life is rising, surprising.*
> *The [infidels] are high-rising, talking, advising, chastising, advising.*
> *We got a plan finalizing.*
> *Crystallizing, Muslims realizing.*
> *Ain't no disguisin', we're on the horizon.*[88]

The combination of a familiar youth-oriented format with American speakers proved to be a powerful recruiting tool. Additional videos were produced, including one showing Hammami leading an event on behalf of children whose fathers had died fighting for Shabab. The male children were given toy guns and encouraged to play "mujahideen."[89]

Abu Mansour's stock continued to rise with a wider and more diverse audience, thanks to the influence of online American friends such as Daniel Maldonado. Somalia was fast becoming a cause célèbre for a new breed of jihadist recruits.

JIHAD JANE

Perhaps no case illustrates the incredible diversity of the American jihadist community better than the story of Colleen LaRose, better known as "Jihad Jane."

Jihad is mostly a boy's game, both in the United States and abroad. From time to time, jihadist organizations will trumpet the formation of a women's brigade, equipped with Kalashnikovs and modest, body-covering uniforms, but these are the exception rather than the rule. A handful of women have also volunteered as suicide bombers, mostly to exploit the security hole created by expectations that a terrorist will be male. In the United States, women jihadists have mostly been confined to the sidelines, raising small amounts of money for groups like Al Shabab and providing moral support to jihadist husbands. [90]

So when a blue-eyed, blonde woman from Pennsylvania emerged as an accused terrorist, it made headlines across the country. Colleen LaRose was born in 1963 and lived a life "like a country music song," as one investigator told the *Philadelphia Inquirer*. She grew up in Texas, married at sixteen, divorced, married again eight years later, then divorced again. Her life was dotted with fights, drunken escapades, bad checks, and at least one suicide attempt.[91]

Moving to Pennsburg, Pennsylvania, in 2002, she continued to struggle with her inner demons, finally converting to Islam late in life with little fanfare. She didn't stop drinking and brawling, but she did start surfing the Web. Her Internet postings—under the username "JihadJane"—were a strange combination of love and hate. On the one hand, she was desperately seeking a Muslim husband (unbeknownst to her live-in boyfriend in Pennsburg), but on the other, she steadily posted scenes of jihadist violence on YouTube. [92]

Through connections made online, LaRose met like-minded people in Europe and Asia. One of them promised to marry her if she just took care of one little task—find and kill a Swedish cartoonist whose work had been deemed offensive to Islam. In August 2009, investigators alleged, LaRose flew to Sweden and began stalking the cartoonist but did not complete her mission. When she returned to the United States in October, she was arrested.[93]

One of LaRose's online correspondents was Jamie Paulin-Ramirez, an American woman from Colorado. Paulin-Ramirez had converted to Islam after learning about it online. Using e-mail and chat, she communicated with Muslim men in Europe, hiding her interactions from her family.

LaRose encouraged the Colorado woman to join her for terrorist training in Europe. On September 11, 2009, with her six-year-old son in tow, Paulin-Ramirez got on a plane and flew to Europe. Two days later, she married one of the men she had met online. With her new husband and several other men allegedly linked to the Sweden plot, she moved to Ireland.

In March 2010 investigators in the United States and Europe, following leads from the LaRose investigation, arrested four men and three women in rural Ireland for complicity in the assassination scheme. Paulin-Ramirez was pregnant when she was returned to American soil and indicted.[94] LaRose pleaded guilty to her role in the assassination plot in early 2011. As of this writing, Paulin-Ramirez was awiting trial.

LaRose and Paulin-Ramirez were extremely unusual examples of women involved in operational terrorism, but the manner in which they were radicalized has become disturbingly common. Although American Muslims have made great strides in driving radical recruiters out of bricks-and-mortar mosques, on the Internet, extreme forms of Islam are only a click away.

11
The Keyboard and the Sword

The jihad movement is fueled by propaganda. In the earliest days, it was mostly ephemeral— flyers, newsletters, short handouts, and live English translations of speeches by jihadist figures visiting the United States.

Over time, more sophisticated products began to emerge, including *Al Jihad* magazine from Abdullah Azzam's Services Bureau, the *Al Hussam* newsletter, and the *Islam Report* (see chapter 5). Many of these publications fell by the wayside, due in part to shifting tolerances among American Muslims, as well as the arrest and incarceration of the publishers. By September 11 a significant amount of jihadist propaganda already had moved online; this accelerated after the attack.

For many years jihadists' use of the Internet and computer technology had tracked closely with the wider world's. Some specific organizations, including al Qaeda, were early adopters, keeping digitized records on computers and using e-mail to communicate by the mid-1990s.

After September 11 and even more after the invasion of Iraq, terrorists began to use the Internet in increasingly innovative ways. The decentralized nature of the Internet offered terrorist leaders real promise as a way to bypass the media and distribute their message on a global scale, far more affordably than through traditional print media. The *Al Hussam* newsletter ran upward of $1,000 per month to publish and distribute.[1] In contrast, a website might cost only a few hundred dollars per year.

For a time, a number of terrorist and jihadist organizations tried to maintain traditional static websites, but starting around 2003, and corresponding to a rise in social media generally, online message boards and forums became the dominant outlet for jihadist talk and propaganda. When a server was knocked offline, the forum's database could be restored quickly on a new site.

The forums also had a democratizing effect on the jihad movement, allowing the audience to participate and bring their own thoughts and opinions to the table. Would-be jihadists and curiosity-seekers could interact directly with leaders of terrorist and jihadist organizations, asking questions, having their dreams interpreted, and requesting fatwas to reinforce their intentions.

Some interesting personalities have emerged over the course of the online jihad, and a smaller percentage of these figures have become involved in more than talk. Terrorism expert Jarret Brachman coined the term "jihobbyist" for those who engage in jihad talk online without taking direct action to become involved in violence. But jihobbyism has increasingly emerged as a gateway to violent action.

It's important to understand the following case studies in context. None of the figures profiled here have a particularly large following or any real credibility as scholars, religious leaders, or fighters. They tend to orbit around more established authority figures, such as Anwar Awlaki or Jamaican cleric Abdullah Al Faisal. They are fringe personalities within American Islam and even within the jihadist movement itself. They are symptoms rather than causes.

But they are not insignificant. They reflect and sometimes amplify and interpret the views of real opinion leaders and are themselves candles around which lesser moths may flit. They are the loudest voices in an angry mob. As such, they help make the mob sound louder and look angrier.

Perhaps most important, they tend to disclose a lot of information about themselves, from which we can learn. They provide a window into what attracts Americans to radical beliefs, and when they move from jihobbyism to jihadism, they leave a trail we can follow.

RISE OF THE FORUMS

After September 11, "official" websites for the Taliban and other jihadist outlets in the West were among the first casualties of the war on terror. One of the most prominent, Azzam.com, was shut down and its London-based operator arrested.[2]

The change in jihad media during the last decade reflects the change in the broader media. Organizational strength has been eroded by Web 2.0—media outlets are more disjointed, and individual voices can be dramatically amplified. Most jihadist organizations online have abandoned static websites in favor of anonymously administrated Web forums that allow for "official" announcements, along with direct user interaction.

Any Internet user with average to high skills can create an online message board quickly and with relative anonymity. Visitors to the site can read messages or register as users to post their own comments, news, or files. A host of jihadist and jihad-accepting forums have sprung up since September 11, most of which are strictly fan sites. A smaller number of these forums operate with the direct involvement of active jihadists such as al Qaeda, al Qaeda in the Arabian Peninsula, Al Shabab, the Taliban, Chechen mujahideen, and so on.

In addition to hosting conversations by individuals around the world who are interested in jihad, these officially sanctioned forums—usually run by noncombatants in nonconflict zones—frequently post official communications from their affiliated groups. This allows readers to feel confident that they are reading authentic messages from jihadist figures, who range from the famous to the obscure.

The top-tier forums have password-protected sections that active jihadists can use to communicate and where those who are interested in moving from talk to action can contact jihadists abroad and sometimes arrange to join them.

The most important forums operate mostly in Arabic, but a few have English sections or separate forums for English-language users. The Al Ansar forum, which has Arabic, English and German versions, and the Somali-language forum Al Qimmah, which features an English section, have some of the closest ties to jihadists in the field.

A larger number of English-language forums, static websites, and blogs espouse jihadist thought and encourage radical or extremist conversations but are careful to stay within the limits of American First Amendment protections. The number of these sites is estimated to be between the hundreds and the low thousands.

Within the last couple of years, these English-language outlets have become important incubators for the radicalization of American Muslims. They have also caused fundamental changes in the patterns of radicalization, which, combined with the U.S. war on terrorism, have led to shifts in the profile of American jihadists generally and American terrorists in particular.

ISLAMIC AWAKENING

IslamicAwakening.com is jihad for beginners. It describes its aim as "correcting" Muslims who have gone astray, fighting off the "ideological onslaught" against Muslims, and "[reviving] the abandoned and forgotten obligations without which the victory to the Ummah remains impossible"—a reference to jihad, which often called the "forgotten duty."[3]

The site has an extensive news and commentary section and a lively forum. Much of the discussion is devoted to Islamic life, culture, and jurisprudence, but the most active area by far is the "Politics, Jihad and Current Affairs" forum.[4] Participants in the IA forums skirt the edge of legality but rarely cross over. Moderators keep a lid on discussions about committing terrorism or threats of violence. Within those parameters, participants on the site are palpably angry.

One forum topic, which the moderators keep at the top of the first page of posts, is titled "America is a sick place" and consists of links to news stories showing various immoral acts by Americans, such as murder, child abuse, and sexual promiscuity.[5] (The fact that Muslim countries such as Yemen and Saudi Arabia have similar problems, including a massive trade in child slaves who are often sexually abused, does not have its own topic.[6])

Other topics, selected from a range over time, included

- Fatwas from Anwar Awlaki
- "Are we Muslims or *Munafiqeen* [hypocrites]?"
- "Long live the Mujahideen!"
- "Atrocities of the real terrorists" (meaning Americans)
- "Israel using nude female soldiers to seduce Palestinian youth"
- "Where to find jihad videos?"
- "Fatwa on jihad in Chechnya"

Some of this material is repurposed from other, more aggressive jihadist sites; other topics are based on news stories. In some cases, topics reprint individual letters and e-mails from jihadist clerics such as Anwar Awlaki or from Muslim prisoners accused or convicted of terrorism.

The overall effect of all this posting by users based mostly in the United Kingdom and the United States is to create a giant echo chamber of complaints of

Muslim victimization, as well as explicit jihadist incitement, including overt examples and "precursor" rhetoric such as comments on the misdeeds of Americans, both individually and collectively. Disliking America does not make one a jihadist sympathizer, but virtually all jihadist sympathizers dislike America.

The forum boasts of such celebrity members as the American founders of the radical website Revolution Muslim, al Qaeda propagandist Samir Khan, and would-be jihadists Zach Chesser, Daniel Maldonado, and Tarek Mehanna.

REVOLUTION MUSLIM

When you widen the circle out from the members of the Islamic Awakening forum, it doesn't take long to arrive at Revolution Muslim.

Spun off from a British extremist group, Revolution Muslim and its lesser-known offline affiliate, the Islamic Thinkers Society (ITS), are based in and around New York City, with supporters and members scattered throughout the country.[7] The core group is usually fewer than twenty people, and the names often change, due to vicious "office politics" and backbiting among key members.[8] Adherents and fans are believed to number in the thousands.[9]

Both groups claim to be nonviolent political organizations that oppose U.S. policies and corrupt Arab regimes, while promulgating an aggressive version of Islam. Both have been widely condemned by mainstream Muslims. And both organizations are predominantly American.

"We're all just regular kids in New York City," said Ariful Islam, a spokesman for ITS, in 2005. "We grew up here."[10]

ITS is the original group, operating in New York as early as 1986. Revolution Muslim is a more recent and wide-reaching spin-off, centered around an active and controversial blog that promotes English-speaking jihadist ideologues such as Syrian Omar Bakri Muhammad, American citizen Anwar Awlaki, and Abdullah Al Faisal, a Jamaican-born cleric. All of them have large followings in the West.[11]

Faisal plays a direct role in counseling the site's operators and takes part in regular online chats with Revolution Muslim's readers. He was convicted in the UK in 2003 of inciting racial hatred and soliciting murder for speeches in which he told adherents that they would go to heaven for killing non-Muslims. After serving four years in prison, he was deported back to Jamaica.[12]

RM was founded by Yousef Al Khattab, a Brooklyn Jew turned Muslim convert who was born in 1968 with the name Joseph Cohen, and Younus Abdullah Muhammad, a younger Caucasian American born Jesse Morton.

Deeply engaged with his Judaism, Cohen turned to Orthodoxy in his twenties and moved to Israel with his wife and children in 1998, but he became frustrated with the complexity and inconsistency of competing rabbinical interpretations of the religion.

Like many converts, he found simplicity in Islam. "In the Koran, it says not to ask so many questions," he explained to a reporter in 2003.[13] Many converts to Islam are attracted to an impression of simplicity and absolutism, although in reality the history of disputation and interpretation in Islam is at least comparable to that of other religions.[14]

Revolution Muslim's content is mostly tedious. Postings alternate between pedestrian news items that describe—or can be interpreted as describing—the persecution of Muslims in various contexts, and discussions of Islamic law and tradition that range from esoteric to obscurantist, in an effort to establish the site's religious credibility.[15]

The site enjoyed bursts of notoriety for praising terrorists. Khattab famously told CNN that he "loved Osama bin Laden," a video clip that was replayed endlessly as Revolution Muslim and its associates became more and more known for their extremism.[16] In 2009 Khattab wrote a post praising Nidal Hasan, the Fort Hood shooter, shortly after the attack.

> An officer and a gentleman was injured while partaking in a pre-emptive attack. Get well soon Major Nidal. We love you. [. . .] Rest assured the slain terrorists at Fort Hood are in the eternal hellfire.[17]

Khattab dropped out of the organization in 2009, when he moved from the United States to Morocco with his family and, by his account, experienced a change of heart regarding the use of violence in Islam—at least up to a point. According to Khattab, he had come around to the view that Muslims should use "the democratic process" to advance the spread of Islam. According to a post on his personal blog,

> I denounce my previous misunderstanding that the rulers and tyrants that reign over the Muslim lands should be killed. I prefer less bloodshed and establishment of Islam via schools, media, and medical facilities etc. This does NOT mean I love the rulers, no it means that I will try to hold the higher moral ground & change by example rather than by bloodshed.[18]

Khattab passed the baton to another Revolution Muslim blogger, who was subsequently forced out by cofounder Younus Abdullah Muhammad, to Khattab's displeasure. The two founders had a very public falling out, with Khattab accusing Muhammad of luring young Muslims into situations that would lead to their arrest, and Muhammad claiming to have fired Khattab and accusing his former colleague of trying to get him arrested.[19]

Muhammad became the main public face of Revolution Muslim, appearing as a speaker at its functions and in regularly staged "street *dawah*" events in New York City. During these events, which are usually videotaped, RM members accost passersby, both Muslim and non-Muslim, with a barrage of anti-American rhetoric. Barack Obama is one of Muhammad's favorite targets:

> As Barack Obama slaughters Muslims in Afghanistan, you remain silent. You are supposed, this is the change we're supposed to believe in. This is the change that you all believed in. This is the change the imams, the so-called leaders of this community, stood up at the pulpit and told you to go and vote for. This is what you believed in and this is what you got.
>
> This is what you got. The change that the Muslim must believe in must be Islam, it must be shariah. It must be *jihad fe sabeelillah* [military jihad, that is, violence]. This is the change for the Muslims. And only if Barack Obama adheres to these terms of peace will there be peace. Anything else will be his destruction by the hands of the Muslims.[20]

It's difficult to pin down Muhammad's views, because they shift with the wind. Under media or government scrutiny, Muhammad backs away from his more extreme statements and attempts to recast himself as the victim of distortion. Yet in event after event, as well as on the site, Muhammad clearly works the jihadist side of the aisle.

> All over the Muslim world, in Afghanistan, in Iraq, everywhere, that are waging *jihad fe sabeelillah* against the American occupiers should be supported. Why will they not tell you to support the mujahideen? Why will they tell you that jihad does not mean to fight, that jihad means to go to university, so you can get jobs living in their system supporting the promotion of American empire?[21]

In 2010 Younus Abdullah Muhammad was the latest casualty of Revolution Muslim's infighting, apparently pushed aside as a wave of British extremists took center stage. The new crew used Revolution Muslim's American mailing address in an effort to avoid British laws against inciting violence. It didn't work; its Internet service provider shut down the site after new blogger Bilal Ahmed posted a "hit list" of British parliament members who had voted to go to war in Iraq. Ahmed himself was arrested.

In the meantime Muhammad had started a new site, Islampolicy.com, which he said would work to develop a blueprint for new Islamic states rather than promote jihad. The commitment to nonviolence was short lived. Days after RevolutionMuslim.com went offline, Muhammed posted that Islam Policy was the old site's "new home" and soon reverted to form, featuring communiqués from Osama bin Laden, Anwar Awlaki, and other al Qaeda leaders. Revolution Muslim's website might have been dead, but its media operation continued with barely a hiccup.[22]

Despite the problems that plagued Revolution Muslim—infighting, inconsistency, and relative lack of religious sophistication—the group and its members have proved capable of radicalizing American Muslims.

Mahmood Alessa, a Palestinian American born in the United States, and Carlos Eduardo Almonte, a naturalized citizen of Dominican descent, were seen at several Revolution Muslim events in the company of Younus Abdullah Muhammad. At one event, Almonte (not the sharpest knife in the drawer) brandished a sign that read "Death to all Zionist Juice."[23]

Alessa and Almonte were fans of Anwar Awlaki who devoured jihadist content online and trained in combat techniques with an eye toward joining Al Shabab in Somalia. Of course, if that didn't work out, they were prepared to settle. Alessa was recorded by the FBI while holding forth on his philosophy:

> I'm gonna get a gun. I'm the type of person to use it at any time. But, if I would've had a gun, I can't—I can't even I'll, I'll have more bodies on it than—than the than the hairs on my beard. You know what I'm saying? It's already enough, you don't worship Allah, so, that's a reason for you to die. [W]e're being pushed by every corner of the earth, [meaning], they only fear you when you have a gun and when you—when you start killing them, and when you—when you take their head, and you go like this, and you behead it on camera, and you—you have to be ruthless, bro.
>
> I swear to God, bro. Enough of this punk shit. It's that everyone has to be ruthless to—with these people. We'll start doing killing here, if I can't do it over there. I'm gonna get locked up in the airport? Then you're gonna die here, then. That's how it is. Freaking Major-Nidal-shaved-face-Palestinian-crazy guy, he's not better than me. I'll do twice what he did.[24]

The FBI recorded hours of such scintillating conversation, placing an informant near the two and arresting them before they could do any damage. People become involved with jihadism for many reasons, among them a simple predisposition toward violence. Alessa and Almonte may not have been the most sophisticated followers of Revolution Muslim and the Islamic Thinkers Society, but others would surpass them.

BRYANT VINAS

Bryant Vinas was a Latino American from Long Island. He was raised Catholic, but his life was thrown into chaos when his parents divorced shortly before he entered high school. He became so unruly that his exasperated mother sent him to live with his father. When he left high school, he enrolled in the military but washed out of boot camp. A friend's brother introduced him to Islam.

During the next couple of years, Vinas drifted into the orbit of the Islamic Thinkers Society and met Revolution Muslim cofounder Yousef Al Khattab on several occasions.

In Afghanistan during the 1980s and later in Bosnia, many jihadists were drawn in by specific acts of aggression. Vinas was attracted by the paradigm that had been spreading like wildfire since the September 11 attacks—that America was at war with Islam. Vinas went further still, believing that America was behind the September 11 attacks and that FEMA (the Federal Emergency Management Agency) was building concentration camps for Muslims.[25]

But Vinas was not like Alessa. He was smart and engaged with ideology, eventually coming to define himself as a Salafi, part of a strict movement that seeks to emulate the early days of Islam.[26] Many jihadists call themselves Salafis, but not all Salafis are jihadists.

Friends said his anger simmered and finally began to dominate his personality.[27] He explored the jihadist Internet, increasingly frustrated with the ITS, which he believed was all talk. With assistance from a friend at ITS, Vinas decided to act. He went to Lahore and met with Pakistani militants in the porous border region with Afghanistan.[28] Vinas later said that someone in New York helped arrange an introduction.[29]

Vinas volunteered to be a suicide bomber. He was trained, but he washed out when his handlers decided that he wasn't up to the task and recommended additional religious training. There is only one case of an American suicide bomber in the public record, possibly due to cultural predispositions, but also because U.S. citizens—and their passports—are extremely valuable to terrorist networks.

Disappointed with his progress, Vinas decided to separate from the Pakistani group and seek out al Qaeda by wandering the wild, lawless region of Pakistan along the border with Afghanistan, where the terrorist group's top leaders are believed to be hiding.

It is a testament to both his determination and his capabilities that he succeeded in this task without getting killed. In early 2008 Vinas was inducted into al Qaeda as a formal member, swearing *bayat*, the Islamic oath of allegiance.[30]

Housed with other Western recruits, he lobbied to fight U.S. forces on the front lines in Afghanistan and was sent on a few unsuccessful missions during which he fired rockets at American troops. Yet despite his failure to destroy the target, he had proved his commitment, and it was time for the next phase. Under the watchful eye of senior al Qaeda leaders—including Mustafa Abu Al Yazid, one of the group's founders—Vinas was taught assassination techniques and how to build bombs, including suicide belts.[31]

Vinas briefed his supervisors on the Long Island Rail Road, which he had ridden as a young man, and an operation to bomb the commuter hub was initiated, although it remained in the planning stages. During this process Vinas made a trip to Peshawar to use the Internet, buy supplies, and look for a wife. By this time U.S. intelligence services were looking for him. Vinas was arrested by Pakistani authorities and extradited to the United States.[32] Like many captured jihadists, Vinas began to talk, giving rare and extensive intelligence on al Qaeda's reconfiguration after the invasion of Afghanistan.

"For informing on the people that are fighting in Afghanistan, I call him a coward," said Revolution Muslim's cofounder Yousef Al Khattab.[33] Unfortunately for Revolution Muslim, Vinas would not be the only collaborator.

ABU TALHA AL AMRIKI

Zach Chesser was born in Virginia in 1989. Much of his youth was unremarkable, at least on the surface. He played football and basketball and later signed up for crew.[34] He was a joiner, jumping from obsession to obsession, whether it was Marilyn Manson or breakdancing.[35]

There were other Muslims at his high school, but he didn't embrace Islam until his senior year.[36] It didn't take him long to discover the jihadist Web. With all the enthusiasm and arrogance of a new convert, he christened himself Abu Talha Al Amrikee and began to dispatch unsolicited advice to his fellow Muslims and to the seniors of the jihadist movement as a self-appointed expert in everything from economics to espionage.

In many ways, Abu Talha was the epitome of a jihobbyist. Armed with virtually no real knowledge of Islam, the history of the theological schools that he promoted, or the practical aspects of terrorism, Chesser became a ubiquitous Web presence, tirelessly aping the online propaganda he consumed voraciously while jumping from theme to theme and project to project in a manner suggestive of attention deficit disorder. Yousef Al Khattab described his output as "Tourette's *Dawa* [preaching]."[37]

Chesser went through a series of platforms, including a YouTube account and a blog, along with an active membership on the Islamic Awakening forum. Then he joined Revolution Muslim, where he posted for a few months, spending time with the site's cofounder Younus Abdullah Muhammad.[38] Chesser next moved on to official jihadist forums such as Al Fallujah and Al Qimmah, a Somali jihadist site linked to the Al Shabab militia.

Abu Talha may have lacked focus and knowledge, but like many bloggers both inside and out of the jihad subculture, he tried to make up for these lapses with self-confidence, enthusiasm, and sheer volume. A typical post featured Chesser—who had been a Muslim for less than two years—hectoring other Muslims about their failure to do right by the mujahideen.

> Are you doing your part to support your Brothers and Sisters in Somalia? Have you given *d'ua* [prayers] for brothers like Abu Mansour Al Amriki and other brothers lately? It may be time brothers and sisters to not only agree with the actions of The Lions of *Tawheed* [Monotheism], but also do something to support your brothers in Somalia and other places where Al Islam is being attacked. This is a call to action and a call to fulfill your obligation as a Muslim to defend your brothers and sisters. As your brothers and sister in Somalia are raped and killed by the Ethiopian Puppets from Addis Ababa and the Somalia slaves of the United States, will you be like Brother Mohamoud Hassan or Brother Abu Mansour [two Americans who fought in Somalia] and answer the call to Jihad? For Allah (SWT) knows best and will reward those who sacrificed on the Day of Judgment.[39]

Chesser described his motivations in a June 2010 interview with Aaron Y. Zelin, then a graduate student in Islamic and Middle Eastern studies at Brandeis University, who runs the Jihadology blog. Although Chesser wasn't above playing the classic Muslim victimization card (as in the previous excerpt), his ideological bent and interest in jihad were mostly on the broadest level:

> I hope to take part in the creation of an Islamic state where the shariah is applied *inshallah* [God willing] with no exceptions of general matters of which there is a consensus. That is the bare minimum. After that I would hope that it is a just society where the law is applied and where the people are treated fairly.[40]

For most of his career, Chesser's ruminations on jihad were strictly "inside baseball," of interest primarily to a handful of terrorism and jihadism researchers whose attention he virtually demanded. For instance, a series of blog postings on "Counter-Counter-Terrorism" proposed luring terrorism researchers (including the author of this book) into political arguments with each other in order to create divisions. Other entries in the series focused on law enforcement, suggesting that jihadist sympathizers should create a flood of false reports of suspicious packages so that authorities would be lulled when a real bomb was left on a street corner.[41]

Yet in April 2010, he managed to stumble into the big time with a post on Revolution Muslim about the Comedy Central animated TV show *South Park*, which was scheduled to air an episode satirizing the controversy over depicting the Prophet Mohammed.

Beneath a picture of the dead body of Theo Van Gogh, a Dutch film director who was killed after producing a film critical of Islam, Chesser posted address information for South Park producers Matt Stone and Trey Parker, writing,

> We have to warn Matt and Trey that what they are doing is stupid and they will probably wind up like Theo Van Gogh for airing this show. This is not a threat, but a warning of the reality of what will likely happen to them.[42]

Of course, it was a threat, no matter how finely Chesser tried to parse his definitions in the interests of staying out of jail. A follow-up posting featured audio of Anwar Awlaki explaining that mockery of Mohammed was punishable by death. The threats garnered an avalanche of national attention, putting scrutiny on Revolution Muslim, sparking general outrage, and ultimately resulting in the episode being censored by its distributor Comedy Central.[43] Chesser and his family received death threats, and his parents stopped speaking to him.[44]

Overwhelmed by the attention, Chesser went silent after the *South Park* incident, but he was not idle. He started to make preparations to travel to Somalia and join the al Qaeda–linked Al Shabab militia, which had already hosted a number of American fighters (see chapter 10).

Or rather, he put on a show of making preparations. Although Chesser went through the motions of trying to get to Somalia, something always seemed to get in the way. His first effort failed when he lost his very first battle in the jihad—convincing his mother-in-law to return his wife's passport, which she had hidden to keep her daughter from leaving the country. Chesser tried again in July 2010, with his infant son in his arms. He figured that U.S. authorities wouldn't believe he was taking his baby into a war zone. It wasn't clear what he planned to do with the child once he arrived in Somalia.

He was turned away by airport security because his name had been added to a no-fly list. Rather than keep trying, he called the FBI and said he wanted to provide information on Al Shabab. News of a Shabab suicide bombing in Uganda had prompted another one of his now-famous changes of heart, he explained, to the growing exasperation of the FBI.[45] Perhaps simply to shut him up, FBI agents arrested Chesser in July and charged him with material support for terrorism in relation to his efforts to join Al Shabab.[46]

When a Western jihadist is arrested, the jihobbyists tend to circle the wagons, lining up to show support on the forums and "make *dua*" (pray) for the person arrested. It is a sign of Chesser's polarizing character that very few stepped up to post on his behalf. Revolution Muslim never even bothered to acknowledge the arrest. On the forums, some noted that "the brother [had] loose lips."

Yousef Al Khattab, the Revolution Muslim founder who by this point claimed to have abandoned his commitment to al Qaeda and violent jihad, offered a particularly harsh critique.

> Just because we are Muslim or their [sic] is no [Islamic caliphate] does not give us a carte blanche to behave like pre Islamic barbarians and give unconditional support to those that dig their own graves.[47]

SAMIR KHAN

Like Zach Chesser, Samir Khan was another young American Muslim with an attitude and Internet access. Khan was born in Saudi Arabia, and his parents were moderate Muslims who moved the family to Queens when he was seven.

Khan began blogging as a teenager, shortly after attending a Muslim summer camp sponsored by a little-known fundamentalist group called the Islamic Organization of North America that was devoted to the nonviolent establishment of the Islamic way of life in America.[48] Soon after, Khan discovered the Islamic Thinkers Society.

Although his early blog entries didn't address the issue of jihad, they were unquestionably conservative. He wrote about the need to purify American society and signs of the End Days and generally presented a fairly chipper vision of a devout, intense Muslim who was not in the mainstream but perhaps not far from it either.

> Humanity is in need of a Just Social Order; a way of life that protects men and women from the deceptions that this world can trap one into. In order to truly bring about this "Renaissance" within the fixed area of man's existence [sic], we must turn to the root of the different philosophies that man offered to the world; from there do we then choose the revolution which will bring about this great change. For this reason, I am in complete agreement with the Islamic Revolution brought about by Prophet Muhammad (peace be upon him). With his revolution, was the human changed not only externally, but also internally; it was the absolute greatest internal revolution which led to the spreading of Islam, not by the sword, but by the hearts! Conquering a land is easy, but conquering a heart . . . well, you will need one heck of a philosophy![49]

The warning sign, if there was one, was to be found in Khan's username, "inshallahshaheed"—"God willing, a martyr." With the advent and escalation of the war in Iraq, Khan became increasingly militant. He celebrated the deaths of U.S. soldiers in Iraq and dismissed their grieving families as "people of hellfire." His blog linked to al Qaeda videos, and he justified the Islamic doctrine of *takfir* (which attempts to justify the killing of moderate Muslims) while celebrating the writings of Omar Abdel Rahman, Ayman Al Zawahiri, and Anwar Awlaki.[50]

Khan encountered challenges in keeping his blog online due to its controversial content, which violated most Internet service providers' rules on hate speech and the incitement of violence. If one Googles "inshallahshaheed," the result is page after page announcing that the blog has found a new server. All the links are dead.[51] There were other complications as well. On at least one occasion, Khan's parents—in whose basement he lived—cut off his Internet access.[52]

In 2009 Khan upped the ante, producing an online magazine in PDF format called *Jihad Recollections*. The magazine was overproduced—slick but too busy and at times unreadable, loosely inspired by popular American magazines. Its content consisted of a series of articles that included transcriptions of speeches and communiqués by al Qaeda leaders and original pieces by Khan and members of his social circle, such as Revolution Muslim cofounder Younus Abdullah Muhammad. The magazine was distributed through a wide variety of English-language jihadist forums and websites.

Khan published four issues of *Jihad Recollections*, which featured such stories as "The Men behind 9/11 and the Motives That Bound Them," "The Emphasis for an Identity in the Storm of Kufr [apostasy]" and "The Science behind Night Vision Technology." An article titled "Staying in Shape without Weights" was penned by a teenager from Oregon named Mohamed Mohamud, who would be arrested in 2010 for trying to bomb a family-oriented Christmas tree lighting ceremony in Portland. *Jihad Recollections* also included historical and religious pieces, such as a biography of a recently killed al Qaeda trainer and an adaptation of an Anwar Awlaki lecture on one of the Prophet Muhammad's companions.[53]

The final issue of *Jihad Recollections* was published in September 2009. That's when Samir Khan got the call to join the big leagues. In October he left the United States for Yemen, where he met with Awlaki. In November Nidal Hasan went on his killing spree at Fort Hood, and the backlash forced Awlaki underground.

Khan resurfaced in July 2010, when al Qaeda in the Arabian Peninsula released *Inspire*, an English-language jihadist magazine whose design relationship to *Jihad Recollections* was unmistakable. Everyone who had read *Recollections* immediately concluded that the new magazine was the work of Samir Khan, and media reports soon confirmed it.[54]

The new magazine was nearly identical in format and content to the old one, with the exception of its official imprimatur and an original article written by Awlaki especially for *Inspire*. A page collecting memorable quotes featured Revolution Muslim cofounder Yousef Al Khattab and a quote by a counterterrorism analyst about the effectiveness of the Islamic Thinkers Society.[55]

As of this writing, Inspire had published two more issues, one very similar to the first, and a "special edition" commemorating an AQAP attempt to bomb two cargo planes bound for the United States. The special edition, which included a detailed description of the plot and its objectives, commanded notice from U.S. intelligence and terrorism analysts as conclusive evidence that Khan—and likely Awlaki—had direct access to AQAP's operational team, and perhaps even full membership.[56]

BACK IN BOSTON

Tarek Mehanna was an American Muslim of Egyptian descent. He earned a doctorate from the Massachusetts College of Pharmacy in Boston and subsequently moved to nearby Sudbury, where he attended the Islamic Center of New England mosque in Sharon, Massachusetts.[57]

After September 11 Mehanna obsessively surfed the Internet looking for material related to the al Qaeda attack, referring to the hijackers as the "19 martyrs." He shared videos and propaganda with friends, both online and in the real world. One of his childhood friends was particularly receptive. Ahmad Abousamra was the son of a local doctor and a Syrian American born and raised in Massachusetts.[58]

They tried to find other Muslims in the Boston area who would support their jihadist cause, but few were interested. Despite these frustrations, they kept trying and drew potential recruits aside for one-on-one talks, slipping them CDs with copies of al Qaeda recruitment videos.[59]

They had some successes amid many failures. Abousamra met a recent white convert to Islam from northern Massachusetts named Daniel Maldonado, whom he introduced to Mehanna.[60]

A friend recalled later, "I met Danny the week he converted. He was cool. He dressed in T-shirts and jeans and didn't hide any of his tattoos. His hair was in dreadlocks. He was eager, and he had a lot of questions."

Soon after his conversion, Maldonado became decidedly less cool. He adopted an increasingly strict view of Islam and, like many converts who become jihadist recruits, began to affect an Arab style of dress. His wife began to wear a full burka, and they covered the head of their baby daughter (which is not required in Islam).[61]

Mehanna and Abousamra filled Maldonado's head with jihadist ideology, including justifications for killing civilians and suicide bombings, and the three would get together to devour hours of jihadist video propaganda found online.

Mehanna and Maldonado participated robustly in online jihadist communities, such as the Islamic Awakening forums, where both men were well known. Maldonado was also heavily involved with other sites, including the Islamic Network and Clear Guidance. They followed popular jihadist clerics such as Muhammad Al Maqdisi of Jordan and Anwar Awlaki.

The three young men talked incessantly about seeking out military training in Pakistan so that they could join the jihad overseas. But unlike many online jihobbyists, they took concrete steps to translate talk into reality, contacting an associate with connections for information about how to find and enroll in a training program.[62]

In 2002 Abousamra was the first to make a go of it. With a few hundred dollars given to him by a sympathetic friend, he traveled to Pakistan in 2002 and again in 2003, looking for training to join Afghan insurgents in battle against U.S. forces. He tried unsuccessfully to enlist with Lashkar-e-Tayyiba. Then he tried the Taliban, which also refused his assistance (supposedly due to his "lack of experience").[63] Rebuffed, he returned to the United States to seek more advice.

So desperate was Abousamra to make the trip that he shelled out $5,000 to someone he thought could make an introduction. Abousamra and Maldonado were itching to see combat; Mehanna seemed less enthused, but he went through the motions. In 2004 Mehanna, Abousamra, and a childhood friend of Mehanna's flew to Yemen for training, this time with the intention of continuing on to fight U.S. forces in Iraq.[64]

They had set a high bar for themselves. For reasons that are not clear, almost no Americans had managed to enter Iraq and join the jihadists fighting U.S. forces there.[65] Once again, the young hopefuls failed to find a training camp. Everyone was either in jail or in hiding.[66] Discouraged, Mehanna returned to the United States after two weeks.[67]

But Abousamra was committed. He went on to Fallujah and became the only American clearly documented as reaching Iraq to take part in jihad. He remained there for about fifteen days. He told a friend that he had met with insurgents during the trip but said they would not allow him to participate because he was an American.[68]

Maldonado too felt the call of jihad, packing up his family and moving first to Egypt and then to Somalia in 2006. Like Zach Chesser, Maldonado described a desire to be part of a political movement. Although Maldonado had a tendency to alter his story depending on his audience, the fixation on an Islamic state is consistent in all of his accounts. In a letter posted to jihadist forums, Maldonado wrote,

> Once my wife (may Allah accept her) and I found out that an Islamic State was established in Somalia, especially after the taking of Mogadishu, we decided to go and make Hijra (migration) from Egypt.[69]

Yet in a handwritten letter filled with spelling mistakes submitted in court after his arrest, he tried to recast his migration as the result of persecution in America and Egypt.

> [I] moved my family to Somalia because I wished to live as a Muslim without a problem with the way I or my family practice our religion (beard, veil, going to mosque much, wearing Islamic garb and so on). After September 11, the U.S. was a hard place to live as a Muslim, and I felt that I should not have to change my looks or way I practice 'cause some other Muslims did wrong. [. . .] It seemed that if they really made a true Islamic state that was practicing Islam as the law, it would be the perfect place for a family like mine.[70]

It's extremely difficult to credit Maldonado's claim that practicing Islam in America was so difficult that it would be easier in an active war zone. Elsewhere in the court letter, he claimed he had heard "business was booming" in Somalia. One day after his first letter to the court, Maldonado wrote a second letter in which he admitted to "many dishonest statements."

In the new letter, he claimed he had been eying jihad all along. The decision to go to Somalia had emerged during discussions with a friend named Omar Hammami, who was married to a Somali woman. They "talked about possibly joining the jihad if we went. We decided that he would go first and I would go later with my family." He also admitted that he had sought out and participated in jihadist training, including instruction on how to build improvised explosive devices.[71]

There were al Qaeda members among the jihadists. When Maldonado arrived, the primary Islamic faction fighting to take control of Somalia was the Islamic Courts Union (ICU). Maldonado observed that the al Qaeda members he met received more respect than the ICU fighters. Soon after Maldonado's departure, many of the more extreme members of the ICU—including Maldonado's American friend Omar Hammami—would break away to join the even more militant Al Shabab militia (see chapter 10).

Despite his stated dream of taking part in an Islamic state, Maldonado's trip quickly turned dark. At one point, he took part in the interrogation of a supposed spy—a flight attendant who had the temerity to take a picture of jihadists arriving in Somalia by plane. The man was beaten. Maldonado pointed a gun at the man's head and threatened to kill him if he didn't talk. The flight attendant—almost certainly an innocent bystander—ended up dead.[72]

Maldonado's accounts of his trip to Somalia were telling but divergent:

Internet Letter

> Knowing that the Ethiopians were coming and the women were about to leave, [my wife] thought that there was a great possibility I would be killed. So we had a nice, long beautiful talk as she prepared. We expressed our love and admiration for each other. She thanked me by saying: "You are the greatest teacher I have ever had! You are the only man who has stuck around in my life! [. . .] You are a real man! I love you so much!"[73]

First Court Letter

> [My wife and I] went to a house. We were told that we could rest in an empty room. We woke up the next day to be told we would not be able to go to the border together, [because] I am white and very obvious to anyone that may wish harm. They said that many things were getting out of hand. I told them that they could give me a gun, and I would go..[. . .] I wanted to be with my family. They explained it would be much harm and that no one would hurt a woman, especially seeing that my wife is black. [. . .] I finally agreed.[74]

His letter to his coreligionists online described a valiant battle, followed by a powerful survival ordeal in the jungle. His letter to the court described a man trying desperately to flee Somalia. Both stories ended the same way—with Maldonado getting arrested by the Kenyan military while trying to escape in early 2007.[75] While he was going through this process, his wife died of malaria. Maldonado considered her a martyr.[76]

Meanwhile, Tarek Mehanna's childhood friend—who had gone with him to Yemen—had started informing to the FBI about the circle of jihadists. At the end of 2006, the FBI showed up on Mehanna's doorstep, asking about Maldonado. Mehanna said he had no idea where his friend was, although the two had stayed in contact over the phone.

Maldonado had urged Mehanna to join him in Somalia, but Mehanna continued to hedge.[77] He had been slower than his peers to translate his ideology into fighting, but he had not been idle. On his blog, Mehanna translated a blizzard of jihadist propaganda, from the writings of Abdullah Azzam to poems and historical Islamic texts. Nearly all of this material pertained to extremely conservative interpretations of Islam, and much of it dealt with jihad.[78]

It was relatively unusual for Mehanna to contribute material he had written himself, although he posted regularly to the forums, poking here and there at examples that he felt showed the victimization of Muslims.[79]

He also indulged in the occasional outburst of poetry. One of his efforts, titled "Make Martyrdom What You Seek," invoked the traditional jihadist's reward of seventy-two virgins:

You turn and behold! The voices are singing
Coming from Maidens so fair and enchanting,
These are the [Houris] with round and firm chests
Pure untouched virgins, they're better than the best,
Seventy-two in all, with large eyes of dark hue
Each one created especially for you.

Mehanna's friends had surpassed him in their commitment to physically taking part in jihad, but Mehanna had an ugly, voyeuristic obsession with violence that often seemed to be a greater inspiration than his interest in Islam. He joked with a friend that New York was no longer the "Land of the Two Towers" (a play on a jihadist reference to Iraq, the "Land of the Two Rivers"). Instead, he suggested that it be called the "land of rape." With friends in tow, Mehanna visited Ground Zero. A photo taken at the site shows him grinning and pointing at the sky.

He circulated videos depicting the mutilation of the body of an American soldier in Iraq, referring to it as "Texas BBQ." (The soldier was supposedly killed as retaliation for the alleged rape of a Muslim woman by a U.S. serviceman.)[80] In online chat sessions with a friend, he joked about beheadings. In a chat with Abousamra, he suggested that a female Muslim leader who had spoken out against extremism "needs to be raped with a broomstick." Referring to Mahdi Bray, a leader of the Muslim American Society, Mehanna said, "I wish I could [. . .] cut off his testicles."[81]

In short, Tarek Mehanna was a nasty piece of work. He was arrested in 2009 for lying to the FBI about Maldonado then indicted for material support of terrorism. Abousamra was also indicted, but he had already fled the country after he was interrogated by the FBI in 2006. He is today believed to be living in Syria, where he has family ties.[82]

Despite the ugliness of his private rhetoric, Mehanna became a cause célèbre, both within the local community in Boston and online, particularly on the Islamic Awakening forum. Mehanna's letters from prison, including poems and drawings, were posted online by IA members who knew him before his arrest. Campaigns were organized through the forum to write letters and provide other shows of support, including a savvy social networking effort mounted by Mehanna's brother.[83]

All of these efforts together have built a mythic picture of Mehanna as a political prisoner, drowning out the sordid details that were laid out in page after page of court documents. At the time of this writing, his case had not yet gone to trial, but it seems unlikely that further revelations will make a dent in the narrative created by his defenders, especially given the absence of overt violence in the charges against him. The most serious allegation was that he had appointed himself the "media wing" of al Qaeda in Iraq, but as of this writing, no evidence had emerged to suggest he had a direct connection to the terrorist organization.[84]

SERIOUS BUSINESS

Evaluating the threat posed by jihobbyists online is a game that journalists often play to extremes. Either they ignore it, or they hype it to the skies. For example, Revolution Muslim has been around for years but garnered only sporadic coverage until the *South Park* incident, which inspired an explosion of stories lacking context.

The release of Samir Khan's *Inspire* in July 2010 prompted an incredible wave of hysterical and wildly inaccurate coverage from normally responsible news outlets, including stories claiming that the magazine was a website (it wasn't), that it had been published on glossy paper (it wasn't), and that it was the first English-language publication targeting Western recruits (it wasn't). None of the reporters and few quoted analysts had even heard of *Al Hussam* or the four issues of *Jihad Reflections* published just months earlier. In fact almost none of the reporters had even read *Inspire*—the PDF was corrupted when it was first uploaded, prompting jihadists and journalists alike to panic and assume that the file contained a virus (it didn't).[85]

Given the series of setbacks and failures described in this chapter, it might be tempting to dismiss the online jihad as a comedy of errors, a gang that couldn't shoot straight. It's easy enough to underestimate the significance of the jihadist Web, especially when so many of its celebrities are young and inept like Zach Chesser, or when they don't appear to be taking direct action toward violence, as in the case of Tarek Mehanna. But there are several levels on which these forums and websites are fundamentally transforming the face of American jihadists.

It's not simply a question of volume, at least not yet. Although the data set is sketchy, it appears the number of American jihadists and jihad sympathizers in 2010 is not exponentially higher than it was at the end of the 1980s. The perception of an increase is due, in part, to the fact that Americans are paying more attention now than they were then. And the jihadists themselves are far more visible to outsiders, thanks to the Internet.

There are also considerably more Muslims in America today than there were in 1990. Reliable figures on the number of U.S. Muslims are hard to come by, but even the most conservative estimate (1.3 million, almost certainly too low) shows the Muslim population more than doubled from 1990 to 2008.

That creates a bigger pool from which jihadists can recruit, but it doesn't mean that the number of jihadists, as a percentage of the American Muslim population, has increased by leaps and bounds. It should be stressed that only a tiny percentage of American Muslims are drawn into violent extremism, but it should also be recognized that Muslims represent the pool in which jihadists cast their lines. Based on the admittedly incomplete data, it appears likely that the percentage of American Muslims drawn into jihadist activity has increased somewhat but is not dramatically higher than it was in 1990.

The odds of developing credible data covering the last thirty years are slim, so the numbers game becomes something of a dead end. But we can observe, much more directly, that the Internet is creating a significant change in the patterns of radicalization and the types of people who make the decision to go from talk to action.

During the 1980s and the 1990s, recruits for jihad overseas most often entered combat from the perspective of defending Muslims from fairly unambiguous acts of aggression by non-Muslims, and they tended to be selected by recruiters or self-selected on the basis that they would be good in a fight—for instance, if they had military training. Candidates were usually filtered through a network of recruiters who helped screen volunteers and direct them to settings where they could be most useful.

For many, perhaps most, of these first-phase recruits, sophisticated ideological structures came only after they had decided to become combatants. When they arrived at the camps, itching for combat, they were instead subjected to days or weeks of religious indoctrination before they were allowed to take part in military training, let alone fight.

That's not to say that pre-9/11 recruits were oblivious to more advanced jihadist ideas—for instance, the ambition to create Islamic states or *takfiri* ideas about killing infidels (even when the infidels were Muslims). Some were preconditioned with these ideas, through exposure to ideologues such as Omar Abdel Rahman, but others were simply attracted to the miracles described by Abdullah Azzam or moved by mainstream media reporting about atrocities in Bosnia. Even those who had a more thorough grounding in abstract jihadist theology were absorbing those lessons through a relatively limited number of sources.

Religious indoctrination at the camps was tightly controlled by al Qaeda and a handful of loosely related organizations working from more or less the same playbook, including Lashar-e-Tayyiba and the Islamic Group. Instruction was delivered within a controlled environment, where cultlike indoctrination techniques such as dislocation and isolation helped reinforce the message. This more structured environment created jihadists who were, generally speaking, more formidable and more consistent in their beliefs.

In the post-9/11 era, two major changes worked together to dramatically alter the model. First, the invasion of Afghanistan virtually destroyed the existing network of al Qaeda training camps and drove non-Qaeda camps deep underground. It became much harder (though far from impossible) to travel to the fields of jihad and receive a decent education. The reconstituted camps in Pakistan operated under a cloak of extreme secrecy in a much more restrictive environment than before. In the United States, the environment for recruiters deteriorated in a corresponding manner, with mosques clamping down on the public airing of extremist rhetoric.

At the same time, the use of the Internet launched a decade of sustained and often explosive growth, not only for jihadists but for everyone. Internet access became ubiquitous, costs came down, and software and websites became easier to use. The advent of Web 2.0 led to a proliferation of blogs and message boards, and e-mail became the preferred method of communication. All these tools spread within the jihadist community at much the same pace that they did in the general population.

The chief effect of these two changes was to reverse the old paradigm. With the rise of the jihadist Web, religious indoctrination now tends to come first, and the decision to take part in combat comes second, if at all.

Would-be jihadists are today able to immerse themselves in a dizzying array of radical Islamic literature. They can feast on hundreds or thousands of hours of video and audio lectures by established clerics, as well as enthusiastic amateurs.

Among the amateurs, many lack a sophisticated Islamic outlook, but they excel at the Wikipedia approach to expertise. Anyone armed with Google can convince himself (and a certain number of others) that he is an expert in nearly any topic with a few weeks of concerted effort. Islamic jurisprudence may be especially vulnerable to this cut-and-paste mentality, due to its dense complexity and lack of a central religious authority to settle disputes.

Eventually, aspiring jihadists convince themselves that they too are experts, capable of deciding religious questions that have life-and-death consequences. All this can happen before the jihobbyist steps one foot overseas, as it did with Samir Khan and Zach Chesser.

Where the jihobbyists start to run into trouble is when they attempt to make the transition from talk to action. The clear passages to physical jihad are long gone, and those who wish to fight are left to their own devices.

Some succeed, but many more fail. Bryant Vinas nearly got himself killed trying to reach al Qaeda. In late 2009 five young men from the Washington, D.C., area demonstrated that not everyone is as lucky or competent as Vinas. They got arrested about a week after getting off the plane.[86]

Before 9/11 someone who selected himself for jihad usually did so because he was pretty damn tough. After 9/11 someone who selected himself was more likely to be a voracious reader.

When you're fighting a war, you need foot soldiers more than poets. Whether through lack of aptitude or lack of desire, many jihobbyists simply don't make it to the front lines. Tarek Mehanna never found a connection, if he was even trying. Ahmed Abousamra managed to get to Iraq only to return after two weeks. Yousef Al Khattab apparently just dropped out. Zach Chesser couldn't even make it onto a plane.

12
The Future of American Jihad

The journey of the American jihadist spans continents and decades. Americans of every race and cultural background have made the decision to take up arms in the name of Islam and strike a blow for what they believed to be justice.

Many who embarked on this journey took their first steps for the noblest of reasons—to lay their lives on the line in defense of people who seemed defenseless. But some chose to act for baser reasons—anger, hatred of the "other," desire for power, or an urge toward violence.

In the early days of the movement, it was possible to be a jihadist and still be a "good" American. Fighting the Soviets in Afghanistan was seen as admirable in many quarters, including the American right—the same political movement that today harshly criticizes mainstream Muslims who are slow to condemn Hamas. Both the right and the left united to support the Muslims of Bosnia (in principle, at least), and there was no effort to police volunteers who would help them with weapons or their lives.

But there were flaws in the program. The Afghan jihad gave birth to al Qaeda, and the Bosnian jihad was deeply infiltrated by al Qaeda and other terrorist networks.

In each country, jihadists primarily (if not exclusively) targeted soldiers of an opposing military force. Today's jihadists rarely confine themselves to military targets. They also intentionally kill civilians, including increasing numbers of Muslims, and many stage attacks outside of war zones and call those acts of violence "jihad." Because of this, the concept of military jihad has today been almost irrevocably welded to violent extremism and terrorism.

Modern jihad presents a clear threat to the national interest of the United States and to the safety of its citizens at home and abroad, as well as to countless innocent civilians of other nations. These countries include Pakistan, Afghanistan, Iraq, Yemen and Somalia, where Sunni extremists have targeted Shia Muslims, other Muslim sects they consider to be apostate, and any Muslim of any sect who dares take a stand against them.

We cannot interdict the behavior of individuals or popular masses on a global scale, but we can and must deal with the problem when it strikes closest to home. American jihadists present a unique threat to their homeland. Understanding the problem is the first step toward finding solutions.

The observations that follow pertain to the specific, peculiarly American path to jihad. On the global level, the question of radicalization and jihadism is more complex and interwoven with local political and cultural issues, but some of these points still apply.

PORTRAIT OF AN AMERICAN JIHADIST

Many jihadist ideologues are motivated by the desire to recreate some form of Islamic caliphate in the Middle East, Asia, Africa, and elsewhere in the Eastern hemisphere, whether regionally or in individual countries. Others seek to expand that caliphate on a global scale, with the intent to absorb Western society into a world-spanning Islamic state ruled by a strict, often brutal, interpretation of the shariah (Islamic law).

Although such motives have a place in public discourse concerning global policy, they are nearly irrelevant to the question of radicalization, especially the radicalization of Americans. Those who take up the jihadist path often end up embracing such global ambitions at a later stage, but very few Americans simply wake up one morning with a desire to impose shariah on the world.

Radicalization starts most often quietly and usually with a specific grievance. Many elements lead American Muslims to take up the banner of jihad, and some of these will be examined in the following passages, but the first element is almost always the same.

Whatever else lies in their hearts, virtually all American jihadists share an urgent feeling that Muslims are under attack. The most important religious and political justifications for jihad are based on the idea of self-defense, striking back against aggressors and protecting the members of the global Muslim community, known in Arabic as the *Ummah*.

Therein lies a sticky, painful problem. The narrative of Muslim victimization does not originate with al Qaeda. It is a pervasive theme that is deeply entrenched in mainstream Muslim thought, both in America and abroad.

In preparing for this book, I read nearly two hundred issues of the monthly English-language magazine published by the Saudi-supported Muslim World League, arguably the single most influential Muslim organization in the world. Month after month, the magazine trumpets the alarm: Islam is under attack from enemies everywhere. Islam is misunderstood because of vicious lies by its enemies. Muslims are persecuted and discriminated against on the global stage and in individual countries.

This isn't only a Saudi predilection. It can be found, to a greater and lesser extent, around the world. In the United States, the most visible example is the Council on American-Islamic Relations, a Washington, D.C., nonprofit whose daily e-mail newsletter enumerates grievance after grievance, from workplace discrimination to alleged hate crimes, which can be anything from a nasty word to murder or arson. CAIR's message is more carefully calibrated than that of the MWL, but it contributes to the echo chamber.

Some of the specific complaints aired by both organizations are entirely valid. Muslims in the United States and around the world suffer their share of travails and persecution, sometimes more than their share in a given time and place.

Muslim advocates absolutely deserve to have a voice, but they must also ask themselves whether they are—sometimes inadvertently—helping to perpetuate a counterproductive narrative about how the United States collectively treats Muslims.

CAIR follows in the footsteps of the American Muslim Council, founded by Abdurrahman Alamoudi. AMC was, in its day, as prominent as CAIR is today, but it faded from the scene after Alamoudi's arrest for trying to assassinate the Saudi crown prince Abdullah. During his time in the spotlight, Alamoudi gave voice to the same litany of grievances and the same sometimes-explicit argument that America, as it currently exists, is fundamentally inhospitable to Muslims.

This dynamic is made more complicated by the fact that all three of the aforementioned organizations have meaningful ties to jihadist movements. The

Muslim World League was Abdullah Azzam's employer (see chapter 1), and its personnel have been linked to al Qaeda and a number of terrorist plots. Abdurrahman Alamoudi was funneling money from Osama bin Laden to Omar Abdel Rahman even as he advocated for American Muslims as head of AMC (chapter 4). And CAIR's incorporators can be found in the personnel rolls of Hamas support groups in North America during the early 1990s.[1]

While acknowledging the deep complexity of this issue and the clear need for advocacy by and on behalf of American Muslims, it is important to realize that the path to radicalization begins with a rock-solid belief that Muslims are a victim class. Potential radicals do not have to look far to find reinforcement for this view. I will not belabor the point, because I think Muslims must resolve the issue themselves, and excessive input by outsiders can heighten the problem rather than ease it (as will be discussed later in this chapter). But those who encourage American Muslims to see themselves as disenfranchised victims must accept some degree of responsibility for the result.

Almost every jihadist profiled in this book started on his path with the idea that Muslims are being attacked by non-Muslims, whether in a specific circumstance or on a global level. The line that must be crossed to proceed to military jihad requires defining those attacks as a "war on Islam" (although not everyone who uses that language means to endorse jihad). War must be met by war, and by that logic, people move from angry talk to violent action.

Jihadist recruiters cynically exploit aggression and atrocities committed against Muslims, as in Bosnia. Once drawn in, recruits often find the sphere of attacks on Muslims that justify an armed response quickly expands. The list of provocations starts with military violence but grows to include "economic oppression," which is blamed for poverty in Muslim nations; the "immodest" display of women's bodies on television, which is blamed for corrupting Muslims' morals; and even simple insults or criticisms of Islam.

Accepting that someone, or everyone, is engaged in a war with Islam is only a precondition to the radicalization process. To complete the transaction, American jihadists will usually need one or more of the following traits:

Idealism/altruism: Many American jihadists act—in the beginning, at least—out of good intentions and the simple belief that their actions can bring about a positive change in the world. Ismail Royer is an example of someone who defends his actions with an intellectualized appeal to the better angels of our nature. Abdullah Rashid, in a simpler way, continually calls back to the basic idea of doing good. For both men, the complexity of the real world (and their real personalities) outpaced the simplicity of the stories they like to tell about themselves. Idealism burns brightly in the heart, and it is often impervious to reality.

Violent tendencies or an obsession with violence: Military jihad and terrorism are inherently violent activities. Those who become jihadists must come to terms with that violence, and some fully embrace it. In certain cases, violent impulses are the primary driver that leads someone to jihad, even more than the defensive rationale. Tarek Mehanna watched and cheered videos of gory beheadings the way other Americans watch football. Isa Abdullah Ali, the veteran of Lebanon and Bosnia, is riveting when he describes himself as a professional soldier and killing machine. His adoption of jihad seems at times like an effort to ennoble a preexisting attraction to violence. Sometimes people seek out a convenient rationalization for their worst impulses, and sometimes that rationalization happens to be jihad.

Ideology: As discussed in previous chapters, the role of ideology has changed significantly in the last thirty years. During the 1980s people were often recruited to jihad out of a sense of adventure or due to the personal charisma of leaders such as Abdullah Azzam, only becoming seriously indoctrinated with religious rationales after they arrived in Afghanistan or other fields of jihad. Today, the Internet offers a path to ideological radicalization before action. Recruits such as Tarek Mehanna and Zach Chesser absorbed the philosophy of politicized Islam and more advanced radical belief structures, like *takfir*, before ever taking action.

Identity politics: On paper, Islam is color-blind. In practice, Muslims can be as racist as anyone else, and radical American movements like Al Fuqra—whose members are mostly black separatists—have a strong component of racial and identity politics. Islam itself can also be experienced as an exclusive political or social identity. Some American jihadists, such as Jose Padilla, have a history of gang identification prior to converting to Islam. The allure of joining a seemingly empowered social network should not be underestimated.

Alienation: In Europe, social alienation is seen as a significant driver of radicalization among Muslims, but American Muslims tend to be more assimilated than their European counterparts. Nevertheless, some American Muslims—such as Daniel Maldonado—took steps toward radicalism because of a feeling that they could not practice Islam in the United States due to social pressures. Millions of American Muslims would disagree with Maldonado on this point, but it should be recognized as a potential risk factor.

Fetishization of sex and women: The psychology of sex and gender is incredibly complicated, and I will not attempt a detailed deconstruction here. Yet it's worth noting that sex often makes an appearance in these stories. Many American jihadists, such as Nidal Hasan and Omar Hammami, were described by friends as "desperate" to get married but only to extraordinarily chaste women. Some jihadist clerics even allow followers to have sex outside of marriage as part of their recruitment pitch.[2] Jihadists can also show clear signs of sexual dysfunction, such as Anwar Awlaki's penchant for hanging around schoolyards and patronizing teenage prostitutes. The ubiquitous use of rape stories in jihadist propaganda also points toward a fetishized view of sex and women. It's admirable to act to prevent rape and assist its victims, but the recurring tales of jihadists whose dreams are haunted by the screaming of Muslim women raise some questions worthy of deeper consideration.

The mix of these qualities is fluid and has changed over time. For instance, the number of jihadist recruits who start from the broad platform of politicized Islam has increased, compared to those who react to specific situations of clearly defined aggression. The motivation of creating an Islamic state is more visible among Americans who want to fight in Somalia but have no ethnic ties to the conflict, to pick the most obvious example.

The ready availability of sometimes shockingly brutal jihadist propaganda on the Internet also attracts a large cheering section of bottom-feeders: violence junkies, anti-Semites, and small men gripped by hate and self-loathing who lack the will to act themselves but are willing to provide a social context for those who would.

EVALUATING THE THREAT

In the 1980s and well into the 1990s, being a jihadist did not by definition alone make someone an enemy of the United States. But since September 11, the practice of military jihad has been criminalized and inextricably linked to terrorism.

Even those who would take part in jihad overseas, forgoing American targets, are subject to prosecution or death by drone. The most active jihadists overseas are declared enemies of the United States, even when their concerns are primarily local. The participation of American citizens and long-term residents in any sort of jihadist activity is now treated as a security threat in itself, regardless of the nature of that activity.

Several factors have contributed to that change, aside from the broad shift in American attitudes after September 11. U.S. diplomatic and intelligence efforts have deliberately linked jihadism to terrorism in the sphere of international relations, with a considerable amount of success.[3]

And the jihadists themselves have almost universally come to define America as the enemy. Although this war was launched by al Qaeda in almost every meaningful sense, the subsequent invasion of Iraq on the basis of unfounded claims about weapons of mass destruction has provided jihadist ideologues with all the ammunition they need to deflect and avoid the question of "who started it." No future change in the course of U.S. policy can fully erase the impact of that mistake.

In Iraq and Afghanistan today, U.S. military forces are directly fighting jihadists on the battlefield. In Somalia and Yemen, the "hidden hand" of U.S. military and political influence is seen as manipulating events on the ground, not without some justification.

For better or worse, America is embroiled in a global war with jihadism, and there is no immediately foreseeable end to that conflict. The ultimate direction of that war is beyond the scope of this book. The goal here is evaluating the threat from the self-styled jihadists in our midst. There are three major considerations:

Quality of entry-level recruits: As noted in chapter 11, early jihadist recruits generally had relevant skills, often some kind of traditional military training. As the Internet replaced the real-world network of recruiters and personal connections, jihadist volunteers began to reflect a different demographic. The most rabid supporters of jihad today are very young converts with little practical experience in Islam, fighting, or life. They're often not even particularly good at using the Internet securely. Abdullah Azzam, writing in 1988, complained about the immaturity and the shallow Islamic learning of his followers.[4] He would likely have been horrified to see the state of jihad in 2010.

Numbers: Offsetting the low quality of many of these volunteers is the Internet's reach. Before 9/11 you had to find and engage a real world social network in order to learn about and eventually win an invitation to jihad. Now anyone with a computer can find himself hip-deep in jihad-friendly social circles in no time flat and can e-mail someone like Anwar Awlaki for encouragement and instructions on how to proceed with mayhem. The pool of people with more than a casual interest in jihad is much larger, and it's easier for them to find social reinforcement to go deeper. There are more traps and dead ends for aspiring jihadists online than there were for someone walking down Atlantic Avenue in Brooklyn in 1990, but generally anyone with enough persistence can move from talk to action with active support from serious players met online. A 2010 report claiming that three hundred Americans had trained with al Qaeda in the Arabian Peninsula raises alarm bells.[5] I'm a bit skeptical about this estimate, but if it's true, that could be more Americans than took part in the wars in 1980s Afghanistan and 1990s Bosnia combined.

Lack of training: The devastation wrought on al Qaeda's training camps in Afghanistan has paid dividends to U.S. national security. No one has ever come close to replicating the success of al Qaeda's training network, in terms of length of training, quality of graduates, and relative ease of access. It's not uncommon for modern-day American recruits to try several times before gaining access to any terrorist training camp, if they make it at all. Once they get there, their handlers are usually in a hurry to give them a bare minimum of instruction and send them off on an attack. As seen most memorably in the attempted Times Square bombing, inadequate training has a tendency to lead to failure.

In light of these considerations, the danger posed by American jihadists cannot be measured on a linear scale over time. During the 1990s jihadists based in the United States were relatively professional: more experienced, better trained, and likely to have a military background. Their schemes—such as the World Trade Center bombing and the "Day of Terror" plot—were carefully planned, fairly well financed, and staffed by more people.

In the years since September 11 and especially since 2008 and the rise of Anwar Awlaki, a new pattern has emerged. The attacks are more frequent and less complex. The attackers are more and more often radicalized young people, acting in small groups or alone, with minimal funds and even less training. Awlaki's *Inspire* magazine has explicitly encouraged American Muslims to act alone using simple tactics, and al Qaeda Central has echoed that call in messages from Adam Gadahn and others.[6]

Counterterrorism officials worry about the prospect that U.S. terrorists will exploit their knowledge of American life and psychology to wreak terrible damage. It's a valid concern, but Americans who join jihad movements often start by abandoning the trappings of their native culture, losing some of their competitive edge in the process.

At-risk converts often adopt Arab dress and customs, even though such affectations have little to do with Islam per se. Those who join jihadist organizations are often so eager to assimilate that they affect or acquire vaguely Arabic-sounding accents, as in the cases of Omar Hammami and Adam Gadahn.

From a Westerner's perspective, this is a good thing. It makes them less effective at speaking to Americans in propaganda, and so far, it has also rendered them less effective at crafting uniquely American forms of attack. When someone is inducted into what is essentially a cult, he is likely to follow rather than lead.

There are exceptions. People who grew up with a foot in both worlds—such as Anwar Awlaki and perhaps Adnan Shukrijumah—appear more successful at adapting their messages and tactics for Westerners. Awlaki has proved his ability to speak effectively to Westerners using their own idioms. Awlaki's student Nidal Hasan struck out in a very American manner, with guns blazing. Another of Awlaki's students, Samir Khan, produces the West-friendly *Inspire* magazine.

Shukrijumah is more of a cipher. His ultimate impact on al Qaeda's tactics is still shrouded in secrecy as of this writing, but if the volume of the FBI's statements about him is any indication, there is cause for concern. Adam Gadahn made an impact on al Qaeda's propaganda operations, but his more Westernized ideas, like the *Voice of the Caliphate* newscast, have faded away in favor of traditional talking-head communiqués.

The potential game-changer that lurks ahead is the question of whether the American jihad movement can achieve critical mass and become a force in its own right, rather than a toolbox for jihadists abroad. Until now, most Americans have only been a commodity to foreign jihadists such as al Qaeda and, in recent years, an expendable commodity. They have been thrown away on missions doomed to fail or absorbed so thoroughly into a foreign culture that their uniquely American qualities become secondary to new allegiances.

In May 2010 someone—probably Revolution Muslim blogger Zach Chesser—set up a Twitter account called "AQNorthAmerica." Although Chesser was something of a running joke in the counterterrorism community, it didn't take long for my e-mail to start pinging with incredulous comments from colleagues about the account (which has been silent since Chesser's arrest).

While the Twitter account was undoubtedly nothing more than some ill-considered posing, it points to the future. If the ranks of radicalized Muslims in America continue to grow at the current pace or even faster, prodded by political events or a surge in anti-Muslim rhetoric in the United States, could they achieve enough critical mass to create a genuine al Qaeda franchise worthy of the name in North America?

Most al Qaeda franchises and close allies overseas count their membership in the hundreds or higher. Assembling such a team in the United States without being discovered by law enforcement would have been difficult in 1990. The dozens of jihadists in Brooklyn and New Jersey certainly didn't manage it. They were discovered by law enforcement—more than once—before arrests were made. But agents and officers at street level were dealing with a Washington, D.C., culture that had little appetite for investigating religious extremism.

That culture has obviously changed. With rare exceptions, domestic terrorist cells broken up since September 11 have consisted of six or fewer members, mostly with little or no support from overseas. Mosques have become much less hospitable to extremists, and the online forums where would-be terrorists congregate have been profoundly compromised by law enforcement and intelligence agencies.

While at least thousands of Muslims in the United States are engaged to a greater or lesser extent in jihadist chatter online and in the real world, they remain a very small percentage of the American Muslim population. Very few of these talkers are anywhere close to action. With a caveat for inadequate data, the number of American Muslims who have picked up a gun, a knife, or a bomb with the intention of using it against another human being under the heading of jihad is almost certainly less than 1 percent of the total American Muslim population.

Those most prone to act are also most likely to have attracted law enforcement scrutiny. Simply gathering a dozen aspiring amateurs in one place for a terrorist operation is tempting fate. In the short-term future, it is likely that these conditions will continue to make major coordinated terrorist activity by homegrown American terrorists extremely difficult, but something short of impossible.

Because of all these factors, the new breed of American jihadists has almost uniformly failed to execute mass-casualty terrorist attacks on U.S. soil. Unfortunately, that is nearly certain to change, perhaps by the time this book reaches print, perhaps a few months or years into the future. Whether by learning from failure or by simple luck, it is highly likely that the American jihadist movement will eventually succeed in a spectacular attack and cost hundreds or more American lives in the process.

There is also a greatly heightened threat of less conceptually ambitious terrorist attacks that can be staged by individuals or very small groups with little or no preparation or training, such as Nidal Hassan's shooting rampage. Anwar Awlaki and his followers are actively pursuing this tactic. While there are serious questions about the strategy's long-term viability, the prospects are unfortunately strong for near-term chaos caused by such small-scale attacks.

Evolution is the greatest danger and the biggest wild card. The history of American jihadists is one of constant, dynamic change. The jihadists of today are profoundly different from those of yesterday. They are younger and wilder, less predictable, and faster to act.

The American jihadists of the future will learn from their predecessors. Some will learn patience, and others will learn the tradecraft of terrorism. Some will be trained and receive money from terrorist networks abroad. Some will become extraordinarily dangerous. They may find ways to unify their efforts. Will there ever be a viable "al Qaeda in North America"? Forming a cohesive and capable organization would be a big challenge, but it's not impossible.

As the players change, their methods will change, and the rules will change. The most immediate risk factors include:

Countermeasures: Zach Chesser's jihadist career was less than exemplary, but he publicly articulated a subject that is certainly being discussed in private—

how to foil established counterterrorism tactics. Jihadists have not caught up with advances in law enforcement and intelligence techniques, but we can't assume we will retain the edge, particularly as it regards online security. Al Qaeda and its allies have almost always operated on an open-source basis, especially since September 11. Jihadist forums have until recently put a premium on accessibility over security. Arrests based on online intelligence gathering may inspire jihadists to get creative about protecting themselves and the identities of the forums' members.[7] Small steps have already been taken in that direction. In 2008, for example, al Qaeda–linked militants introduced military-grade encryption software customized for terrorist use.[8] A few talented terrorist hackers could conceivably change the balance of power online. For now, though, the advantage remains decisively with the West. Another concern is that as new technologies continually roll out, unforeseen innovations may appear that render surveillance more difficult.

Reconstitution of al Qaeda's training camps: Al Qaeda's training camp structure was severely disrupted by the invasion of Afghanistan, but there are troubling signs that these camps may be enjoying a renaissance on the Afghanistan-Pakistan border, in Yemen under the auspices of al Qaeda in the Arabian Peninsula, and in Somalia, in coordination with both Al Shabab and the core al Qaeda.[9] Rank amateurism was a defining characteristic for the wave of American jihadists exposed in 2009 and 2010. Even an incremental improvement in the training and the professionalism of the current generation of American terrorists could exponentially increase their destructive power. On the plus side, it's very difficult to travel to a region where advanced terrorist training takes place without popping up on somebody's intelligence radar screen.

The numbers game: No one really knows how many Americans have been genuinely radicalized through online and other sources. All of our best estimates are simply guesses, but the number is almost certainly measured in thousands. Not all of those who have been radicalized would directly support an act of violence. As the stories in this book show, there's no single factor most likely to precipitate a radical thinker into a radical actor. An event of sufficient magnitude—along the lines of the Bosnia war—could tip a large number of these talkers into actors in a very short amount of time. Even allowing for continued amateurism in the ranks of American terrorists, this has the potential to unleash chaos. Nine times out of ten, a trained sniper on the rooftop will kill more people than a lunatic with a shotgun running down the street, but the lunatic is still dangerous. And ten lunatics on the sidewalk at one time are more dangerous than the sniper.

As we move forward, we must do so with an understanding of how American jihadists are created and how they develop over time. It's easy to reduce these men to caricatures, to demonize them without listening to them, and to ignore what they say when their words do not fit our expectations. To listen carefully and critically, to acknowledge their stories, is not to excuse their actions. Understanding why Americans take up the banner of jihad is the first step to finding solutions.

As the extremists evolve, so too must the relationship between Americans and mainstream American Muslims. America's most valuable asset in combating extremism has been truth. Jihadist idealogues—and even some mainstream American Muslim leaders—insist the United States has declared war against Islam. That claim has proved false, even in the dark days immediately after September 11.

But ten years later, we find the nation poised at a perilous juncture. The 2010 controversy over a proposed Islamic center in New York, a few blocks from Ground Zero, put an exclamation point on a rising tide of anti-Muslim sentiment in this country that has the potential to fuel extremism and discourage reformers.

During the summer of that year, prominent mainstream politicians on the right compared the Islamic center's organizers—and Muslims writ large—to Nazis and other historic wartime enemies of the United States in comments that too often went unchallenged by members of the media and other politicians. Newt Gingrich, former speaker of the house, was the most visible and most mainstream voice to make this comparison:

> Nazis don't have the right to put up a sign next to the Holocaust museum in Washington," [...] We would never accept the Japanese putting up a site next to Pearl Harbor. [...] There is no reason for us to accept a mosque next to the World Trade Center.[10]

Whatever one's views on appropriateness of the center, the fact is that such extreme and indiscriminate anti-Muslim rhetoric helps to validate the worldview of our enemies—the premise that America's wars are indeed wars against Islam. I said earlier in this chapter that Muslims who perpetuate a victimization mentality must accept some responsibility for the result. Non-Muslims who wish to define the entire religion of Islam as America's enemy must also carry their share of that burden. You cannot tell someone, "You are my enemy," and then blame them for believing you.

This in no way justifies or rationalizes the actions of those who translate their anger into violence, particularly terrorist violence, which is especially reprehensible for its focus on intentionally indiscriminate killing. The responsibility for such acts lies primarily with the individuals who commit them and those who explicitly encourage them to do so. The decision to step over the line and commit murder is inexcusable—but that doesn't mean it has to be incomprehensible.

It's fair game to challenge American Muslim leaders if they enable, excuse, or try to ignore the problem of radicalization—and some do—but those challenges must be thoughtful and made with an eye toward consequences, constructive dialogue, and moving through the impasse instead of deepening it. In turn, Muslim leaders must rise to the challenge of these times by directly confronting the problem of military jihadism rather than denying it exists or seeking to silence discussion with charges of Islamophobia and bigotry.

There must be an exit strategy for this discussion. We must preserve the constitutional rights and basic human respect due to American Muslims while changing the playing field to create conditions in which extremism cannot thrive. Those goals are not mutually exclusive—they are interdependent.

If principle and pragmatism are not enough reason to change the tone of the conversation, there is one more thing to consider. It would be not only dangerous but shameful to prove that our enemies were right about us all along.

ACKNOWLEDGMENTS

It took a lot of help to make this book possible, and this list will certainly omit people who deserve to be thanked. For that I apologize in advance. I want to thank everyone who agreed to speak with me, but especially Tom Corrigan, formerly of the Joint Terrorism Task Force, who was generous not only with his time but also with crucial documentation that allowed me to present the words of the jihadists profiled herein. Former CIA analyst Mike Scheuer and former FBI agent Chris Voss, who now runs the Black Swan Group, helped stitch often-disparate threads together into a coherent whole. Alia Rashid sat down for two interviews—which were arranged with the help of Rashid's attorney, Ken Wasserman—as did Ray Royer. Bilal Philips persisted through days of phone tag with a fourteen-hour time difference during Ramadan so that we could speak. There were many more, and each provided unique value. A number of people consented to speak on a not-for-attribution basis who could not have spoken otherwise.

Much of my work is based on documents, and many people were generous in sharing the primary source material that forms the core of the narrative. The Motley Rice law firm in Mount Pleasant, South Carolina, working to represent the families of the victims of September 11, has created an unparalleled resource on al Qaeda and Islamic extremism, and its lawyers shared material with me that would never have seen the light of day without their efforts. The U.S. Attorney's office in Boston endured a great deal of hassle in making documents from the Boston Al Kifah Center available to me, and I want to thank Aloke Chakravarty and Christina Dilorio-Sterling for their help and their patience. Terrorism investigators J. C. Brisard and Evan Kohlmann generously provided key information and documents relating to Bosnia. Peter Lance provided transcripts of the World Trade Center bombing and the "Day of Terror" court cases.

Several people helped on the back end of the book as well. David Hebditch and Ola Flyum, the makers of the television documentary *Sarajevo Ricochet*, gave me the opportunity to go to Bosnia and to conduct on film several of the interviews used in this book. The outstanding Bosnian Muslim journalist Esad Hecimovic shared both information and insight. Jody Jenkins, the writer and the producer of the *American Jihadist* documentary, helped with advice on sources at various points and with a screener copy of the excellent film, which was directed by Mark Claywell. Roxanne Euben and Aaron Zelin provided me with invaluable help in understanding the complexities of jihadist ideology, and Aaron also provides notes on an early draft of the manuscript. Thanks are also due to Lawrence Wright and Marissa Allison for facilitating conversations with some of their own valued sources.

Chris Heffelfinger, of the Combating Terrorism Center at West Point, introduced me to Hilary Claggett of Potomac Books, Inc., who gave me the chance to write this book. She and Katie Neubauer of Potomac helped turn it around fast.

Anne Berger transcribed hours of audio with amazing accuracy, expending extraordinary effort to get down often-obscure Arabic terms, sift through accents, and enhance source files that were often less than ideal. At various points, she enlisted most of the rest of my family to assist in this effort.

Geneva Berger has read probably tens of thousands of pages of things I have written over the years, always providing support and encouragement, even when the material never made it out of my desk drawer, and I am incredibly grateful for that.

Rachel Milton helped in more ways than I can count, talking out difficult issues, developing ideas, providing source material, and remembering who was who and who did what to whom, and she was always available with a phone number or e-mail address of someone I needed to talk to.

Finally, this book literally could not have been written without the assistance of Janet Walsh. Through a very long haul, she offered nothing but faith, support, and incredible patience. She helped me talk through problems and issues, listened to stories, read through drafts, and allowed me the freedom to carve out a niche in a very challenging profession, even when it seemed like a long shot. Not to mention the marathon editing session in 95-degree heat. I can't express how much I appreciate all of this and more.

NOTES

Introduction

1. State Department Cable, "Execution of Mosque Attackers," JIDDA 00210, January 10, 1980; Yaroslav Trofimov, *The Siege of Mecca* (New York: Doubleday, 2007), 240–241.
2. Trofimov, *The Siege of Mecca*; J. M. Berger, ed., *The Siege at Mecca Sourcebook* (Intelwire Press, 2006), ii–iii.
3. State Department Cable, STATE 012300, no subject specified, January 16, 1980.
4. Steve Emerson, "Abdullah Assam: The Man before Osama Bin Laden," International Association for Counterterrorism and Security Professionals, retrieved August 25, 2010, http://www.iacsp.com/itobli3.html.

Chapter 1. The Early Years

1. Yvonne Yazbeck Haddad and Jane Idleman Smith, eds., *Muslim Communities in North America* (Albany: SUNY Press, 1994), 31.
2. Jonathan Curiel, "Muslim Roots, U.S. Blues," *Saudi Aramco World*, July–August 2006, retrieved August 10, 2010, http://www.saudiaramcoworld.com/issue/200604/muslim.roots.u.s.blues.htm.
3. Akbar Ahmed, *Journey into America: The Challenge of Islam* (Washington, DC: Brookings Institution Press, 2010), Kindle edition, locations 2335–2341.
4. Curiel, "Muslim Roots, U.S. Blues."
5. See http://www.moorishsciencetempleofamericainc.com/MoorishHistory.html, retrieved August 16, 2010.
6. Yvonne Yazbeck Haddad, ed., *The Muslims of America* (New York: Oxford University Press, 1993), 111–123; author analysis of documents from DePaul University Archives: Islam in America: Muslim Students' Association collection; and Noreen S. Ahmed-Ullah, Sam Roe, and Laurie Cohen, "A Rare Look at Secretive Brotherhood in America," *Chicago Tribune*, September 19, 2004.
7. Ian Johnson, *A Mosque in Munich: Nazis, the CIA, and the Muslim Brotherhood in the West* (New York: Houghton Mifflin Harcourt, 2010), 89.

8. More than twenty years of *Muslim World League Journal* publications in English were reviewed by the author from 1977 through 2003. The issues were provided by Motley Rice law firm.
9. John W. King, *The Breeding of Contempt* (Xlibris, 2002); Pierre Tristam, "What Was the 1977 Hanafi Siege in Washington, D.C.?" About.com, retrieved August 18, 2010 http://middleeast.about.com/od/religionsectarianism/f/me090310a.htm.
10. "Islamic Organizations' Conference, Newark, USA—A Report," *Muslim World League Journal* (May 1977); *Proceedings of the First Islamic Conference of North America* (Muslim World League, 1977).
11. For an overview, see Yaroslav Trofimov, *The Siege of Mecca* (New York: Doubleday, 2007); Steve Coll, *Ghost Wars: The Secret History of the CIA, Afghanistan, and Bin Laden, from the Soviet Invasion to September 10, 2001* (New York: Penguin Press, 2004); *Encyclopedia Britannica*, "Iran Hostage Crisis," retrieved August 18, 2010, http://www.britannica.com/EBchecked/topic/272687/Iran-hostage-crisis.
12. Trofimov, *The Siege of Mecca*; J. M. Berger, ed., *The Siege at Mecca Sourcebook* (Intelwire Press, 2006); State Department cables were obtained by the author through the Freedom of Information Act (FOIA), including all cables cited in the following notes.
13. State Department Cable, "Execution of Mosque Attackers," JIDDA 00210, January 10, 1980.
14. State Department Cable, no subject specified, STATE 012300, January 16, 1980.
15. Trofimov, *The Siege of Mecca*, 240–241.
16. State Department Cable, "Booklet Attributed to Perpetrators of Grand Mosque Incident," KUWAIT 05422, November 29, 1979.
17. Confidential interview, March 2007; Peter Bergen, *The Osama bin Laden I Know* (New York: Simon & Schuster, 2006), 16.
18. Vincent Jauvert, "Oui, la CIA est entrée en Afghanistan avant les Russes . . . ," *Le Nouvel Observateur*, January 15, 1998, retrieved August 17, 2010, http://hebdo.nouvelobs.com/sommaire/documents/008877/oui-la-cia-est-entree-en-afghanistan-avant-les-russes.html .
19. Video: *We Are Afghanistan*, U.S. Information Agency (State Department), obtained from the National Archives.
20. Greg Krikorian, "Singlaub to Lead Anti-Communist Group," *San Diego Union-Tribune*, September 4, 1984; Orr Kelly, "How Americans Help Finance Foreign Wars," *U.S. News & World Report*, September 23, 1985.
21. "Rabita Delegation Visits to South-East Asia," *Muslim World League Journal* (March 1980). Rabita al-Alam al-Islami is the Arabic name of the Muslim World League.
22. Charles R. Babcock, "Dallas Hosts Anti-Communist League; Diverse Group Hears Insurgents Plead for 'No-Strings' Funding," *Washington Post*, September 17, 1985.
23. Peter L. Bergen, *Holy War, Inc: Inside the Secret World of Osama bin Laden* (New York: Simon & Schuster, 2002), 55.
24. DePaul University Archives: Islam in America: Muslim Students' Association collection: "Muslim Scholars Visit ITC," *Islamic Teaching Center News*, February

1978. The Islamic Teaching Center was a spin-off controlled by the Muslim Students Association. One of the people Azzam met with was former MSA president Eltigani Abugidieri, who was also linked to the Muslim World League.

25. Najwa and Omar Bin Laden, *Growing Up Bin Laden: Osama's Wife and Son Take Us inside Their Secret World* (New York: Macmillan, 2009), 24–26; see also "Osama in America: The Final Answer," *New Yorker*, June 30, 2009, http://www.newyorker.com/online/blogs/stevecoll/2009/06/osama-in-america-the-final-answer.html.
26. *The 9-11 Commission Report: Final Report of the National Commission on Terrorist Attacks upon the United States, Official Government Edition* (Washington, DC: U.S. Government Printing Office, 2004), 58.
27. *An Interview with Tamim Adnani, Director of the Mujahideen Service Office in Afghanistan* (Lawrence Islamic Video, 1988), obtained by the author.
28. Mark Ensalaco, *Middle Eastern Terrorism: From Black September to September 11* (Philadelphia: University of Pennsylvania Press, 2008), 131.
29. Bergen, *The Osama bin Laden I Know*, 27.
30. Undated Abdullah Azzam video, circulated online by al Qaeda, obtained by the author.
31. Abdullah Azzam, *Join the Caravan* (Boston: Care International, 1995).
32. *USA v. Omar Abdel Rahman et al.*, S5 93 Cr. 181, court transcript, July 13, 1995, Testimony of Khaled Ibrahim.
33. Hampton-El's biography is based on the following sources except where otherwise noted: author interviews with Alia Rashid, June 26, 2008, and October 23, 2008; *USA v. Omar Abdel Rahman et al.*, S5 93 Cr. 181, August 1, 1995, and August 2, 1995, Testimony of Clement Hampton-El.
34. *USA v. Omar Abdel Rahman*, S5 93 Cr. 181, court transcript, June 5, 1995, citation of surveillance audio.
35. *USA v. Abdel Rahman*, S5 93 Cr. 181, case heading; author interviews with Tom Corrigan, June 24, 2008, through June 23, 2010, inclusive; and author interview with Islamic cleric Bilal Philips, August 25, 2010.
36. Author e-mail interview with Clement Hampton-El, conducted during several months in 2010.
37. Hampton-El propaganda video, provided to the author by former JTTF investigator Tom Corrigan.
38. *USA v. Fawaz Damrah*, No. 04-4216, Sixth Circuit Court of Appeals Opinion, March 15, 2005.
39. *USA v. Omar Abdel Rahman et al.*, S5 93 Cr. 181, court transcript, August 2–3, 1995, Testimony of Clement Hampton-El (Abdullah Rashid).
40. Interview with counterterrorism expert Evan Kohlmann, June 23, 2008; physical description of Zaki from images in *The Martyrs of Bosnia* propaganda videotape obtained by the author; and biographical data derived from court exhibits obtained by the author from *U.S. v. Muhamed Mubayyid, Emadeddin Muntasser, and Samir Al Monla*, Criminal Action No. 05-40026-FDS (2007).
41. *USA v. Omar Abdel Rahman et al.*, S5 93 Cr. 181, Hampton-El propaganda video.
42. Author interviews with Alia Rashid, June 26, 2008, and October 23, 2008.
43. *USA v. Omar Abdel Rahman et al.*, S5 93 Cr. 181, Hampton-El propaganda video.

44. Ibid.
45. Author interviews with Alia Rashid, June 26, 2008, and October 23, 2008.
46. *USA v. Omar Abdel Rahman et al.*, S5 93 Cr. 181, Hampton-El Testimony.
47. Ibid.; author interviews with Tom Corrigan, June 24, 2008, through June 23, 2010, inclusive.

Chapter 2. Al Qaeda's Americans

1. Lawrence Wright, *The Looming Tower: Al Qaeda and the Road to 9/11* (New York: Knopf, 2006), 131–132. Bayazid was contacted with a request for an interview but stopped responding during discussions.
2. Tony Rizzo, "KC Man Linked to Al Qaeda," *Kansas City Star*, September 9, 2006.
3. Wright, *The Looming Tower*, 109–110.
4. *USA v. Omar Abdel Rahman et al.*, S5 93 Cr. 181, July 13, 1995, Testimony of Khaled Ibrahim.
5. *An Interview with Tamim Adnani, Director of the Mujahideen Service Office in Afghanistan* (Lawrence Islamic Video, 1988), obtained by the author.
6. Wright, *The Looming Tower*, 110.
7. Letter from Osama bin Laden to Abu Ridah Al Suri, spring 1987. The letter was part of a collection of al Qaeda documents known as the "Tareekh Osama" file, which were recovered from an al Qaeda hard drive seized by the FBI in Bosnia and obtained by the author.
8. Wright, *The Looming Tower*, 115–117.
9. Minutes of an August 11, 1988, meeting, formation of al Qaeda, Tareekh Osama files. See also Wright, *The Looming Tower*, 131–132, 402n. Bayazid denied attending the meeting, but the denial must be measured against the document evidence, including the handwritten meeting minutes, obtained by the author. Wright notes Bayazid's denial, but his account describes Bayazid as being present at the meeting and recording the minutes.
10. Peter Bergen, *The Osama bin Laden I Know* (New York: Free Press, 2006), 92.
11. Steve Coll, *Ghost Wars: The Secret History of the CIA, Afghanistan, and Bin Laden, from the Soviet Invasion to September 10, 2001* (New York: Penguin Press, 2004), 204.
12. Minutes of an August 11, 1988, meeting, formation of al Qaeda, Tareekh Osama files.
13. Minutes of an August 20, 1988, meeting, formation of al Qaeda, Tareekh Osama files.
14. *US v. Usama bin Laden et al.*, S(7) 98 Cr. 1023, Indictment, November 5, 1998, Superseding Indictment, S(10) 98 Cr. 1023 (LBS), undated.
15. Undated El Hage al Qaeda application, Tareekh Osama files. The document lists El Hage's age as twenty-eight, which puts the application around 1988, making El Hage one of the first members.
16. FBI FD-302 Record of Interrogation, Wadih El Hage, September 23, 1997.
17. Oriana Zill, "A Portrait of Wadih El Hage, Accused Terrorist," *PBS Frontline* website, http://www.pbs.org/wgbh/pages/frontline/shows/binladen/upclose/elhage.html, retrieved June 17, 2010; Kevin Peraino and Evan Thomas, "Odys-

sey into Jihad," *Newsweek*, January 14, 2002; and undated El Hage al Qaeda application, Tareekh Osama files.

18. *USA v. Usama bin Laden*, S(7) 98 Cr. 1023, February 6, 2001, and subsequent days, Testimony of Jamal Al Fadl.
19. Wright, *The Looming Tower*, 110.
20. Photographs retrieved from an al Qaeda computer seized in Bosnia, obtained by the author.
21. *USA v. Daniel Patrick Boyd, et al.*, 5:09cr216-1FL, Indictment, July 22, 2009.
22. Surveillance audio, retrieved June 17, 2010, http://www.investigativeproject.org/1357/05-20-2009-140800-141005mp3.
23. Surveillance audio, retrieved June 17, 2010, http://www.investigativeproject.org/1359/06-10-2009-124355-124600mp3.
24. Tom Hays and Sharon Theimer, "Egyptian Agent Worked with Green Berets, bin Laden," *Associated Press*, December 31, 2001.
25. *USA v Ali Mohamed*, S(7) 98 Cr. 1023 (LBS), Plea Hearing, October 20, 2000.
26. Montasser Al Zayat, *The Road to Al Qaeda: The Story of Bin Laden's Right-Hand Man* (Sterling, Virginia: Pluto Press, 2003), 45, 54.
27. This analysis runs counter to some conventional wisdom, which holds that al Qaeda and EIJ merged at a much later date. Yet the testimony of Jamal Al Fadl and other al Qaeda members clearly shows how closely intertwined the two organizations were. It may be helpful to think of EIJ as al Qaeda's special forces branch—in some respects, a distinct operation but still clearly part of the same army.
28. Benjamin Weiser and James Risen, "The Masking of a Militant: A Special Report," *New York Times*, December 1, 1998.
29. Interviews with former CIA analyst Michael Scheuer, October 27, 2008, and August 18, 2009; *Triple-Cross: Bin Laden's Spy in America* (National Geographic Video, 2007). The author was the lead researcher for this television documentary, and a small amount of unpublished material from that project is referenced throughout under this citation.
30. Weiser and Risen, "The Masking of a Militant: A Special Report."
31. Andrew Martin and Michael J. Berens, "Terrorists Evolved in U.S.: 2 Egyptians Set Stage for Attacks," *Chicago Tribune*, December 11, 2001.
32. Bergen, *The Osama bin Laden I Know*, 103.
33. *Triple Cross* (video).
34. Ibid.; Weiser and Risen, "The Masking of a Militant: A Special Report."
35. *USA v. Rahman*, S5 93 Cr. 181, Nosair Exhibit JJJ-1 (Ali Mohamed video).
36. *USA v Ali Abdelseoud Mohamed*, Affidavit of Daniel Coleman, September 1998.
37. Al Zayat, *The Road to Al Qaeda*, 37; Wright, *The Looming Tower*, 409n; and T5 B7 Analysis of Immigration Status of Pre-9-11 Terrorists Fdr-Entire Contents 196, retrieved July 18, 2010, http://www.scribd.com/doc/16729114/T5-B7-Analysis-of-Immigration-Status-of-Pre911-Terrorists-Fdr-Entire-Contents-196.
38. *USA v. Rahman*, S5 93 Cr. 181, multiple exhibits.
39. *The Al Qaeda Manual*, retrieved June 19, 2010, http://www.justice.gov/ag/manualpart1_1.pdf, Paul Butler, PDASD (SO/LIC), *Briefing on Detainee Operations at Guantanamo Bay*, U.S. Department of Defense, Office of the Assistant Secretary

of Defense (Public Affairs), retrieved June 19, 2010, http://www.defense.gov/transcripts/transcript.aspx?transcriptid=2071.

40. *USA v. Omar Abdel Rahman et al.*, S5 93 Cr. 181, Testimony of Khaled Ibrahim.
41. John Miller and Michael Stone with Chris Mitchell, *The Cell: Inside the 9/11 Plot and Why the FBI and CIA Failed to Stop It* (New York: Hyperion, 2003), 48–49; Nexis address search. By coincidence, the author lived in the same neighborhood at approximately the same time.
42. Author interviews with Tom Corrigan, June 24, 2008, through June 23, 2010, inclusive.
43. Author interviews with Alia Rashid, June 26, 2008, and October 23, 2008.
44. *US v. Usama bin Laden et al.*, S(7) 98 Cr. 1023, February 15, 2001.
45. Zak Ebrahim speech at the 2010 Student Peace Alliance National Conference, February 26, 2010, Southwestern University, Georgetown, Texas, retrieved August 20, 2010, http://www.youtube.com/watch?v=VnDHorm0DjM.
46. *USA v. Omar Abdel Rahman et al.*, S5 93 Cr. 181, Testimony of Khaled Ibrahim.
47. *USA v. El Atriss*, no case number, bail hearing (sealed), November 19, 2002, Testimony of Det. Sgt. Fred Ernst. Transcript provided by attorney Louis Pashman, representing New Jersey media plaintiffs. Nexis address search for 2828 Kennedy Ave., Jersey City, N.J.
48. Miller and Stone, *The Cell*, 51.
49. Scattered reports have indicated that the United States may have brought some of these mujahideen to the United States and covertly sponsored or facilitated their training. I have not been able to authenticate these reports; however, Jamal Al Fadl claimed to have traveled to the United States in 1985 for "Islamic military training." This fact was stipulated to by prosecutors in *US v. Usama bin Laden*, presumably to keep the details from coming out in open court. *US v. Usama bin Laden, et al.*, S(7) 98 Cr. 1023, April 30, 2001, Stipulation.
50. Author interview with retired FBI agent Robert Stauffer, June 10, 2010.
51. Confidential interview with retired FBI agent, June 21, 2010.
52. Author interviews with Tom Corrigan, June 24, 2008, through June 23, 2010, inclusive.
53. Ibid.; interview with former FBI agent Christopher Voss, June 20, 2008; and *USA v. Rahman*, S5 93 Cr. 181, court transcript, February 7, 1995, and others.

Chapter 3. The Death Dealers

1. See http://www.baseball-reference.com/bullpen/Sam_Khalifa, retrieved August 23, 2010.
2. Abu Ameenah Bilal Philips, *The Quran's Numerical Miracle, 19 Hoax and Heresy* (Jeddah, Saudi Arabia: Abul Qasin Publications, 1987); Zahir Uddin Siddiqui, "Ye Who Believe!" *Muslim World League Journal* (November 1977).
3. Philips, *The Quran's Numerical Miracle, 19 Hoax and Heresy*.
4. Abdullah Bin Baz et al., *In Defence of the Quran and Sunnah* (Canada: Maglis of Al Haq Publication Society, 1985).
5. FBI FD-302 Record of Interrogation, Wadih El Hage, September 23, 1997.
6. Jamie Komarnicki, "Accused Not Reliably Linked to Crime Scene of Imam, Court Hears," *Edmonton (Alberta) Journal*, September 5, 2009.

7. Daryl Slade, "Alleged Murderer Ordered Deported; Charged with Killing Imam in 1990," *Calgary (Alberta) Herald*, October 17, 2009.
8. Grand Jury Testimony, Wadih El Hage, New York City, September 24, 1997, read into court record during *USA v. bin Laden*, S(7) 98 Cr. 1023, February 15, 2001.
9. Colorado Attorney General, "Information Regarding Colorado's Investigation and Prosecution of Members of Jamaat Ul Fuqra," retrieved July 22, 2010, http://web.archive.org/web/20080718193618/http://www.ago.state.co.us/pr/121001_link.cfm.html, Eric Sagara, "Man Arrested in '90 Slaying of Religious Leader at Local Mosque," *Tucson Citizen*, April 29, 2009.
10. John Kane and April Wall, "Identifying the Links between White-Collar Crime and Terrorism," study written with a grant from the U.S. Department of Justice, National Institute of Justice, September 2004, 29.
11. Kevin Martin and Nadia Moharib, "DNA Links Suspect to Calgary; Community Residents Shocked to Hear They Lived Near Accused Killer of Arizona Scholar," *Calgary (Alberta) Sun*, July 22, 2010.
12. Colorado Attorney General, "Information Regarding Colorado's Investigation and Prosecution of Members of Jamaat Ul Fuqra."
13. Author interviews with Tom Corrigan, June 24, 2008, through June 23, 2010, inclusive.
14. *Patterns of Global Terrorism 1999*, Department of State, Office of the Coordinator for Counterterrorism (Washington, DC: Department of State Publications, April 2000); David Kohn, "Sheik Gilani: CBS' Man in Pakistan Tracks Him Down," *60 Minutes* website, March 13, 2002, retrieved September 6, 2010, http://www.cbsnews.com/stories/2002/03/13/60II/main503644.shtml.
15. Lee Berthiaume, "The Untold Story of Hasanville's Shadowy Past," *Ottawa (Ontario) Citizen*, May 4, 2002.
16. Christopher Heffelfinger, "Evaluating the Terrorist Threat Posed by African-American Muslim Groups," *CTC Sentinel*, May 2008.
17. Interviews with former CIA analyst Michael Scheuer, October 27, 2008, and August 18, 2009.
18. Author interviews with Tom Corrigan, June 24, 2008, through June 23, 2010, inclusive.
19. Colorado Attorney General, "Information Regarding Colorado's Investigation and Prosecution of Members of Jamaat Ul Fuqra."
20. Kane and Wall, "Identifying the Links between White-Collar Crime and Terrorism."
21. Interviews with former CIA analyst Michael Scheuer, October 27, 2008, and August 18, 2009; author interviews with Tom Corrigan, June 24, 2008, through June 23, 2010, inclusive.
22. T5 B7 Analysis of Immigration Status of Pre-9-11 Terrorists Fdr- Entire Contents 196, retrieved July 18, 2010, http://www.scribd.com/doc/16729114/T5-B7-Analysis-of-Immigration-Status-of-Pre911-Terrorists-Fdr-Entire-Contents-196.
23. *USA v. Rahman*, S5 93 Cr. 181, court transcript, Testimony of Ali Shinawy, July 11, 1995.
24. *USA v. Rahman*, S5 93 Cr. 181, court transcript, April 3, 1995; see also John Miller and Michael Stone with Chris Mitchell, *The Cell: Inside the 9/11 Plot and Why the FBI and CIA Failed to Stop It* (New York: Hyperion, 2003).

25. Neil MacFarquhar, "In Jail or Out, Sheik Preaches Views of Islam," *New York Times*, October 2, 1995.
26. Montasser Al Zayat, *The Road to Al Qaeda: The Story of Bin Laden's Right-Hand Man* (Sterling, Virgnia: Pluto Press, 2003), 27 et al.
27. Richard Bernstein, *Out of the Blue: The Story of September 11, 2001, from Jihad to Ground Zero* (New York: Macmillan, 2002), 438.
28. Omar Abdel Rahman, *The Present Rulers and Islam: Are They Muslims or Not?* (Kuwait: 1988).
29. State Department Cable, "Summary of Conversations with a Member of 'The Islamic Group' AKA Al Jihad," CAIRO 09476, dated April 25, 1989, obtained by the author through the Freedom of Information Act.
30. Interview with Frank Wisner, former U.S. ambassador to Cairo, July 1, 2010.
31. Douglas Jehl, "'C.I.A. Officer Signed Visa for Sheik,' U.S. Says," *New York Times*, July 14, 1993.
32. Andrew C. McCarthy, *Willful Blindness: A Memoir of the Jihad* (New York: Encounter Books, 2008), 15–16.
33. Author interviews with Tom Corrigan, June 24, 2008, through June 23, 2010, inclusive; McCarthy, *Willful Blindness*, 125; and Miller and Stone, *The Cell*, 64
34. Abullah Azzam, *Join the Caravan* (Boston: CARE International, 2nd ed., 1989), introduction.
35. *U.S. v. Muhamed Mubayyid, Emadeddin Muntasser, and Samir Al Monla*, Criminal Action No. 05-40026-FDS (2007), Exhibit 266.
36. Maktab al Khidmat (Abdullah Azzam's organization), arbitration records dated November 25, 1988, and December 29, 1988, Tareekh Osama files.
37. Author interviews with Tom Corrigan, June 24, 2008, through June 23, 2010, inclusive ; profile of Abdullah Azzam, retrieved June 17, 2010; http://www.ummah.com/forum/showthread.php?5062-Profiles-of-Ash-Shuhadaa, and Steve Coll, *Ghost Wars: The Secret History of the CIA, Afghanistan, and Bin Laden, from the Soviet Invasion to September 10, 2001* (New York: Penguin Press, 2004), 204.
38. Coll, *Ghost Wars*; Aryn Baker, "Who Killed Abdullah Azzam?" *Time Magazine*, June 18, 2009, retrieved August 24, 2010, http://www.time.com/time/specials/packages/printout/z0,29239,1902809_1902810_1905173,00.html.
39. *Al Jihad Magazine*, November/December 1990.
40. *USA v Ali Abdelseoud Mohamed*, S(7) 98 Cr. 1023 (LBS), Sealed Complaint, September 1998 (Affidavit of Daniel Coleman).
41. *USA v. Rahman*, S5 93 Cr. 181, court transcript, May 3, 1995, Testimony of Abdo Haggag. The quote was related by Haggag, whose English was imperfect and has been paraphrased slightly for grammatical purposes.
42. *Terrorists Among Us—Jihad in America* (DVD, SAE Productions, Nov. 11, 2001).
43. Zak Ebrahim speech at the 2010 Student Peace Alliance National Conference, February 26, 2010, Southwestern University, Georgetown, Texas, retrieved August 20, 2010, http://www.youtube.com/watch?v=VnDHorm0DjM .
44. Meir Kahane FBI investigative files, obtained by the author through the Freedom of Information Act; Joel Brinkley, "Israel Bans Kahane Party from Election," *New York Times*, October 6, 1988.
45. FBI FD-302 Record of Interrogation, name redacted, October 27, 1992; FBI FD-

302 Record of Interrogation, Name Redacted (2), October 27, 1992; and FBI Letterhead Memorandum, September 18, 1992, "El Sayyed A. Nosair."

46. FBI FD-302, Record of Interrogation, name redacted, October 28, 1992.
47. Ronald Sullivan, "Trade Center Blast Prompts Kahane Case Review," *New York Times*, March 13, 1993.
48. Greg B. Smith, "Bin Laden Bankrolled Kahane Killer Defense," *New York Daily News*, October 9, 2002; Chitra Ragavan, Nancy L. Bentrup, Ann M. Wakefield, Sheila Thalhimer, and Monica M. Ekman, "Tracing Terror's Roots," *U.S. News & World Report*, February 24, 2003,
49. Peter Bergen, *Holy War Inc.* (New York: Free Press, 2001), 134; author interviews with Tom Corrigan, June 24, 2008, through June 23, 2010, inclusive; and McCarthy, *Willful Blindness*, 192–193.
50. Author interviews with Tom Corrigan, June 24, 2008, through June 23, 2010, inclusive.
51. Ibid.; Gerald Posner, *Why America Slept* (New York: Random House, 2003), 6; Jailan Halawi, "Jihad Implicated in US Embassy Bombings," *Al Ahram Weekly*, May 27, 1999; and McCarthy, *Willful Blindness*, 193.
52. Mary B. W. Tabor, "Slaying in Brooklyn Linked to Militants," *New York Times*, April 11, 1993.
53. Ibid.
54. *Triple Cross* (video).
55. Grand Jury Testimony, Wadih El Hage, New York City, September 24, 1997, read into court record during *USA v. bin Laden*, S(7) 98 Cr. 1023, February 15, 2001.
56. FBI FD-302, Interrogation of Nidal Ayyad, December 27, 2005, http://www.peterlance.com/FBI_302_12_28_05_Nidal_Ayyad_pages_1-2.pdf, retrieved August 6, 2010; Peter Lance, "The Spy Who Came in for the Heat," *Playboy*, August 2010.
57. Author interviews with Tom Corrigan, June 24, 2008, through June 23, 2010, inclusive; confidential interview with retired FBI agent, June 2010.
58. FBI FD-302, Nidal Ayyad; Lance, "The Spy Who Came in for the Heat."
59. Grand Jury Testimony, Wadih El Hage, New York City, September 24, 1997.
60. Author interviews with Tom Corrigan, June 24, 2008, through June 23, 2010, inclusive.
61. Ibid.; Miller and Stone, *The Cell*, 76.
62. *USA v. Ramzi Ahmed Yousef and Eyad Ismoil*, S12 93 CR 180 (KTD), court transcript, August 11, 1997.
63. *The 9-11 Commission Report: Final Report of the National Commission on Terrorist Attacks upon the United States, Official Government Edition* (Washington, DC: U.S. Government Printing Office, 2004), 71–73 (hereafter *9/11 Commission Report*); *USA v. Abdel Rahman*, S5 93 Cr. 181, court transcripts, various dates; *US v. Mohammad A. Salameh et al.*, S593CR.180(KTD), various dates; and Simon Reeve, *The New Jackals: Ramzi Yousef, Osama bin Laden and the Future of Terrorism* (Boston, Massachussets: Northeastern, 2002), 120.
64. *USA v. Abdel Rahman*, S5 93 Cr. 181, court transcript, February 7, 1995; *USA v. Abdel Rahman*, S5 93 Cr. 181, court transcript, July 17, 1995.
65. *USA v Ali Abdelseoud Mohamed*, Affidavit of Daniel Coleman, September 1998;

USA v. Abdel Rahman, S5 93 Cr. 181, court transcript, July 17, 1995; *US v. Usama bin Laden*, S(7) 98 Cr. 1023, court transcript, February 23, 2002, Testimony of L'Houssaine Kherchtou; *USA v Ali Mohamed*, S(7) 98 Cr. 1023 (LBS), plea hearing, October 20, 2000; *US v Salameh*, S593CR.180(KTD), November 10, 1993, Government Exhibits 2781 through 2786; *USA v. Abdel Rahman*, S5 93 Cr. 181, September 11, 1995; and *USA v. Abdel Rahman*, July 13, 1995.

66. Author interviews with Tom Corrigan, June 24, 2008, through June 23, 2010, inclusive; McCarthy, *Willful Blindness*, 109
67. James C. McKinley Jr., "Fingerprints Link Suspect to Bombing, Officials Say," *New York Times*, August 5, 1995; "Bloomington Native Linked to '93 Bombing," *Indianapolis Star*, October 11, 2001, http://www2.indystar.com/library/factfiles/crime/national/2001/sept11/yasin.html, retrieved August 24, 2010.
68. Miller and Stone, *The Cell*, 90–96; "FBI 100th Anniversary, First Strike: Global Terror in America," Federal Bureau of Investigation website, February 26, 2008, retrieved August 25, 2010; http://www.fbi.gov/page2/feb08/tradebom_022608.html, and Reeve, *The New Jackals*, 8–12.
69. Richard Bernstein, "Trade Center Witness Tells of Manuals on Bombs," *New York Times*, November 10, 1993; "FBI 100th Anniversary, First Strike: Global Terror in America," FBI website; Joseph P. Fried, "U.S. Says Man Helped Brother Flee in Trade Center Bombing," *New York Times*, September 19, 1996; and Michael Isikoff, "Saddam's Files; They Show Terror Plots, but Raise New Questions about Some U.S. Claims," *Newsweek*, March 31, 2008.

Chapter 4. Project Bosnia

1. Audio: Bilal Philips, "My Way to Islam," circa 2007; Emmanuel Sivan, *Radical Islam: Medieval Theology and Modern Politics* (Binghamton, NY: Yale University, 1985).
2. See http://www.famousmuslims.com/bilal%20Philips.htm, retrieved August 28, 2010; also see http://www.way-to-allah.com/en/journey/philips.html, retrieved August 28, 2010; Philips audio, "My Way to Islam."
3. Author interview with Bilal Philips, August 25, 2010; Philips audio, "My Way to Islam."
4. John Mintz and Gregory L. Vistica, "Muslim Troops Loyalty a Delicate Question," *Washington Post*, November 2, 2003.
5. Author interview with Bilal Philips, August 25, 2010.
6. Mahmud Khalil, "Jamaican-Born Canadian Interviewed on Islamic Missionary Work among US Troops," *Al Majallah* via *Global News Wire*, August 3, 2003.
7. Ibid.
8. Author interview with Bilal Philips, August 25, 2010.; Philips audio, "My Way to Islam"; and James Yee, *For God and Country: Faith and Patriotism under Fire* (New York: PublicAffairs, 2005), 24–25.
9. FBI FD-302, Interrogation of Jamal Al Fadl (Gamal Ahmed Mohamed Al Fedel), November 10, 1991, http://www.scribd.com/doc/16981234/T1-B24-Various-Interrogation-Reports-Fdr-11898-FBI-Investigation-Gamal; Peter Lance, "First Blood: Was Meir Kahane's Murder al-Qaida's Earliest Attack on U.S. Soil?" *Tablet*, September 1, 2010.

10. Author interview with Bilal Philips, August 25, 2010.
11. Karen Branch-Brioso, "Muslims in U.S. Military Reassert Their Patriotism," *Port St. Lucie/Fort Pierce* (*Florida Tribune*), April 3, 2003.
12. Author interview with Bilal Philips, August 25, 2010.
13. Interview with Peter Galbraith, May 2009; interview with Tony Lake, May 2009; and interview with Fotini Christia, assistant professor of political science, Massachusetts Institute of Technology, May 2009.
14. Interviews with Esad Hecimovic, a Bosnian journalist, June 2008 through August 2010, inclusive; video: *Sarajevo Ricochet* (Fenris Film, 2010), review of documents obtained for documentary, including Bosnian intelligence records of mujahideen.
15. *The Martyrs of Bosnia*, Bosnian mujahideen propaganda video; interview with Evan Kohlmann, June 2009; interviews with Esad Hecimovic, a Bosnian journalist, June 2008 through August 2010, inclusive.
16. *The Martyrs of Bosnia*, Bosnian mujahideen propaganda video.
17. E-mail interview through an intermediary with Yamin Ramzi, a former jihadist cleric, October 2009; Bosnian intelligence document, *Report on Afro-Asian Citizens and Institutions in Bosnia*, November 19, 1995.
18. Abdullahi Sheikh Muhammed, "Force against Serbia: Will OIC Go It Alone?" *Muslim World League Journal* (January 1993).
19. Author interviews with Tom Corrigan, June 24, 2008, through June 23, 2010, inclusive.
20. Abdurahman Alamoudi, "Bosnia—from the Muslim Perspective," *Washington Times*, August 7, 1995.
21. Interview with George Rivera, former *ABC News* reporter in Bosnia, October 23, 2008; Susan Gonzalez, "Unbiased Reporting Is Not Always Noble, CNN Journalist Say," *Yale Bulletin*, April 22, 2005, http://www.yale.edu/opa/arc-ybc/v33.n27/story8.html.
22. Interview with Tony Lake, May 2009; interview with Peter Galbraith, May 2009.
23. Transcript, "News Conference with the American Task Force for Bosnia (ATFB)," *Federal News Service*, August 6, 1993.
24. David Binder, "Alija Izetbegovic, Muslim Who Led Bosnia, Dies at 78," *New York Times*, October 20, 2003.
25. *Al Hussam* newsletter, October 30, 1992.
26. *USA v. Omar Abdel Rahman et al.*, S5 93 Cr. 181, Exhibit 450/451, transcript of speech.
27. Evan Kohlmann, *Al-Qaida's Jihad in Europe: The Afghan-Bosnian Network* (Berg Publishers, 2004), 38–39
28. "Muslims In Yugoslavia: Victims of Political And Economic Discrimination," *Muslim World League Journal* (July 1983); Kerim Reis, "Islamic Education Spreads in Yugoslavia," *Muslim World League Journal* (April 1984).
29. Interrogation of Jamal Al Fadl (Gamal Ahmed Mohamed Al Fedel), November 10, 1991.
30. Interview with Javid Ali, former TWRA employee, December 5, 2008; *Expert Report Concerning the Area Financial Investigations*, Third World Relief Agency, International Criminal Tribunal for the former Yugoslavia (ICTY); and records

of German police investigation of the Third World Relief Agency, provided to the author.

31. Surveillance tape transcript, Omar Abdel Rahman, February 25, 1993, Reel 7, Call 26; *Expert Report Concerning the Area Financial Investigations*, ICTY report; author interviews with Tom Corrigan, June 24, 2008, through June 23, 2010, inclusive.
32. Author interview with Bilal Philips, August 25, 2010.
33. Ibid.; *USA v. Rahman*, S5 93 Cr. 181, court transcript, May 17, 1995.
34. American Forces Press Service, "Muslim Troops Highlight Nation's Diversity," *American Forces Information Service (Defense Department)*, January 1999; Laurie Goodstein, "For Muslims in the Military, a Chaplain of Their Own," *Washington Post*, December 4, 1993.
35. Branch-Brioso, "Muslims in U.S. Military Reassert Their Patriotism"; Philips audio, "My Way to Islam"; author interview with Bilal Philips, August 25, 2010; and *USA v. Rahman*, S5 93 Cr. 181, court transcript, August 2–3, 1995, Testimony of Clement Hampton-El (Abdullah Rashid).
36. Author interview with Bilal Philips, August 25, 2010.
37. Bryan Brumley, "Bosnian Mujahedeen Will Welcome, Not Threaten, U.S. Soldiers," *Associated Press*, December 4, 1995; "Tuzla Air Base," retrieved August 31, 2010, http://www.globalsecurity.org/military/facility/tuzla.htm.
38. Interrogation of Jamal Al Fadl (Gamal Ahmed Mohamed Al Fedel), November 10, 1991; confidential interview with source close to the investigation, August 5, 2010.
39. FBI FD-302, Interrogation of El Sayyid Nosair, December 27, 2005, http://www.scribd.com/doc/35687185/FBI-302-El-Sayyid-Nosair-12-20-05; interrogation of Jamal Al Fadl (Gamal Ahmed Mohamed Al Fedel), November 10, 1991.
40. Author interview with Bilal Philips, August 25, 2010.
41. Confidential interview with source close to the investigation, August 5, 2010; interrogation of Jamal Al Fadl (Gamal Ahmed Mohamed Al Fedel), November 10, 1991; and *USA v. Rahman*, S5 93 Cr. 181, court transcripts, May 17, 1995, and August 2, 1995. Tahir's name is alternately spelled Tahir, Tehar, and Taher, but all three refer to the same person.
42. *USA v. Rahman*, S5 93 Cr. 181, court transcript, August 2–3, 1995, Testimony of Clement Hampton-El (Abdullah Rashid).
43. Ibid.; Hampton-El e-mails to the author, 2009 to 2010, inclusive; author interview with Bilal Philips, August 25, 2010.
44. *USA v. Rahman*, S5 93 Cr. 181, court transcript, August 2–3, 1995, Testimony of Clement Hampton-El (Abdullah Rashid); author interview with Bilal Philips, August 25, 2010.
45. *USA v. Rahman*, S5 93 Cr. 181, court transcript, August 2–3, 1995, Testimony of Clement Hampton-El (Abdullah Rashid); author interview with Bilal Philips, August 25, 2010.
46. Author interview with Bilal Philips, August 25, 2010.
47. Interview with Muradif Pajt, former business associate of the Third World Relief Agency, July 9, 2008; confidential interview with former senior Bosnian government official, October 2008; surveillance tape, Siddig Ali, May 31, 1993, Tape

CM-29; author interview with Bilal Philips, August 25, 2010; and *USA v. Rahman*, S5 93 Cr. 181, court transcript, August 2–3, 1995, Testimony of Clement Hampton-El (Abdullah Rashid). Saffet Catovic did not respond to repeated requests for an interview.

48. *USA v. Rahman*, S5 93 Cr. 181, court transcripts, May 11, 1995.
49. Surveillance tape, Siddig Ibrahim Ali, Cassette 41, undated.
50. *USA v. Rahman*, S5 93 Cr. 181, court transcripts, May 18, 1995.
51. *USA v. Rahman*, S5 93 Cr. 181, court transcripts, March 21, 1995, and April 4, 1995.
52. *USA v. Rahman*, S5 93 Cr. 181, court transcripts, September 5, 1995.
53. Interview with Muhammad Filipovic, July 2008.
54. Interview with Muradif Pajt, former business associate of the Third World Relief Agency, July 9, 2008; *USA v. Rahman*, S5 93 Cr. 181, court transcript, August 2–3, 1995, Testimony of Clement Hampton-El (Abdullah Rashid).
55. *USA v. Rahman*, S5 93 Cr. 181, court transcript, August 2–3, 1995, Testimony of Clement Hampton-El (Abdullah Rashid).
56. Interview with Ken Wasserman, Hampton-El's defense attorney, June 2008.
57. Author interviews with Tom Corrigan, June 24, 2008, through June 23, 2010, inclusive.
58. Author interview with Bilal Philips, August 25, 2010.
59. Ibid.
60. *USA v. Rahman*, S5 93 Cr. 181, court transcript, August 2–3, 1995, Testimony of Clement Hampton-El (Abdullah Rashid); *USA v. Rahman*, S5 93 Cr. 181, court transcripts, July 31, 1995.
61. *USA v. Rahman*, S5 93 Cr. 181, court transcripts, January 30, 1995, and others; author interviews with Tom Corrigan, June 24, 2008, through June 23, 2010, inclusive; and safe house video surveillance tape provided by Tom Corrigan.
62. Andrew C. McCarthy, *Willful Blindness: A Memoir of the Jihad* (New York: Encounter Books, 2008), 257.
63. Khalil, "Jamaican-Born Canadian Interviewed on Islamic Missionary Work among US Troops."
64. Author interview with Bilal Philips, August 25, 2010.
65. *USA v. Rahman*, S5 93 Cr. 181, court transcript, August 2–3, 1995, Testimony of Clement Hampton-El (Abdullah Rashid); interview with former FBI agent Christopher Voss, June 20, 2008; author interviews with Tom Corrigan, June 24, 2008, through June 23, 2010, inclusive; and interviews with former CIA analyst Michael Scheuer, October 27, 2008, and August 18, 2009.
66. Mike Barber, "Muslims in the U.S. Military Are as Loyal as Any, Chaplain Says," *Seattle Post-Intelligencer*, October 20, 2001; Qaseem Uqdah, Memorandum, "Islamic Observance of Ramadan and Eid-Ul-Fitr," American Muslim Armed Forces and Veterans Affairs Council, retrieved September 1, 2010, http://www.uscg.mil/lantarea/docs/AMAF%20and%20VAC%20Ramadan%202010%20ltr.pdf.
67. Author e-mail interview with Clement Hampton-El, 2009 and 2010.
68. Surveillance tape, Siddig Ali, May 31, 1993, Tape CM-29; Evan Kohlmann, *Al-Qaida's Jihad in Europe: The Afghan-Bosnian Network* (New York: Berg Publishers, 2004), 38–39.

69. Montasser Al Zayat, *The Road to Al Qaeda: The Story of Bin Laden's Right-Hand Man* (Sterling, Virginia: Pluto Press, 2003), 62.
70. *USA v. Rahman*, S5 93 Cr. 181, court transcripts, Sept. 5, 1995.
71. Interview with former FBI agent Christopher Voss, June 20, 2008.

Chapter 5. Rebuilding The Network

1. *U.S. v. Muhamed Mubayyid, Emadeddin Muntasser, and Samir Al Monla*, Criminal Action No. 05-40026-FDS (2007), Affidavit of FBI Special Agent James T. Martinelli, April 5, 2005.
2. Ibid.
3. *Al Hussam* newsletter, March 3, 1993.
4. *Al Hussam* newsletter, December 17, 1993.
5. *Al Hussam* newsletter, January 28, 1994.
6. *Al Hussam* newsletter, August 26, 1994.
7. Ibid.
8. *U.S. v. Muhamed Mubayyid, Emadeddin Muntasser, and Samir Al Monla*, Criminal Action No. 05-40026-FDS (2007), FBI wiretap, January 19, 1996, conversation between Imad Muntasser, Kassem Daher, and Adham Hassoun.
9. *Al Hussam* newsletter, March 24, 1995.
10. *Al Hussam* newsletter, April 16, 1993; *U.S. v. Muhamed Mubayyid, Emadeddin Muntasser, and Samir Al Monla*, Criminal Action No. 05-40026-FDS (2007), Exhibit 448A.
11. *Al Hussam* newsletter, March 15, 1996.
12. *Al Hussam* newsletter, July 28, 1995.
13. *U.S. v. Muhamed Mubayyid, Emadeddin Muntasser, and Samir Al Monla*, Criminal Action No. 05-40026-FDS (2007), Exhibit 285, letter to Hekmatyar, Exhibit 283, meeting minutes, Exhibits 266, 283.
14. *The Martyrs of Bosnia*, Bosnian mujahideen propaganda video; *U.S. v. Muhamed Mubayyid, Emadeddin Muntasser, and Samir Al Monla*, Criminal Action No. 05-40026-FDS (2007), Exhibit 270.
15. *U.S. v. Muhamed Mubayyid, Emadeddin Muntasser, and Samir Al Monla*, Criminal Action No. 05-40026-FDS (2007), Exhibit 556.
16. Interview with Aloke Chakravarty, Assistant U.S. Attorney in Boston, June 2008; *U.S. v. Muhamed Mubayyid, Emadeddin Muntasser, and Samir Al Monla*, Criminal Action No. 05-40026-FDS (2007), various financial exhibits.
17. Interview with Aloke Chakravarty, Assistant U.S. Attorney in Boston, June 2008.
18. *Al Hussam* newsletter, June 16, 1995.
19. *U.S. v. Muhamed Mubayyid, Emadeddin Muntasser, and Samir Al Monla*, Criminal Action No. 05-40026-FDS (2007), Exhibit 436, CARE International flyers, April 4, 1997; Esad Hecimovic, "Mysteries Surround 1997 B-H Murder Victim Misidentified as Terrorist Hisham Diab," *Dani*, January 14, 2005.
20. *U.S. v. Muhamed Mubayyid, Emadeddin Muntasser, and Samir Al Monla*, Criminal Action No. 05-40026-FDS (2007), Exhibit 510A, transcript of November 19, 1994 wiretap.
21. *The Martyrs of Bosnia*, (video); *Al Hussam* newsletter, June 16, 1995.
22. *Al Hussam* newsletter, June 2, 1995; *U.S. v. Muhamed Mubayyid, Emadeddin*

Muntasser, and Samir Al Monla, Criminal Action No. 05-40026-FDS (2007), Exhibit 436, American Islamic Group flyer.

23. E-mail interview through an intermediary with Yamin Ramzi, a former jihadist cleric, October 2009; confidential e-mail interview with an American mujahid in Bosnia through an intermediary; and Bryan Brumley, "Bosnian Mujahedeen Will Welcome, Not Threaten, U.S. Soldiers," *Associated Press*, December 4, 1995.
24. Jody Jenkins and Mark Claywell, *American Jihadist*, independent film, 2010. All Isa Ali quotes and information are taken from the documentary except as otherwise cited.
25. William Branigin, "U.S. Sniper in Beirut: Abdullah from D.C. Hunts Israeli Targets," *Washington Post*, July 29, 1982.
26. Jenkins and Claywell, *American Jihadist.*
27. Branigin, "U.S. Sniper in Beirut."
28. Jenkins and Claywell, *American Jihadist.*
29. Ibid.
30. Ibid.
31. Ibid.
32. Ibid.
33. Ibid.
34. Letter from Randall Royer to Judge Leonie Brinkema, March 31, 2004.
35. Interview with Ray Royer, October 2008.
36. Karen Branch-Brioso, "Islam Set Direction of Area Man's Life; He Is Charged with Conspiring to Fight with Muslim Groups Abroad," *St. Louis Post-Dispatch*, June 29, 2003.
37. Ibid.
38. Letter from Randall Royer to Judge Leonie Brinkema, March 31, 2004.
39. Branch-Brioso, "Islam Set Direction of Area Man's Life; He Is Charged with Conspiring to Fight with Muslim Groups Abroad."
40. Interview with Ray Royer, October 2008.
41. Letter from Randall Royer to Judge Leonie Brinkema, March 31, 2004.
42. "1994: Market Massacre in Sarajevo," *BBC News*, retrieved July 19, 2010, http://news.bbc.co.uk/onthisday/hi/dates/stories/february/5/newsid_2535000/2535435.stm.
43. See http://ismailroyer.blogspot.com/2002_09_15_archive.html.
44. Propaganda video and photographs obtained by the author during a trip to Bosnia; author interview with Tomo Petrovic, the father of one of the victims, July 2008; and interview with Vlado Petrovic, the brother of the victim (no relation to Tomo Petrovic), July 2008.
45. Bosnian Intelligence records showing surveillance of mujahideen phone records were obtained by the author. In addition, a phone record in the same format showing a call from a mujahideen facility to Osama bin Laden was shown to the author by terrorism expert Evan Kohlmann. Additional data from interviews with CIA analyst Michael Scheuer, August 2008, and NSA analyst John Schindler, June 2008.
46. *USA v. Usama bin Laden et al.*, S(7) 98 Cr. 1023, court transcript, February 6, 2001, and subsequent days, Testimony of Jamal Al Fadl; *Expert Report Concerning the Area Financial Investigations*, Third World Relief Agency, International

Criminal Tribunal for the former Yugoslavia (ICTY); contents of al Qaeda hard drive seized in Sarajevo.

47. Letter from Randall Royer to the author, October 31, 2009.
48. E-mail interview through an intermediary with Yamin Ramzi, former jihadist cleric, October 2009.
49. *USA v. Christopher Paul*, 2:07cr:87, Indictment, April 11, 2007; Justice Department press release, "Ohio Man Sentenced to 20 Years for Terrorism Conspiracy to Bomb Targets in Europe and the United States," February 26, 2009, retrieved July 12, 2010, http://www.justice.gov/opa/pr/2009/February/09-nsd-171.html.
50. *USA v. Enaam M. Arnaout*, No. 02 CR 892, Government's Evidentiary Proffer Supporting the Admissibility of Coconspirator Statements, January 6, 2003.
51. Confidential interview with Justice Department official, October 2009.
52. Material from al Qaeda hard drive seized in Sarajevo.
53. Undated CIA cable from Al Qaeda hard drive; interviews with CIA analyst Michael Scheuer, August 2008; and author interview with Evan Kohlmann, terrorism expert, June 23, 2008.
54. *U.S. v. Muhamed Mubayyid, Emadeddin Muntasser, and Samir Al Monla*, Criminal Action No. 05-40026-FDS (2007), multiple CARE International checks introduced as exhibits.
55. *USA v. Kifah Wael Jayyousi and Kassem Daher*, Case No. 04-3565RID, Criminal Complaint; *U.S. v. Muhamed Mubayyid, Emadeddin Muntasser, and Samir Al Monla*, Criminal Action No. 05-40026-FDS (2007), various FBI wiretaps; and *U.S. v. Muhamed Mubayyid, Emadeddin Muntasser, and Samir Al Monla*, Criminal Action No. 05-40026-FDS (2007), Exhibit 272, CARE International letter, April 4, 1997.
56. *U.S. v. Muhamed Mubayyid, Emadeddin Muntasser, and Samir Al Monla*, Criminal Action No. 05-40026-FDS (2007), FBI wiretap, January 19, 1996, conversation between Kifah Jayyousi and Samir Al Monla and various other wiretaps, Exhibits 273 and 273 (flyers).
57. *USA v. Kifah Wael Jayyousi and Kassem Daher*, Case No. 04-3565RID, Criminal Complaint; *USA v. Adham Amin Hassoun et al.*, 04-60001-CR, April 7, 2005, Fourth Superseding Indictment.
58. *USA v. Adham Amin Hassoun et al.*, 04-60001-CR, April 7, 2005, Fourth Superseding Indictment.
59. *U.S. v. Muhamed Mubayyid, Emadeddin Muntasser, and Samir Al Monla*, Criminal Action No. 05-40026-FDS (2007), FBI wiretap, August 3, 1998, conversation between Kifah Jayyousi and Samir Al Monla.
60. *USA v. Kifah Wael Jayyousi and Kassem Daher*, Case No. 04-3565RID, Criminal Complaint; "Former Agent of Islamic Charity Awaiting Deportation Ruling," *Associated Press*, October 9, 2002.
61. *USA v. Adham Amin Hassoun et al.*, 04-60001-CR, April 7, 2005, Fourth Superseding Indictment.
62. Ibid.
63. FBI FD-302, Interrogation of Jose Padilla, May 8, 2002; Michael Grunwald and Amy Goldstein, "An Unusual Odyssey: U.S.-Born Latino Turns Islamic Terror

Suspect," *Washington Post*, June 11, 2002. Various media reports have attributed a bewildering number of different gang affiliations to Padilla.

64. FBI FD-302, Interrogation of Jose Padilla, May 8, 2002.
65. Manuel Roig-Franzia and Amy Goldstein, "A Bomb Suspect's Search for Identity: In Padilla's Metamorphosis into Al Muhajir, Fla. Provided a Turning Point," *Washington Post*, June 15, 2002.
66. Wanda J. Demarzo, Sara Olkon, and Daniel de Vise, "Bomb Suspect Changed His Life in South Florida; Al Qaeda Called Jose Padilla 'the Immigrant,'" *Miami Herald*, June 12, 2002; FBI FD-302, Interrogation of Jose Padilla, May 8, 2002; and *USA v. Adham Amin Hassoun et al.*, 04-60001-CR, April 7, 2005, Sentencing Memorandum, November 29, 2007.
67. FBI FD-302, Interrogation of Jose Padilla, May 8, 2002.
68. *USA v. Binyam Ahmed Muhammad*, military commission charge sheet.
69. David Johnston, "At a Secret Interrogation, Dispute Flared over Tactics," *New York Times*, September 10, 2006.
70. Remarks of Deputy Attorney General James Comey regarding Jose Padilla, June 1, 2004, retrieved September 2, 2010, http://nefafoundation.org/miscellaneous/FeaturedDocs/azizDOJ_Padilla Link.pdf.
71. Kat Long, "American Al Qaeda Leader Was at Home on Brooklyn's Atlantic Avenue," *New York Examiner,* August 9, 2010, retrieved August 9, 2010, http://www.examiner.com/historic-places-in-new-york/american-al-qaeda-leader-was-at-home-on-brooklyn-s-atlantic-avenue.
72. Josh Meyer, "A Mystery Man Who Keeps the FBI up at Night," *Los Angeles Times*, September 3, 2006; David Kocieniewski and Peg Tyre, "Feds: Plotters Taped," *Newsday*, July 2, 1993.
73. Susan Candiotti and Ross Levitt, "From Dishwasher to al Qaeda Leadership: Who Is Adnan Shukrijumah?" CNN.com, August 6, 2010, retrieved August 8, 2010, http://www.cnn.com/2010/CRIME/08/06/terror.qaeda.leader/?hpt=Mid.
74. Lisa J. Huriash, "Former Miramar Man Now Runs al-Qaida, FBI Says. Not True, His Mother Says," *South Florida Sun-Sentinel*, August 7, 2010; Richard Willing, "Pursuit of Al Qaeda Keeps Coming Back to Fla.," *USA Today*, June 15, 2004.
75. Candiotti and Levitt, "From Dishwasher to al Qaeda Leadership: Who Is Adnan Shukrijumah?"; Meyer, "A Mystery Man Who Keeps the FBI up at Night."

Chapter 6. War on America

1. *Triple-Cross: Bin Laden's Spy in America* (National Geographic Video, 2007).
2. *USA v Ali Abdelseoud Mohamed*, S(7) 98 Cr. 1023 (LBS), Sealed Complaint, Affidavit of Daniel Coleman, September 1998.
3. Confidential interview with retired U.S. Army officer, October 25, 2008.
4. Interviews with former CIA analyst Michael Scheuer, October 27, 2008, and August 18, 2009.
5. *USA v. bin Laden et al.*, S(7) 98 Cr. 1023, court transcript, February 6, 2001, and subsequent days, Testimony of Jamal Al Fadl.
6. *USA v Ali Abdelseoud Mohamed*, S(7) 98 Cr. 1023 (LBS), Sealed Complaint, Affidavit of Daniel Coleman, September 1998.

7. *USA v. Usama bin Laden*, S(7) 98 Cr. 1023,court transcript, June 26, 2001; *US v. Usama bin Laden*, court transcript, May 1, 2001.
8. Orlana Zill, "A Portrait of Wadih El Hage, Accused Terrorist," *PBS Frontline*, retrieved August 30, 2010; http://www.pbs.org/wgbh/pages/frontline/shows/binladen/upclose/elhage.html, *USA v. bin Laden*, S(7) 98 Cr. 1023, Indictment, November 5, 1998, Superseding Indictment, undated; *USA v. bin Laden*, S(7) 98 Cr. 1023, court transcript, April 16, 2001, Testimony of Mohammed Odeh; Douglas Farah, "Report Says Africans Harbored Al Qaeda: Terror Assets Hidden in Gem-Buying Spree," *Washington Post*, December 29, 2002; *USA v Ali Abdelseoud Mohamed*, S(7) 98 Cr. 1023 (LBS), Sealed Complaint, Affidavit of Daniel Coleman, September 1998.
9. *USA v. bin Laden*, S(7) 98 Cr. 1023, court transcript, May 1, 2001.
10. Judith Miller, "A Witness against Al Qaeda Says the U.S. Let Him Down," *New York Times*, June 3, 2002.
11. Chuck Murphy, "Pilot Led a Quiet Life in Orlando," *St. Petersburg Times*, October 28, 2001.
12. *9/11 Commission Report*, 224; Phil Hirschkorn, "Roommate: Moussaoui Saw Jihad as Way to Paradise," CNN.com, March 21, 2006, retrieved August 1, 2010, http://www.cnn.com/2006/LAW/03/21/moussaoui.trial/index.html.
13. Lance Williams, "Bin Laden's Bay Area Recruiter," *San Francisco Chronicle*, November 21, 2001.
14. Estanislao Oziewicz and Tu Thanh Ha, "Canada Freed Top Al Qaeda Operative: Mounties Released Him after Call to FBI," *Globe and Mail*, November 22, 2001; *USA v Ali Abdelseoud Mohamed*, S(7) 98 Cr. 1023 (LBS), Sealed Complaint, Affidavit of Daniel Coleman, September 1998; and *USA v Ali Mohamed*, S(7) 98 Cr. 1023 (LBS), court transcript, Plea Hearing, October 20, 2000, via http://cryptome.org/usa-v-mohamed.htm.
15. *USA v. bin Laden et al.*, S(7) 98 Cr. 1023, court transcript, February 6, 2001, and subsequent days, Testimony of Jamal Al Fadl.
16. *USA v Ali Mohamed*, S(7) 98 Cr. 1023 (LBS), Plea Hearing; Statement of Patrick J. Fitzgerald, United States Attorney, Northern District of Illinois, National Commission on Terrorist Attacks upon the United States (9/11 Commission), June 16, 2004; and *USA v. bin Laden*, S(7) 98 Cr. 1023, court transcript, February 21, 2001, Testimony of L'Houssaine Kherchtou.
17. Lawrence Wright, *The Looming Tower: Al Qaeda and the Road to 9/11* (New York: Knopf, 2006), 411n.
18. *USA v. bin Laden et al.*, S(7) 98 Cr. 1023, court transcript, February 6, 2001, and subsequent days, Testimony of Jamal Al Fadl.; *USA v. Enaam M. Arnaout*, No. 02 CR 892, Government's Evidentiary Proffer Supporting the Admissibility of Coconspirator Statements, January 6, 2003.
19. Wright, *The Looming Tower*, 222n; *USA v. bin Laden*, S(7) 98 Cr. 1023, court transcript, February 21, 2001, Testimony of L'Houssaine Kherchtou.
20. Wright, *The Looming Tower*, 183; Williams, "Bin Laden's Bay Area Recruiter." The exact date of Zawahiri's trip is disputed.
21. *USA v. bin Laden*, S(7) 98 Cr. 1023, court transcript, February 21, 2001, Testimony of L'Houssaine Kherchtou.

22. Susan Sachs, "An Investigation in Egypt Illustrates Al Qaeda's Web," *New York Times*, November 21, 2001; *USA v Ali Abdelseoud Mohamed*, S(7) 98 Cr. 1023 (LBS), Sealed Complaint, Affidavit of Daniel Coleman, September 1998; and Andrew C. McCarthy, *Willful Blindness: A Memoir of the Jihad* (New York: Encounter Books, 2008), 94–95.
23. McCarthy, *Willful Blindness*, 94–95.
24. *USA v Ali Abdelseoud Mohamed*, S(7) 98 Cr. 1023 (LBS), Sealed Complaint, Affidavit of Daniel Coleman, September 1998; McCarthy, *Willful Blindness*, 301.
25. McCarthy, *Willful Blindness*, 304; *Triple-Cross* (National Geographic Video, 2007).
26. *USA v Ali Abdelseoud Mohamed*, S(7) 98 Cr. 1023 (LBS), Sealed Complaint, Affidavit of Daniel Coleman, September 1998; *USA v. bin Laden*, S(7) 98 Cr. 1023, Indictment and Superseding Indictment.
27. *USA v. bin Laden et al.*, S(7) 98 Cr. 1023, court transcript, February 6, 2001, and subsequent days, Testimony of Jamal Al Fadl.
28. Ibid.
29. Author interviews with Tom Corrigan, June 24, 2008, through June 23, 2010, inclusive.
30. *USA v. bin Laden*, S(7) 98 Cr. 1023, court transcript, April 17, 2001.
31. *9/11 Commission Report*, 480.
32. "Bin Laden's Fatwa," *PBS News Hour*, retrieved August 4, 2010, http://www.pbs.org/newshour/terrorism/international/fatwa_1996.html.
33. Wright, *The Looming Tower*, 265; *USA v. bin Laden*, S(7) 98 Cr. 1023, court transcript, May 3, 2001; and Murphy, "Pilot Led a Quiet Life in Orlando."
34. *USA v. bin Laden*, S(7) 98 Cr. 1023, court transcript, May 1, 2001.
35. Ibid., court transcript, February 21, 2001; Kevin Peraino and Evan Thomas, "Odyssey into Jihad," *Newsweek*, January 14, 2002; Zill, "A Portrait of Wadih El Hage, Accused Terrorist."
36. *USA v. bin Laden*, S(7) 98 Cr. 1023, court transcripts, February 21, 2001, and May 1, 2001; Zill, "A Portrait of Wadih El Hage, Accused Terrorist."
37. *USA v. bin Laden*, S(7) 98 Cr. 1023, court transcripts, March 22, 2001, and May 1, 2001; *USA v. bin Laden*, S(7) 98 Cr. 1023, Indictment and Superseding Indictment.
38. *USA v Ali Abdelseoud Mohamed*, S(7) 98 Cr. 1023 (LBS), Sealed Complaint, Affidavit of Daniel Coleman, September 1998.
39. Benjamin Weiser, "Prosecutors Portray the Strands of a Bin Laden Web of Terror," *New York Times*, January 23, 2000; *USA v. bin Laden*, S(7) 98 Cr. 1023, Exhibit 358.
40. *USA v. bin Laden*, S(7) 98 Cr. 1023, court transcript, May 3, 2001. At one point it was also speculated that O'Sam was Mohammed Atef, the military chief of al Qaeda at that time. Atef was killed in November 2001 during the U.S. invasion of Afghanistan.
41. "Jihad against Jews and Crusaders," World Islamic Front Statement, February 23, 1998, retrieved August 4, 2010, http://www.fas.org/irp/world/para/docs/980223-fatwa.htm.
42. Interview, Osama bin Laden, *PBS Frontline*, May 1998, http://www.pbs.org/wgbh/pages/frontline/shows/binladen/who/interview.html.

43. FBI Executive Summary of Findings, International Bulletin, November 18, 1998, retrieved August 4, 2010, http://www.pbs.org/wgbh/pages/frontline/shows/binladen/bombings/summary.html.
44. *USA v Ali Abdelseoud Mohamed*, S(7) 98 Cr. 1023 (LBS), Sealed Complaint, Affidavit of Daniel Coleman, September 1998.
45. *USA v. bin Laden*, S(7) 98 Cr. 1023, court transcript, March 20, 2001.
46. Ibid.
47. *USA v. bin Laden*, S(7) 98 Cr. 1023, court transcript, March 22, 2001; *USA v. bin Laden*, Indictment and Superseding Indictment.
48. *USA v. bin Laden*, S(7) 98 Cr. 1023, court transcript, March 22, 2001; *USA v. bin Laden*, Indictment and Superseding Indictment; *Triple-Cross* (National Geographic Video, 2007); and statement of Patrick J. Fitzgerald, United States Attorney, Northern District of Illinois, National Commission on Terrorist Attacks upon the United States (9/11 Commission), June 16, 2004.
49. Murphy, "Pilot Led a Quiet Life in Orlando."
50. Tony Rizzo, "KC Man Linked to Early al-Qaida," *Kansas City Star*, September 9, 2006.

Chapter 7. The Rise of Anwar Awlaki

1. "Las Cruces History," *Las Cruces Convention & Visitors Bureau*, retrieved August 25, 2010, http://www.lascrucescvb.org/html/las_cruces__new_mexico_history.html.
2. Tom Sharpe, "Radical Iman Traces Roots to N.M.," *Santa Fe New Mexican*, November 15, 2009.
3. Bobby Ghosh, "How Dangerous Is the Cleric Anwar Al Awlaki?" *Time*, January 13, 2010.
4. Scott Shane and Souad Mekhennet, "From Condemning Terror to Preaching Jihad," *New York Times*, May 9, 2010.
5. Catherine Herridge, "Radical Muslim Cleric Lied to Qualify for U.S.-Funded College Scholarship," *Fox News*, April 12, 2010.
6. Aamer Madhani, "Cleric Al Awlaki Dubbed 'bin Laden of the Internet,'" *USA Today*, August 25, 2010; *CNN American Morning*, August 2, 2010, transcript, retrieved August 6, 2010, http://transcripts.cnn.com/TRANSCRIPTS/1008/02/ltm.03.html.
7. Ghosh, "How Dangerous Is the Cleric Anwar Al Awlaki?"; "The Islamic Education of Anwar Awlaki," retrieved March 14, 2010, http://themujahidblog.com/2009/12/30/the-islamic-education-of-shaykh-anwar-al-awlaki/; Hassan Al Ahdal, "Media Terrorism," *Muslim World League Journal* (January 1999); and Hassan Al Ahdal, "Kosovo Crisis," *Muslim World League Journal* (May 1999).
8. Bruce Finley, "Muslim Cleric Targeted by U.S. Made Little Impression during Colorado Years," *Denver Post*, April 11, 2010.
9. Ibid.
10. 9/11 Commission, Memorandum for the Record, Telephone Interview of Lincoln Higgie, November 19, 2003.
11. 9/11 Commission, Memorandum for the Record, Interview of Special Agent [name redacted], November 18, 2003.

12. Audio recording, "CIA Islam—Sheikh Faisal's Takfeer of Anwar Awlaki," Abdullah Faisal, undated.
13. Audio recording, "CIA Islam."
14. Audio: Anwar Awlaki, "Al Akhirah (The Afterlife)," *Al Basheer Audio*.
15. Ibid.
16. Audio: Anwar Awlaki, "The Life of Muhammad (Mecca Period)."
17. Susan Schmidt, "Imam from Va. Mosque Now Thought to Have Aided Al Qaeda," *Washington Post*, February 27, 2008.
18. "Yemen Cleric Zindani Warns against 'Foreign Occupation,'" *BBC News*, January 11, 2010, retrieved August 25, 2010, http://news.bbc.co.uk/2/hi/middle_east/8453025.stm?CFID=17638234&CFTOKEN=54261596.
19. Jordanian Court Record, Confession of Abdullah Kamil Abdullah Al Sharida, February 9, 1994; Memorandum, Muslim World League, International Islamic Relief Organization, "Meeting between Abu Abdallah, Dr. Abdallah Naseef and Sheikh Abdel Majeed Zindani," from the Tareekh Osama files.
20. Mustafa Hamid, "Battle of Torghar," al Qaeda historical document, 1990 (from the Harmony collection); Tom Downey, "Khalid Sheikh Mohammed's 'Old Friend' from the Bosnian War Talks of 16-Year Journey of 'Jihads,'" *Guardian Unlimited*, April 23, 2006; Schmidt, "Imam from Va. Mosque Now Thought to Have Aided Al Qaeda"; *The Martyrs of Bosnia*, Bosnian mujahideen propaganda video, obtained by the author; and John Miller, Michael Stone, and Chris Mitchell, *The Cell: Inside the 9/11 Plot, and Why the FBI and CIA Failed to Stop It* (New York: Hyperion, 2003), 82.
21. *USA v. Numan Muflahi*, 1:03-cr-00412-NG, Defense Memorandum, July 31, 2005.
22. "U.S. Department of Labor Awards More Than $58 Million to Eliminate Exploitive Child Labor around the World," *U.S. Newswire*, October 1, 2008; e-mail interview with Jamal Al Haddi, Program Manager, Charitable Society for Social Welfare, June 2, 2010, and June 23, 2010; documents available at J. M. Berger, "Exclusive: U.S. Gave Millions to Charity Linked to Al Qaeda, Anwar Awlaki," Intelwire.com, April 14, 2010, updated June 23, 2010, retrieved August 27, 2010, http://news.intelwire.com/2010/04/us-gave-millions-to-charity-linked-to.html.
23. Interview with Ray Royer, October 16, 2008; Bruce Finley, "War Divides Colorado Arabs," *Denver Post*, January 27, 1991; Schmidt, "Imam from Va. Mosque Now Thought to Have Aided Al Qaeda"; and *USA v. Usama bin Laden et al.*, S(7) 98 Cr. 1023, court transcript, May 1, 2001.
24. FBI Letterhead Memorandum, "Anwar Nasser Aulaqi," September 26, 2001; Chitra Ragavan, "The Imam's Very Curious Story," *U.S. News and World Report*, June 21, 2004.
25. FBI Letterhead Memorandum, "Anwar Nasser Aulaqi" September 26, 2001; Joe Cantlupe and Dana Wilkie, "Former San Diego Islamic Spiritual Leader Defends Mosque," *Copley News Service*, September 28, 2001.
26. See 9/11 Commission Memorandum for the Record, Interview of Omar Al Bayoumi, October 16–17, 2003.
27. See 9/11 Bayoumi Interview, FBI FD-302, Interrogation of Omar Al Bayoumi, August 18, 2003.

28. See 9/11 Commission Memorandum for the Record, Interview of FBI SA Daniel Gonzales, November 18, 2003.
29. See 9/11 Bayoumi Interview, FBI FD-302, Interrogation of Omar Al Bayoumi, October 16–17, 2003.
30. FBI FD-302, Interrogation of Omer Bakarbashat.
31. FBI FD-302, Investigation of Hijackers' Activities in San Diego Area, January 15, 2002; 9/11 Interview, FBI SA [redacted].
32. *The 9-11 Commission Report: Final Report of the National Commission on Terrorist Attacks upon the United States, Official Government Edition* (Washington, DC: U.S. Government Printing Office, 2004), 218.
33. FBI Summary of Information, Mohdar Abdullah, April 11, 2002.
34. FBI FD-302, Investigation of Hijackers' Activities in San Diego Area, January 15, 2002; *9/11 Commission Report*, 220.
35. Nexis address search for Omer Bakarbashat.
36. *9/11 Commission Report*, 220; Ray Rivera and Matthew Sweeney, "Acquaintance of 2 Hijackers Is Acquitted," *New York Times*, November 18, 2006.
37. Ray Rivera, "Jurors Begin Weighing Perjury Case against Man Who Knew Two Sept. 11 Hijackers," *New York Times*, November 17, 2006; Ian MacLeod, "Algonquin Student Eyed after 9/11; U.S. Prosecutors Discussed Charging Man in Same Case as '20th Hijacker,' Documents Reveal," *Ottawa Citizen*, September 25, 2009; *9/11 Commission Report*, 223.
38. *9/11 Commission Report*, 221.
39. 9/11 Commission Memorandum for the Record, Interview of FBI Special Agent [redacted], November 17, 2003.
40. FBI Letterhead Memorandum, "Anwar Nasser Aulaqi." September 26, 2001.
41. Cantlupe and Wilkie, "Former San Diego Islamic Spiritual Leader Defends Mosque"; 9/11 Commission Memorandum for the Record, Telephone Interview of Lincoln Higgie, November 19, 2003; and FBI Summary of PENTBOM Investigation, Feb. 29, 2004.
42. Audio: Anwar Awlaki, "Abu Bakr Al Siddiq (radiyu al lahu anhu), His Life and Times," *Al Bashir Audio*.
43. Amy Gardner and Anita Kumar, "Va. Muslim Activist Denies Urging Violence; Remarks on YouTube Lead to Resignation," *Washington Post*, September 29, 2007; "Dar Al-Hijrah Hosts Fundraiser For 'Virginia Jihad' Cell Member," *Global Muslim Brotherhood Daily Report*, Feb. 25, 2010, http://globalmbreport.com/?p=2339; Glenn Frankel, "A Fragile Peace; For Northern Virginia's Palestinians, Life in America Is a String of Perils," *Washington Post*, March 1, 1997; and FBI Communication, "PENTBOM; MAJOR CASE 182," August 6, 2002.
44. *PBS NewsHour*, November 12, 2009.
45. Audio: Anwar Awlaki: "The Quran, Book of Tolerance," undated. Awlaki gave a slight variation on this speech at an Islamic Society of North America event just days before September 11, 2001.
46. Audio: Anwar Awlaki, "Mashari Al Ashwaq [The Book of Jihad]," undated.
47. "Milestones: Nidal Malik Hasan: An Interactive Timeline of the Life and Career of Maj. Nidal Malik Hasan, Who Is Charged in the Fort Hood Shootings," *New York Times*, November 7, 2009, retrieved August 25, 2010, http://www.nytimes

.com/interactive/2009/11/07/us/20091107-HASAN-TIMELINE.html; Philip Sherwell and Alex Spillius, "Fort Hood Shooting: Texas Army Killer Linked to September 11 Terrorists," *Daily Telegraph*, November 7, 2009.

48. FBI Communication, "PENTTBOM; Major Case 182," June 30, 2002; *9/11 Commission Report*, 229.
49. *9/11 Commission Report*, 230; 9/11 Commission Memorandum for the Record, Interview of FBI Special Agent Bob Bukowski, November 6, 2003.
50. *9/11 Commission Report*, 221.
51. Ibid., 218.
52. Terry McDermott, *Perfect Soldiers: The 9/11 Hijackers: Who They Were, Why They Did It,* (New York: Harper Collins, 2005), 189–190.
53. Scholars and lecturers who linked from the Ar-Ribat website as of April 18, 2010, included hard-core Salafists such as Ahmed Deedat and Bilal Philips (Chapter 4), and Saudi-sponsored North American scholars such as Jamal Badawi and Siraj Wahhaj. See http://icfoundation.com/new_index.htm, retrieved April 18, 2010; http://www.icfoundation.com/audio_english_islamway.htm, retrieved September 6, 2010; and http://www.icfoundation.com/Brochures/Islamic%20Beliefs%20and%20Practices/authenticity_of_the_quran.htm, retrieved September 6, 2010.
54. *Report of the Joint Inquiry into the Terrorist Attacks of September 11, 2001—By the House Permanent Select Committee on Intelligence and the Senate Select Committee on Intelligence*, December 2002, 59.
55. 9/11 Commission Interview, FBI SA [name redacted], November 18, 2003.
56. Schmidt, "Imam from Va. Mosque Now Thought to Have Aided Al Qaeda."
57. *American Morning*, CNN, August 3, 2010, retrieved August 6, 2010, http://transcripts.cnn.com/TRANS CRIPTS/1008/02/ltm.03.html. Higgie made the same basic statement to the 9/11 Commission. See 9/11 Commission Memorandum for the Record, Telephone Interview of Lincoln Higgie, November 19, 2003. It should be noted that Higgie also told investigators that the "US government and 'the Mossad' knew or should have known about the attacks before they occurred."

Chapter 8. Scenes from September 11

1. Judith Miller and Don Van Natta Jr., "In Years of Plots and Clues, Scope of Qaeda Eluded U.S.," *New York Times*, June 9, 2002.
2. *USA v. Ramzi Yousef and Eyad Ismoil*, S12 93 CR180 (KTD), Government Exhibit 2799-1.
3. Video viewed by the author.
4. CIA and FBI Joint Report, *Arizona Long-Term Nexus For Islamic Extremists*, SECRET, May 15, 2002, obtained by the author through the FOIA. The document was almost entirely redacted except for the title, the date, and the section headers.
5. FBI Letterhead Memorandum, "Zakaria Mustapha Soubra," July 7, 2001.
6. FBI Report, *Working Draft Chronology of Events for Hijackers and Associates*, November 14, 2003, obtained through the Freedom of Information Act.
7. *9/11 Commission Report*, multiple references.
8. "Convicted Terrorists Held on Death Row at Terre Haute Prison," *Associated Press*, March 12, 2002.

9. Author interviews with Alia Rashid, June 26, 2008, and October 23, 2008.
10. Audio: *Democracy Now*, July 31, 2009, retrieved August 11, 2010, http://www.democracynow.org/2009/7/31/exclusive_john_walker_lindhs_parents_discuss; Josh Tyrangiel, "The Taliban Next Door," *Time*, December 9, 2001.
11. Audio: *Democracy Now*, July 31, 2009; Tom Junod, "Innocent," *Esquire*, July 1, 2006; Gregory D. Johnsen, "Profile of Sheikh Abd al-Majid al-Zindani," *Terrorism Monitor*, April 6, 2006.
12. Audio: *Democracy Now*, July 31, 2009.
13. *USA v. John Philip Walker Lindh*, CR 02-37a, Indictment, February 5, 2002.
14. Evelyn Nieves, "A U.S. Convert's Path from Suburbia to a Gory Jail for Taliban," *New York Times*, December 4, 2001.
15. Susan Candiotti and Ross Levitt, "From Dishwasher to al Qaeda Leadership: Who Is Adnan Shukrijumah?" CNN.com, August 6, 2010, retrieved August 7, 2010, http://www.cnn.com/2010/CRIME/08/06/terror.qaeda.leader/indexhtml?hpt=C2.
16. Interview with Ray Royer, October 16, 2008.
17. *USA v. Randall Royer et al.*, CR 03-296-A, Grand Jury indictment, June 2003 term, undated.
18. *USA v. Muhammed Aatique*, CR 03-296-A, Plea Agreement, September 22, 2003.
19. *Triple-Cross: Bin Laden's Spy in America* (National Geographic Video, 2007); *USA v Omar Abdel Rahman, et al.*, S5 93 Cr. 181 (MBM), Testimony of Emad Salem, March 21, 1995.

Chapter 9. The Descent of Anwar Awlaki

1. William Branigin, "When Terror Hits Close to Home," *Washington Post*, September 20, 2001.
2. Debbi Wilgoren and Ann O'Hanlon, "Worship and Worry: Fear for Other Muslims Mixes with Support for U.S.," *Washington Post*, September 22, 2001.
3. Susan Morse, "First Source of Comfort; When Events Overwhelm, Clergy, Not Doctors, Are on the Front Lines, *Washington Post*, September 18, 2001.
4. Wilgoren and O'Hanlon, "Worship and Worry; Fear for Other Muslims Mixes with Support for U.S."
5. FBI Letterhead Memorandum, "Anwar Nasser Aulaqi," September 26, 2001.
6. *9/11 Commission Report*, various dates. Binalshibh interacted primarily with the Hamburg cell members. He was aware of the other hijackers but dealt mainly with Atta.
7. FBI Letterhead Memorandum, "Anwar Nasser Aulaqi," September 26, 2001.
8. Matthew Barakat, "FBI Tries to Track Northern Virginia Connection to Five Hijackers," *Associated Press*, September 21, 2001.
9. Chitra Ragavan, "The Imam's Very Curious Story," *US News and World Report*, June 21, 2004; "Awlaki's Sordid Personal Life," *Fox News* video, May 22, 2010, retrieved August 25, 2010, http://video.foxnews.com/v/4208057/al-awlakis-sordid-personal-life/.
10. Ray Suarez, "Ray Suarez: My Post-9/11 Interview with Anwar Al Awlaki," *PBS Newshour*, http://www.pbs.org/newshour/updates/religion/july-dec09/alawlaki_11-11.html, with video from an Awlaki sermon given on October 30, 2001.
11. Scott Shane, "Terror Cases Lead Back to Cleric; U.S.-Born Muslim's Wit Said

to Have Spurred on Several Extremist Plots," *International Herald Tribune*, November 20, 2009.

12. "Talk of the Nation," *National Public Radio (NPR)*, September 9, 2004.
13. Audio: Anwar Awlaki, "Brutality against Muslims," *khutba*, March 15, 2002.
14. Audio: Anwar Awlaki, "It's a War against Islam," *khutba*, March 22, 2002.
15. Audio: Anwar Awlaki, "Lessons from the Companions Living as a Minority," JIMAS Conference 2002.
16. Joseph Rhee and Mark Schone, "How Anwar Awlaki Got Away; U.S. Attorney's Decision to Cancel Arrest Warrant 'Shocked' Terrorism Investigators," *ABC News*, November 30, 2009, retrieved August 26, 2010, http://abcnews.go.com/print?id=9200720.
17. Rhee and Schone, "How Anwar Awlaki Got Away."
18. Joseph Rhee, "U.S. Attorney Defends Decision to Scrap Awlaki Arrest Warrant," *ABC News*, December 7, 2009.
19. Audio: Anwar Awlaki, "Stop Police Terror," *khutba*, circa 2002.
20. Audio: Anwar Awlaki, "The Enemies of Allah," undated.
21. Duncan Gardham, "Al-Qaeda Leader's Tour of Britain Revealed," *The Telegraph*, November 5, 2010; Sudarsan Raghavan, "Cleric in Fort Hood Probe Grew More Radical in Yemeni Jail," *Washington Post*, December 9, 2009.
22. A Nexis search of national newspaper stories from January 1, 2004, to January 1, 2008, revealed only a handful of stories that specifically focused on Awlaki's role. One of the most ambitious was by a college newspaper. See Katie Rooney, "George Washington U. Ex-Student Tied to 9/11 Hijackers in Report," *The GW Hatchet*, September 7, 2005.
23. Moazzam Begg, "Moazzam Begg Interviews Imam Anwar Al Awlaki," Cageprisoners.com, December 31, 2007, http://old.cageprisoners.com/articles.php?id=22926, retrieved August 6, 2010; Michelle Shephard, "The Powerful Online Voice of Jihad," *Toronto Star*, October 18, 2009.
24. "U.S. Imam Wanted in Yemen over al-Qaida Ties," MSNBC.com, November 10, 2009, retrieved August 6, 2010, http://www.msnbc.msn.com/id/33841279/ns/us_news-tragedy_at_fort_hood/.
25. Begg, "Moazzam Begg Interviews Imam Anwar Al Awlaki."
26. Mirror of Awlaki blog entries, retrieved August 6, 2010, http://www.pureislam.co.za/index.php?option=com_content&task=view&id=644&Itemid=33; and http://www.pureislamco.za/index.php?option=com_content&task=view&id=697&Itemid=33, retrieved August 6, 2010.
27. Mirror of Awlaki blog entry, http://www.pureislam.co.za/index.php?option=com_content&task=view&id=553&Itemid=33, retrieved August 6, 2010, among others.
28. Mirror of Awlaki blog entry, retrieved August 6, 2010, http://www.pureislam.co.za/index.php?option=com_content&task=view&id=394&Itemid=33.
29. Ibid.
30. "Anwar Al Awlaki: 'Salutations to Al Shabab of Somalia,' December 21, 2008," NEFA Foundation, retrieved August 6, 2010, http://www.nefafoundation.org/miscellaneous/FeaturedDocs/awlakishebab1208.pdf.
31. James C. McKinley Jr., "Major Held in Fort Hood Rampage Is Charged with 13 Counts of Murder," *New York Times*, November 12, 2009.

32. James C. McKinley Jr. and James Dao, "Fort Hood Gunman Gave Signals before His Rampage," *New York Times*, November 9, 2009.
33. Thomas Jocelyn, "Getting Serious about Anwar Awlaki," *CBS News*, May 24, 2010, retrieved June 29, 2010, http://www.cbsnews.com/stories/2010/05/24/opinion/main6514380.shtml.
34. McKinley and Dao, "Fort Hood Gunman Gave Signals before His Rampage."
35. Eli Saslow, Philip Rucker, William Wan, and Mary Pat Flaherty, "In Aftermath of Fort Hood, Community Haunted by Clues That Went Unheeded," *Washington Post*, December 31, 2009.
36. "Maj. Nidal M. Hasan's Official Military Record," Newsweek.com, retrieved June 29, 2010, http://www.newsweek.com/blogs/declassified/2009/11/06/maj-nidal-m-hasan-s-officialmilitary-record.html; Saslow, Rucker, Wan, and Flaherty, "In Aftermath of Fort Hood, Community Haunted by Clues That Went Unheeded."
37. Full PowerPoint presentation obtained by the author. Excerpts can be viewed at http://www.washingtonpost.com/wp-dyn/content/gallery/2009/11/10/GA2009111000920.html, retrieved June 29, 2010.
38. Saslow, Rucker, Wan, and Flaherty, "In Aftermath of Fort Hood, Community Haunted by Clues That Went Unheeded"; "Maj. Nidal M. Hasan's Official Military Record," Newsweek.com.
39. Tom Sharpe, "Radical Imam Traces Roots to New Mexico," *New Mexican*, November 14, 2009.
40. Madeleine Gruen, "Backgrounder: Sgt. Hasan Akbar," NEFA Foundation, January 2010, retrieved June 29, 2010, http://www.nefafoundation.org/miscellaneous/nefa_akbarbackgrounder.pdf.
41. Philip Rucker, Carrie Johnson, and Ellen Nakashima, "Hasan E-mails to Cleric Didn't Result in Inquiry," *Washington Post*, November 10, 2009; Ochi J. Dreazen, Peter Spiegel, and Evan Perez, "Hasan to Face Death Penalty," *Wall Street Journal*, November 13, 2009.
42. Brian Ross and Rhonda Schwartz, "Major Hasan's E-Mail: 'I Can't Wait to Join You' in Afterlife," *ABC News*, November 19, 2009, retrieved July 1, 2010, http://abcnews.go.com/Blotter/major-hasans-mail-wait-join-afterlife/story?id=9130339&page=1; Saslow, Rucker, Wan, and Flaherty, "In Aftermath of Fort Hood, Community Haunted by Clues That Went Unheeded."
43. Philip Rucker, "Fort Hood Probe Brings Mosque Unwanted Attention," *Washington Post*, November 24, 2009.
44. Saslow, Rucker, Wan, and Flaherty, "In Aftermath of Fort Hood, Community Haunted by Clues That Went Unheeded."
45. Anwar Awlaki blog, retrieved November 10, 2009, http://www.anwar-alawlaki com/?p=228.
46. Ibid.
47. "Al Jazeera Interview: Anwar Al Awlaki Regarding Malik Nidal Hasan, December 23, 2009," NEFA Foundation, retrieved August 6, 2010, http://www.nefafoundation.org/miscellaneous/NEFAal-Awlaki1209-2.pdf.
48. See http://www.cbsnews.com/htdocs/pdf/Abdulmutallab_Indictment.pdf, retrieved August 6, 2010; James Hider, "Double Life of 'Gifted and Polite' Terror Suspect Umar Farouk Abdulmutallab," *Times of London*, January 1, 2010.

49. For instance, the *Glen Beck Show*, Fox News Network, December 30, 2009; *Campbell Brown*, CNN, December 30, 2009; and numerous other CNN broadcasts in January 2010; "Radical Yemeni Cleric the New bin Laden?" *Washington Times*, April 13, 2010; and others.
50. David S. Cloud, "U.S. Citizen Anwar Awlaki Added to CIA Target List," *Los Angeles Times*, April 6, 2010.
51. "Imam Anwar Al Awlaki, 'A Call to Jihad,' Released: March 17, 2010," NEFA Foundation, retrieved August 6, 2010, http://www.nefafoundation.org/miscellaneous/Al-Awlaki%20Call%20Jihad.pdf.
52. Video: *Exclusive Interview with the Islamic Preacher Anwar Awlaki*, Al Malahim (Al Qaeda in the Arabian Peninsula), obtained May 22, 2010.
53. "Anwar al-Awlaki: 'Do Not Consult Anyone in Killing the Americans,'" Flashpoint Partners, retrieved December 3, 2010, http://www.flashpoint-intel.com/images/documents/pdf/1010/flashpoint_awlaki1110.pdf.
54. Greg Miller, "Muslim Cleric Aulaqi is 1st U.S. Citizen on List of Those CIA is Allowed to Kill," *Washington Post*, April 7, 2010.
55. Christopher Anzalone, "English: Leader of Al Al-Qa'ida in the Arabian Peninsula, Abu Basir Nasir al-Wuhayshi, Vows to Protect Radical American Muslim Preacher Anwar al-'Awlaqi," *Views From The Occident*, June 15, 2010, retrieved November 30, 2010, http://occident.blogspot.com/2010/06/english-leader-of-al-qaida-in-arabian.html.
56. Thomas Hegghammer, "The Case for Chasing al-Awlaki," *Foreign Policy*, November 24, 2010, retrieved November 24, 2010. http://mideast.foreignpolicy.com/posts/2010/11/24/the_case_for_chasing_al_awlaki.
57. Bill Gertz, "Inside the Ring: Al Qaeda-Trained Americans," *Washington Times*, August 25, 2010.

Chapter 10. A Diverse Threat

1. *Department of Justice Inspector General Issues Report on Treatment of Aliens Held on Immigration Charges in Connection with the Investigation of the September 11 Terrorist Attacks*, http://www.justice.gov/oig/special/0306/press.pdf, retrieved August 10, 2010; *Supplemental Report on September 11 Detainees' Allegations of Abuse at the Metropolitan Detention Center in Brooklyn, New York*, retrieved August 10, 2010, http://www.justice.gov/oig/special/0312/final.pdf; retrieved August 10, 2010, http://www.constitutionproject.org/manage/file/57.pdf.
2. "Post-9/11 Detention Policies Hit by Court," *Washington Times*, September 5, 2009.
3. In virtually every interview I conducted with a law enforcement or intelligence official, I asked this question. No one I spoke with could answer it, and all of them said they were unaware of any such record.
4. "Transcript of Attorney General John Ashcroft Regarding Guilty Plea by Enaam Arnaout," February 10, 2003, retrieved August 10, 2010, http://www.justice.gov/archive/ag/speeches/2003/021003agenaamaranouttranscripthtm.htm.
5. Justice Department press release, "Former Officers of a Muslim Charity, Care International, Inc., Convicted," January 11, 2008, retrieved August 10, 2010, http://www.justice.gov/opa/pr/2008/January/08_nsd_021.html; interview with Aloke Chakravarty, Assistant US Attorney in Boston, June 2008.

6. "Federal Jury in Dallas Convicts Holy Land Foundation and Its Leaders for Providing Material Support to Hamas Terrorist Organization," retrieved August 11, 2010, http://www.justice.gov/opa/pr/2008/November/08-nsd-1046.html.
7. *PBS Frontline*, "The Closer: An Al Qaeda Recruiter in the United States," retrieved August 11, 2010, http://www.pbs.org/wgbh/pages/frontline/shows/sleeper/inside/juma.html; and *PBS Frontline*, "Kamal Derwish, the Life and Death of An American Terrorist," http://www.pbs.org/wgbh/pages/frontline/shows/sleeper/inside/derwish.html, retrieved August 11, 2010; and Dina Temple-Raston, *The Jihad Next Door: The Lackawanna Six and Rough Justice in an Age of Terror* (New York: PublicAffairs, 2007).
8. Justice Department press release, "Abdurrahman Alamoudi Sentenced to Jail in Terrorism Financing Case," October 15, 2009, retrieved August 10, 2010, http://www.justice.gov/opa/pr/2004/October/04_crm_698.htm.
9. Ben Jacklet And Janine Robben, "Hawash Regrets 'Worst Decision': Ex-Intel Worker Says He's Sorry as Judge Issues Last Portland 7 Sentences," *Portland Tribune*, February 10, 2004; "October Martinique Lewis Pleads Guilty to Money Laundering Charges in 'Portland Cell' Case," retrieved August 10, 2010, http://www.justice.gov/opa/pr/2003/September/03_crm_532.htm.
10. David Bowermaster, "Man Who Conspired to Aid Taliban Gets Added Prison Term," *Seattle Times*, February 2, 2007; "Seattle Militant to Testify in NY Terror Trial," *Associated Press*, April 27, 2009.
11. Essay: "Becoming Muslim." Yahiye Adam Gadahn, circa 1995.
12. Interview with Roxanne Euben, professor of political science, Wellesley College, June 2, 2010; interview with Alyas Karmani, director of the STREET program (Strategy to Reach, Empower and Educate Teenagers), London, August 10, 2010; and Aayan Hirsi Ali, "Fareed Zakaria GPS," CNN, August 15, 2010.
13. Amy Argetsinger, "Muslim Teen Made Conversion to Fury," *Washington Post*, December 2, 2004.
14. Jeffrey Smith, "A Bosnian Village's Terrorist Ties," *Washington Post*, March 11, 2000; Esad Hecimovic, "Mysteries Surround 1997 B-H Murder Victim Misidentified as Terrorist Hisham Diab," *Sarajevo Dani*, January 14, 2010; George Michael, "Adam Gadahn and Al Qaeda's Internet Strategy," *Middle East Policy* (Fall 2009).
15. Raffi Khatchadourian, "Azzam the American: The Making of an Al Qaeda Homegrown," *New Yorker*, January 22, 2007.
16. Khatchadourian, "Azzam the American"; Michael, "Adam Gadahn and Al Qaeda's Internet Strategy."
17. Khatchadourian, "Azzam the American."
18. *Azzam the American*, al Qaeda propaganda video
19. *Voice of the Caliphate*, al Qaeda propaganda video; Daniel Williams, "*Voice of Caliphate* Web Broadcast Speaks of Joy over US Hurricane," *Washington Post*, September 25, 2005.
20. *The State of the Ummah*, al Qaeda propaganda video.
21. *The 19 Martyrs*, al Qaeda propaganda video.
22. Various al Qaeda propaganda videos.

23. *The Mujahideen Don't Target Muslims*, al Qaeda propaganda video; "Al Qaeda 'Not behind Pakistan Bloodshed': US Militant," AFP, December 12, 2009.
24. Department of Defense, *Summary of Jose Padilla's Activities with Al Qaeda*, May 28, 2004.
25. *USA v. Binyam Ahmed Muhammad*, Military Commission Charge Sheet, undated.
26. Abby Goodnough and Scott Shane, "Padilla Is Guilty on All Charges in Terror Trial," *New York Times*, August 16, 2007.
27. Richard Willing, "Pursuit of Al Qaeda Keeps Coming Back to Fla.," *USA Today*, June 15, 2004; Susan Candiotti and Ross Levitt, "From Dishwasher to al Qaeda Leadership: Who Is Adnan Shukrijumah?" CNN.com, August 6, 2010, retrieved August 8, 2010, http://www.cnn.com/2010/CRIME/08/06/terror.qaeda.leader/?hpt=Mid.
28. Willing, "Pursuit of Al Qaeda Keeps Coming Back to Fla."
29. Chitra Ragavan, "A Hunt for `the Pilot': The FBI Says He's an `Imminent Threat.' But Where Is He?" *US News and World Report*, March 30, 2003.
30. Michael Wilson, "From Smiling Coffee Vendor to Terror Suspect," *New York Times*, September 26, 2009.
31. David Johnston and Al Baker, "Denver Man Admits to a Possible Al Qaeda Connection, Officials Say," *New York Times*, September 19, 2009.
32. Wilson, "From Smiling Coffee Vendor to Terror Suspect."
33. Candiotti and Levitt, "From Dishwasher to al Qaeda leadership: Who Is Adnan Shukrijumah?"
34. Ibid.
35. James Barron and Michael S. Schmidt, "From Suburban Father to a Terrorism Suspect," *New York Times*, May 4, 2010.
36. Andrea Elliott, "Militant's Path from Pakistan to Times Square," *New York Times*, June 22, 2010.
37. See http://documents.nytimes.com/e-mail-from-faisal-shahzad?ref=nyregion, retrieved June 28, 2010.
38. Elliott, "Militant's Path from Pakistan to Times Square."
39. See http://documents.nytimes.com/e-mail-from-faisal-shahzad?ref=nyregion, retrieved June 28, 2010.
40. Syed Shoaib Hasan, "Profile: Islamabad's Red Mosque," *BBC News*, July 27, 2007, retrieved June 28, 2010, http://news.bbc.co.uk/2/hi/south_asia/6503477.stm.
41. "Pakistani Soldiers Storm Mosque," *BBC News*, July 10, 2007, retrieved June 28, 2010, http://news.bbc.co.uk/2/hi/south_asia/6286500.stm.
42. Elliott, "Militant's Path from Pakistan to Times Square."
43. Mark Hosenball, "Mysteries Persist despite Shahzad's Times Square Guilty Plea," Newsweek.com, June 22, 2010, retrieved June 28, 2010, http://www.newsweek.com/blogs/declassified/2010/06/22/mysteries-persist-despite-times-square-guilty-plea.html.
44. *USA v. Faisal Shahzad*, 1:10-mj-00928-UA, Criminal Complaint, May 4, 2010.
45. See http://www.longwarjournal.org/archives/2010/05/pakistani_taliban_cl.php, retrieved June 28, 2010.
46. See http://www.washingtonpost.com/wp-srv/world/kashmir/front.html, retrieved August 15, 2010.

47. Letter from Randall Royer to Judge Leonie Brinkema, March 31, 2004.
48. *USA v. Randall Royer et al.*, CR 03-296-A, Grand Jury Indictment, June 2003 term, undated.
49. Karen Branch-Brioso, "Terrorism Suspect Says He's a Victim of Coincidence, Muslim Stereotypes," *Port St. Lucie/Fort Pierce* (*Florida Tribune*), July 1, 2003.
50. Letter from Randall Royer to Judge Leonie Brinkema, March 31, 2004.
51. Federal Register: March 19, 2002 (Volume 67, Number 53), Notices, Page 12633–12635, retrieved August 16, 2010, http://www.fas.org/irp/news/2002/03/fr031902s.html.
52. *Patterns of Global Terrorism 2000*, Office of the Coordinator for Counterterrorism, April 30, 2001, retrieved August 16, 2010, http://www.state.gov/s/ct/rls/crt/2000/2450.htm; *USA v. Randall Royer et al.*, CR 03-296-A, Grand Jury Indictment, June 2003 term, undated.
53. Letter from Randall Royer to Judge Leonie Brinkema, March 31, 2004.
54. *USA v. Randall Royer et al.*, CR 03-296-A, Grand Jury Indictment, June 2003 term, undated.
55. Laura Sullivan, "11 Terror Suspects Indicted; U.S. Alleges Men Were Planning Possible Attacks Abroad," *Chicago Tribune*, June 28, 2003.
56. U.S. Department of Justice press release, "Defendants Convicted in Northern Virginia 'Jihad' Trial," retrieved August 16, 2010, http://www.justice.gov/opa/pr/2004/March/04_crm_139.htm; "Two Defendants in Virginia Jihad Case Plead Guilty to Weapons Charges, Will Cooperate with Ongoing Investigation," retrieved August 16, 2010, http://www.justice.gov/opa/pr/2004/January/04_crm_030.htm; and Jerry Markon, "Muslim Lecturer Sentenced to Life; Followers Trained for Armed Jihad," *Washington Post*, July 14, 2005.
57. Letter from Randall Royer to Judge Leonie Brinkema, March 31, 2004.
58. Joe Barret, Douglas Belkin, Peter Loftus, and Eric Bellman, "For Terror Suspect, a Life of Contradictions," *Wall Street Journal*, December 12, 2009; Sally A. Downey, "A. Serrill Headley, 68; Owned Phila.'s Khyber Pass Pub," *Philadelphia Inquirer*, January 25, 2008.
59. Barret, Belkin, Loftus, and Bellman, "For Terror Suspect, a Life of Contradictions."
60. Downey, "A. Serrill Headley, 68; Owned Phila.'s Khyber Pass Pub."
61. Barret, Belkin, Loftus, and Bellman, "For Terror Suspect, a Life of Contradictions."
62. *USA v. David Coleman Headley*, 09 CR 830-3, Criminal Complaint, Affidavit of FBI Special Agent Lorenzo Benedict; Jane Perlez, "American Terror Suspect Traveled Unimpeded," *New York Times*, March 26, 2010.
63. Ibid., Plea Agreement, March 13, 2010.
64. Ibid.
65. See http://pib.nic.in/release/release.asp?relid=45446, retrieved July 10, 2010; *USA v. David Coleman Headley*, 09 CR 830-3, Plea Agreement, March 13, 2010.
66. *USA v. David Coleman Headley*, 09 CR 830-3, Criminal Complaint, Affidavit of FBI Special Agent Lorenzo Benedict.
67. Ginger Thompson, "A Terror Suspect with Feet in East and West," *New York Times*, November 22, 2009.

68. *USA v. David Coleman Headley*, 09 CR 830-3, Criminal Complaint, Affidavit of FBI Special Agent Lorenzo Benedict.
69. Ibid.
70. *USA v. David Coleman Headley*, 09 CR 830-3, Plea Agreement, March 13, 2010.
71. "NIA Charge Sheet against David Headley Soon," *Hindustan Times*, July 7, 2010.
72. "David Headley Used Choicest Hindi Expletives for NIA Grillers," *India Today*, July 10, 2010.
73. See https://www.cia.gov/library/publications/the-world-factbook/geos/so.html, retrieved August 11, 2010.
74. Xan Rice, "Somali Hardliner Calls for Foreign Jihadists," *Observer*, December 24, 2006.
75. Mohamed Abdi Farah, "Somalia: ICU Leaders Resign as Ethiopian Army Nears the Capital," *SomaliNet News*, http://web.archive.org/web/20070110230438/http://somalinet.com/news/world/Somalia/6223, retrieved August 11, 2010.
76. Country Reports on Terrorism 2009, U.S. State Department, retrieved August 11, 2010, http://www.state.gov/s/ct/rls/crt/2009/140900.htm.
77. Nir Rosen, "How Did Al Shabab Emerge from the Chaos of Somalia?" *Time*, August 20, 2010.
78. Testimony by Stevan Weine, M.D., professor, Department of Psychiatry, University of Illinois at Chicago, College of Medicine, before the House Committee on Homeland Security, Subcommittee on Intelligence, Information Sharing and Terrorism Risk Assessment, *Hearing on Violent Extremism: How Are People Moved from Constitutionally Protected Thought to Acts of Terrorism?* December 15, 2009.
79. Weine, *Hearing on Violent Extremism;* question by the author to Terrance Ford, director of Intelligence and Knowledge Development, United States Army African Command at a Foreign Policy Research Institute conference on September 27, 2010.
80. Weine, *Hearing on Violent Extremism.*
81. Kristina Davis and Michael Stetz, "Acquaintances Recall Terror Suspect," *San Diego Union-Tribune*, August 7, 2010; *USA v. Jehad Serwan Mostafa*, Case 3:09-cr-03726-WQH, Grand Jury Indictment, October 9, 2009; and Terry Rodgers, "'No War,' Crowds Implore: Thousands Rally at Park against Conflict in Iraq," *San Diego Union-Tribune*, March 17, 2003.
82. The following section is derived mainly from the following two exceptionally reported pieces: Andrea Elliott, "The Jihadist Next Door," *New York Times Magazine*, January 31, 2010; and "American Jihadi," *Vanguard*, Current TV, air date June 30, 2010.
83. *USA v. Daniel Maldonado*, 4:07-mj-00125, Criminal Complaint, Affidavit of Jeremiah A. George.
84. *USA v. Zachary Adam Chesser*, CR 1:10 MS504, Affidavit in Support of Criminal Complaint.
85. *Ambush At Bardal*, Al Shabab propaganda video.
86. Ibid.
87. Ibid.

88. Various nasheeds, Al Shabab propaganda videos.
89. *Festival for the Children of Martyrs*, Al Shabab propaganda video.
90. Nicole Santa Cruz, "San Diego Woman Accused of Aiding Somalia Terrorist Group," *Los Angeles Times*, November 28, 2010.
91. Derrick Nunnally, Kathleen Brady Shea, and Larry King, "'JihadJane's" Life Like a 'Country Music Song,'" *Philadelphia Inquirer*, March 11, 2010.
92. Ian Urbina, "Militant Views Were Expressed Online but Unknown to Neighbors," *New York Times*, March 11, 2010.
93. Carrie Johnson, "JihadJane, an American Woman, Faces Terrorism Charges," *Washington Post*, March 10, 2010.
94. Stephanie Simon, "Paulin-Ramirez's Actions Raised Mother's Concerns," Wall Street Journal, March 13, 2010; Devlin Barrett, "Jamie Paulin-Ramirez Charged In 'Jihad Jane' Case, Plot To Kill Swedish Cartoonist," *Huffington Post*, April 2, 2010, retrieved December 3, 2010, http://www.huffingtonpost.com/2010/04/02/jamie-paulinramirez-will-_n_523648.html.

Chapter 11. The Keyboard and the Sword

1. *U.S. v. Muhamed Mubayyid, Emadeddin Muntasser, and Samir Al Monla*, Criminal Action No. 05-40026-FDS (2007), Exhibit 514A, transcript of phone conversation of January 27, 1996.
2. Andrew North, "Pro-Jihad Website Draws Readers," *BBC News*, February 15, 2002, http://news.bbc.co.uk/2/hi/uk_news/1823045.stm, retrieved July 24, 2010; "The Battle to Banish Babar Ahmad," *BBC News*, November 16, 2005, http://news.bbc.co.uk/2/hi/uk_news/4441680.stm, retrieved July 24, 2010.
3. See http://www.islamicawakening.com/helpus.php, retrieved July 24, 2010; *Al-Jihad: The Neglected Duty*, Muhammad Abdul Salam Faraj (Boston: CARE International, undated).
4. See http://forums.islamicawakening.com/f18/, retrieved July 24, 2010.
5. See http://forums.islamicawakening.com/f18/america-one-sick-place-24585/, retrieved on various dates.
6. See http://www.state.gov/g/drl/rls/hrrpt/2009/nea/136079.htm, and http://www.state.gov/g/drl/rls/hrrpt/2009/nea/136083.htm, retrieved July 26, 2010.
7. Paul Cruickshank and Tim Lister, "Arrested Men Attended Protests Organized by Radical Islamic Group," CNN.com, June 11, 2010.
8. Andrea Elliott, "Queens Muslim Group Says It Opposes Violence, and America," *New York Times*, June 22, 2005; Bradley Hope, "Islamic Thinkers Society Called 'Destructive,'" *New York Sun*, April 25, 2006.
9. Cruickshank and Lister, "Arrested Men Attended Protests Organized by Radical Islamic Group."
10. Elliott, "Queens Muslim Group Says It Opposes Violence, and America."
11. Ibid.; also see http://www.revolutionmuslim.com/2010/07/what-weekend-planed-for-authentic.html, http://www.revolutionmuslim.com/2010/05/sheikh-anwar-al-awlaki-muslim-for-sake.html, retrieved July 30, 2010.
12. See http://forums.islamicawakening.com/f18/feds-arrest-man-behind-south-park-threats-37052/, retrieved July 24, 2010; http://www.revolutionmuslim

.com/p/authentic-tawheed-paltalk.html, retrieved July 30, 2010; Judgment in Appeal of *Crown v. El Faisal*, Supreme Court of Judicature, Court of Appeal, March 4, 2004, http://nefafoundation.org/miscellaneous/FeaturedDocs/RoyalCourts ofJustice_AlFaisal.pdf, retrieved July 30, 2010; "Jamaican Muslim Cleric Back in Kenya Prison," *Xinhua News*, January 11, 2010.

13. "The Brooklyn Jew Who Became a Radical Muslim," *Details*, September 2003.
14. Interview with Roxanne Euben, professor of political science, Wellesley College, June 2, 2010.
15. See http://www.revolutionmuslim.com/, various dates.
16. *American Al Qaeda*, CNN, aired May 15, 2010, and numerous news broadcasts.
17. John Doyle and Janon Fisher, "Sick in the Jihad; America-Hater in Qns. Hails Hood Massacre," *New York Post*, November 8, 2009.
18. Yousef Al Khattab, "Why I Left Revolution Muslim," retrieved August 20, 2010, http://www.yousefalkhattab.com/p/why-i-left-revolution-muslim.html.
19. See http://forums.islamicawakening.com/f18/feds-arrest-man-behind-south-park-threats-37052/, retrieved July 24, 2010.
20. *Revolution Muslim Street Dawah*, March 26, 2010. The video was posted online but subsequently removed by Revolution Muslim. Audio captured by the author.
21. *Revolution Muslim Street Dawah at Muslim Day Parade*, October 2009. The video was posted online but subsequently removed by Revolution Muslim. Audio captured by the author.
22. Aaron Y. Zelin, "Revolution Muslim: Downfall or Respite?," *CTC Sentinel*, November 2010; http://www.islampolicy.com/2010/11/anwar-awlaki-to-make-it-known-and-not.html, retrieved Dec. 3, 2010; http://www.islampolicy.com/2010/12/bin-laden-abdullah-azzam-exposing-saudi.html, retrieved Dec. 3, 2010; and http://www.islampolicy.com/2010/12/whoever-prepares-fighter-has.html, retrieved Dec. 3, 2010.
23. Anti-Defamation League, "Backgrounder: Revolution Muslim," retrieved July 30, 2010, http://www.adl.org/NR/exeres/48925123-070C-411E-A42F-E23160C76E5D,DB7611A2-02CD-43AF-8147-649E26813571,frameless.htm.
24. *USA v. Mohamed Alessa and Carlos E. Almonte*, 2:10-mj-08109-MCA, Criminal Complaint, June 4, 2010.
25. *American Al Qaeda*, CNN; Bryant Vinas timeline, http://www.cnn.com/2010/CRIME/05/11/timeline.bryant.vinas/index.html, retrieved July 30, 2010.
26. Michael Powell, "U.S. Recruit Reveals How Qaeda Trains Foreigners," *New York Times*, July 24, 2009.
27. *American Al Qaeda*, CNN.
28. Ibid..
29. Powell, "U.S. Recruit Reveals How Qaeda Trains Foreigners."
30. *American Al Qaeda*, CNN; Bryant Vinas timeline, retrieved July 30, 2010, http://www.cnn.com/2010/CRIME/05/11/timeline.bryant.vinas/index.html.
31. Powell, "U.S. Recruit Reveals How Qaeda Trains Foreigners."
32. Claire Suddath, "Bryant Neal Vinas: An American in Al Qaeda," Time.com, July 24, 2009; Bryant Vinas timeline, http://www.cnn.com/2010/CRIME/05/11/timeline.bryant.vinas/index.html, retrieved July 30, 2010.

33. Bryant Vinas timeline, retrieved July 30, 2010, http://www.cnn.com/2010/CRIME/05/11/timeline.bryant.vinas/index.html.
34. Wisdom Martin, "Classmate's Shock: 'I Didn't Know How Far He Was Taking It!'" *Channel 5 Fox*, Washington, D.C., retrieved July 23, 2010, http://www.myfoxdc.com/dpp/news/virginia/former-high-school-classmate-discusses-va-man-charged-with-supporting-terror-group-072210.
35. Tara Bahrampour, "Terror Suspect Took His Desire to Belong to the Extreme," *Washington Post*, July 25, 2010.
36. Aaron Zelin, Interview with Abū Talḥah Al Amrīkī, retrieved July 23, 2010, http://azelin.wordpress.com/2010/07/13/exclusive-interview-with-abu-tal%E1%B8%A5ah-al-amriki-of-revolution-muslim/.
37. Yousef Al Khattab, untitled posting, July 23, 2010, http://yousefalkhattab.blogspot.com/2010/07/blog-post_23.html, retrieved July 23, 2010.
38. Anti-Defamation League, "Backgrounder: Revolution Muslim."
39. *USA v. Zachary Adam Chesser*, CR 1:10 MS504, Affidavit of Mary Brandt Kinder; for another example, see Abu Talha Al Amriki, "Counter Counter Terrorism: Misguided Salafis," retrieved August 20, 2010; http://www.jamiahafsaforum.com/forum/showthread.php?t=6412, Anti-Defamation League, "Abu Talhah Al Amrikee: An Extensive Online Footprint," July 23, 2010, retrieved September 6, 2010, http://www.adl.org/NR/exeres/3F7463DE-4DA9-4696-BA38-F6D67881AA7C,DB7611A2-02CD-43AF-8147-649E26813571,frameless.htm; and J. M. Berger, "Counter-Counter-Counter-Terrorism: The Positive Power of Dissent," retrieved April 24, 2010, http://news.intelwire.com/2010/04/counter-counter-counter-terrorism-power.html, Intelwire.com.
40. Zelin, Interview with Abū Talḥah Al Amrīkī.
41. See http://www.revolutionmuslim.com/2010/04/counter-counter-terrorism-8-fomenting.html, retrieved July 23, 2010.
42. Abu Talha Al Amriki, "*South Park* Aired Episode Insulting the Prophet (Salaa Allahu 'Alayhi Wa Salam)," Revolution Muslim, retrieved April 15, 2010; the link was subsequently deleted.
43. Dave Itzkoff, "*South Park* Episode Altered after Muslim Group's Warning," *New York Times*, April 22, 2010.
44. *USA v. Zachary Adam Chesser*, CR 1:10 MS504, Affidavit of Mary Brandt Kinder.
45. Ibid.
46. Spencer S. Hsu and Michael Alison Chandler, "Graduate of Va.'s Oakton High Charged with Trying to Join Terrorist Group," *Washington Post*, July 22, 2010.
47. See http://forums.islamicawakening.com/f18/feds-arrest-man-behind-south-park-threats-37052/, retrieved July 23, 2010. The thread was later deleted by the forum's moderators.
48. Michael Moss and Souad Mekhennet, "An Internet Jihad Aims at U.S. Viewers," *New York Times*, October 15, 2007.
49. Inshallahshahid, "The Destiny of Israel," retrieved July 31, 2010, http://inshallahshaheed.blogspot.com/2005_01_01_archive.html.
50. Moss and Mekhennet, "An Internet Jihad Aims at U.S. Viewers"
51. See http://www.google.com/search?aq=0&oq=inshallahsha&sourceid=chrome&ie=UTF-8&q=inshallahshaheed, retrieved July 30, 2010.

52. Moss and Mekhennet, "An Internet Jihad Aims at U.S. Viewers"; Alison Gendar, "Former New Yorker Samir Khan behind Graphics of New Al Qaeda Recruiting Magazine *Inspire*: Officials," *New York Daily News*, July 18, 2010.
53. *Jihad Recollections*, no. 1, April 2009; *Jihad Recollections*, no. 4, September 2009; "Would-Be Portland Bomber Mohamed Osman Mohamud (a/k/a "Ibn al-Mubarak"): "Getting in Shape Without Weights," *Flashpoint Partners*, retrieved Dec. 2, 2010, http://www.globalterroralert.com/miscellaneous/723-would-be-portland-bomber-mohamed-osman-mohamud-aka-ibn-al-mubarak-getting-in-shape-without-weights.html.
54. Gendar, "Former New Yorker Samir Khan behind Graphics of New Al Qaeda Recruiting Magazine *Inspire*: Officials"; Paul Cruickshank, "U.S. Citizen Believed to Be Writing for al Qaeda Website, Source Says," CNN.com, July 18, 2010, retrieved July 30, 2010, http://www.cnn.com/2010/US/07/18/al.qaeda.magazine/index.html.
55. *Inspire*, Summer 2010, Al Malahem Media (al Qaeda in the Arabian Peninsula).
56. *Inspire,* Issue 3, obtained by the author, November 2010.
57. Shelley Murphy and Milton J. Valencia, "Details Emerge on Plot Suspects: Two Young Men Reportedly Met at Sharon Mosque," *Boston Globe*, October 23, 2009; *USA v. Tarek Mehanna*, Cr. No. 09-10017-GAO, Government's Proffer and Memorandum in Support of Detention.
58. Murphy and Valencia, "Details Emerge on Plot Suspects: Two Young Men Reportedly Met at Sharon Mosque."
59. *USA v. Tarek Mehanna and Ahmad Abousamra*, 1:09-cr-10017-GAO, Second Superseding Indictment, June 17, 2010.
60. Search and Seizure Warrant, Case No. 09-122-LTS, Affidavit of Heidi L. Williams, October 20, 2009.
61. Charles A. Radin, "From N.H. to Somalia: Recalling a Suspect's Zeal," *Boston Globe*, February 17, 2007.
62. *USA v. Tarek Mehanna and Ahmad Abousamra*, 1:09-cr-10017-GAO, Second Superseding Indictment, June 17, 2010.
63. Shelley Murphy, "FBI Calls Sudbury Suspect Inept but Serious Terror Plotter," *Boston Globe*, October 22, 2009; Search and Seizure Warrant, Case No. 09-122-LTS, Affidavit of Heidi L. Williams, October 20, 2009.
64. *USA v. Tarek Mehanna*, 1:09-cr-10017-GAO, Second Superseding Indictment, June 17, 2010.
65. Confidential interview with senior Defense Intelligence Agency analyst, February 19, 2010.
66. Murphy, "FBI Calls Sudbury Suspect Inept but Serious Terror Plotter."
67. *USA v. Tarek Mehanna*, 1:09-cr-10017-GAO, Second Superseding Indictment, June 17, 2010.
68. Search and Seizure Warrant, Case No. 09-122-LTS, Affidavit of Heidi L. Williams, October 20, 2009. Although Abousamra's travel habits suggest that he was serious about joining violent jihadists, it should be noted that his story of continual rejection does not square with the experiences of other American jihadists—consider Bryant Vinas, who managed to get quite far into al Qaeda without an apparent facilitator. According to Abousamra, Lashkar-e-Tayyiba had rejected

him because he was "not an Arab," but the organization had accepted other white Americans—certainly whiter than the ethnically Syrian Abousamra. The Taliban had rejected him for "lack of experience," but other cases suggested that this would not normally be an obstacle.

69. "The Chronicles of Daniel J. Maldonado," retrieved July 29, 2010, http://istighfar.wordpress.com/2007/09/01/the-chronicle-of-daniel-j-maldonado/.
70. *USA v. Daniel Maldonado*, 4:07-mj-00125, Exhibit, handwritten letter from Daniel Maldonado.
71. Exhibit, second handwritten letter from Daniel Maldonado; Criminal Complaint, Affidavit of Jeremiah A. George.
72. Affidavit of Jeremiah A. George.
73. "The Chronicles of Daniel J. Maldonado."
74. *USA v. Daniel Maldonado*, 4:07-mj-00125, Exhibit, handwritten letter from Daniel Maldonado.
75. Ibid., Affidavit of Jeremiah A. George.
76. "The Chronicles of Daniel J. Maldonado."
77. Search and Seizure Warrant, Case No. 09-122-LTS, Affidavit of Heidi L. Williams, October 20, 2009.
78. Tarek Mehanna Blog, retrieved December 11, 2008, http://iskandrani.wordpress.com.
79. For example, http://forums.islamicawakening.com/f47/aafia-siddiqui-i-saw-abu-sabaya-15153/, retrieved December 11, 2008.
80. Search and Seizure Warrant, Case No. 09-122-LTS, Affidavit of Heidi L. Williams, October 20, 2009.
81. *USA v. Tarek Mehanna*, Cr. No. 09-10017-GAO, Government's Proffer and Memorandum in Support of Detention.
82. Search and Seizure Warrant, Case No. 09-122-LTS, Affidavit of Heidi L. Williams, October 20, 2009.
83. See http://forums.islamicawakening.com/f47/, retrieved July 29, 2010, among others; also see http://freetarek.com/, http://www.facebook.com/group.php?gid=159128188381, http://twitter.com/freetarek, retrieved July 29, 2010.
84. *USA v. Tarek Mehanna*, Cr. No. 09-10017-GAO, Second Superseding Indictment.
85. See http://news.intelwire.com/2010/07/aqap-inspire-magazine-is-nothing-new.html, retrieved July 30, 2010; http://news.intelwire.com/2010/07/AlQaedas-new-magazine-or-was-it-web.html, retrieved July 30, 2010.
86. "5 D.C.-Area Men Held in Pakistan," CBS.com, December 9, 2009, http://www.cbsnews.com/stories/2009/12/09/world/main5951110.shtml, retrieved July 30, 2010.

Chapter 12. The Future of American Jihad

1. *USA v. Holy Land Foundation et al.*, Memorandum Opinion Order, July 1, 2009, http://www.scribd.com/doc/43380629/2009-order-on-Holy-Land-Foundation-unindicted-coconspirator-list, retrieved December 4, 2010. CAIR petitioned a federal judge to have its name stricken from a list of unindicted coconspirators in a Hamas financing case. A federal judge rejected CAIR's request, ruling that there is "at least a prima facie case as to CAIR's involvement in a conspiracy to support Hamas."

2. Interview with Alyas Karmani, the director of STREET program (Strategy to Reach, Empower and Educate Teenagers), London, August 10, 2010.
3. Confidential interviews, 2010.
4. Abdullah Azzam, *Join the Caravan* (Boston: Care International, 1995), 12.
5. Bill Gertz, "Inside the Ring: Al Qaeda-Trained Americans," *Washington Times*, August 25, 2010.
6. J.M. Berger, "Gadahn and Awlaki, Together At Last?," Intelwire.com, October 23, 2010, http://news.intelwire.com/2010/10/gadahn-and-awlaki-together-at-last.html, retrieved December 4, 2010.
7. See, among others, Aaron Weisburd, "Ansar Al Mujahideen: Zombie Forum Badly in Need of Brains," Internet Haganah, retrieved September 6, 2010, http://internet-haganah.com/harchives/006972.html#006972.
8. J. M. Berger, "Jihadists Add Strong Encryption to Terrorist Toolbox," Intelwire.com, February 2, 2008. "Mujahideen Secrets 2" encryption software obtained by the author.
9. Gertz, "Inside the Ring: Al Qaeda-Trained Americans"; Sami Yousafzai and Ron Moreau, "Inside Al Qaeda," *Newsweek*, September 4, 2010, retrieved September 6, 2010, http://www.news week.com/2010/09/04/inside-Al Qaeda.html; and Leah Farrall, "Death of a Hoary Old Chestnut?" *All Things Counter Terrorism* blog, September 7, 2010, retrieved September 6, 2010, http://allthingsct.wordpress.com/2010/09/07/death-of-a-hoary-old-chestnut/.
10. Andy Barr, "Newt Gingrich Compares Mosque to Nazis," *Politico*, August 16, 2010, retrieved September 6, 2010, http://www.politico.com/news/stories/0810/41112.html; "Harry Reid: Ground Zero Mosque 'Should Be Built Some Place Else,'" *CBS News*, August 16, 2010, retrieved September 6, 2010, http://www.cbsnews.com/8301-503544_162-20013773-503544.html.

SELECTED BIBLIOGRAPHY

Primary sources for this book include nearly one hundred interviews with former law enforcement, intelligence, and diplomatic officials in both the United States and Bosnia; American jihadists and their families; victims of jihadist violence; and other individuals directly involved in the events described in this book. Document sources include

- Thousands of pages of documents obtained through the Freedom of Information Act, including documents pertaining to the September 11 attacks, the Siege of Mecca, the war in Bosnia, the jihad against the Soviet Union, and Egyptian extremist groups.
- Thousands of pages of documents obtained from the National Archives pertaining to Anwar Awlaki and the activities of the September 11 hijackers in America.
- Court records from dozens of prosecutions of American jihadists, mostly obtained through PACER, as well as several thousand pages of exhibits pertaining to the Al Kifah Center in Boston, obtained from the U.S. Attorney's office in Boston.
- Documents pertaining to al Qaeda and Ali Mohamed that were obtained during the making of the 2007 National Geographic Channel documentary *Triple Cross: Bin Laden's Spy in America.*
- Several thousand pages of intelligence and al Qaeda documents pertain-

ing to the war in Bosnia obtained during the making of the 2010 European television documentary *Sarajevo Ricochet.*

- Court transcripts from major terrorism trials, especially *USA v. bin Laden et al.* (2001) and *USA v. Abdel Rahman et al.* (1995).
- A wide number of books and newspaper reports were consulted during the research process for this book. Especially valuable were reports from the *New York Times*, the *Washington Post*, and the *L.A. Times*. Books to which the author is especially indebted include *The Cell: Inside the 9/11 Plot and Why the FBI and CIA Failed to Stop It*, by John Miller and Michael Stone with Chris Mitchell (Hyperion, 2003), and *The Looming Tower: Al Qaeda and the Road to 9/11*, by Lawrence Wright (Knopf, 2006).

INDEX

ABOUT THE AUTHOR

J. M. Berger has been a journalist for more than twenty years. His writing has appeared in the *Boston Globe* and the *San Francisco Examiner*, and he has produced programming on terrorism and national security for National Public Radio, Public Radio International, and the National Geographic Channel. His recent work includes *Sarajevo Ricochet*, a 2010 European television documentary about the mujahideen in Bosnia. Berger is the founder and the editor of the terrorism news and research website Intelwire.com, based in Cambridge, Massachusetts.